FREE of CHARGE

→) those we encounter — why jist then?

—) giving beyond what we ought

—) how much giving do we need
to do? is it always bad
to say, learn russian poetry,
or learn develop your back hand

—) why the focus or goods/stuff?

FREE OF CHARGE

GIVING AND FORGIVING
IN A CULTURE STRIPPED OF GRACE

MIROSLAV VOLF

ZONDERVAN™

GRAND RAPIDS, MICHIGAN 49530 USA

WWW.ZONDERVAN.COM

ZONDERVAN.COM/
AUTHORTRACKER

ZONDERVAN™

Free of Charge
Copyright © 2005 by Miroslav Volf

Requests for information should be addressed to:
Zondervan, *Grand Rapids, Michigan 49530*

Library of Congress Cataloging-in-Publication Data

Volf, Miroslav
    Free of Charge : giving and forgiving in a culture stripped of grace : the
Archbishop's official 2006 Lent book / Miroslav Volf.
       p. cm.
    Includes bibliographical references.
    ISBN-10: 0-310-26574-6
    ISBN-13: 978-0-310-26574-0
    1. Generosity—Religious aspects—Christianity. 2. Forgiveness—Religious
aspects—Christianity. I. Title: Archbishop's official 2006 Lent book. II. Title.
BV4647.G45V65 2006
241'.4—dc22
{B}
                                             2001017679

Miroslav Volf asserts the moral right to be identified as the author of this work.

Interior design by Michelle Espinoza

Printed in the United States

---

06 07 08 09 10 11 • 19 18 17 16 15 14 13 12 11 10 9 8 7 6 5

To Nathanael and Aaron, my sons –

gifts generously given,
givers adorably giving,
offenders easy to forgive,
forgivers hard to match.

CONTENTS

Foreword by Dr Rowan Williams,
Archbishop of Canterbury   9

Prelude: The Rose   11

1. God the Giver   19

2. How Should We Give?   55

3. How Can We Give?   89

Interlude: Daniel's Death   121

4. God the Forgiver   127

5. How Should We Forgive?   157

6. How Can We Forgive?   193

Postlude: A Conversation with a Skeptic   225

Afterword   235

Acknowledgments   237

Endnotes   241

Foreword by
Dr Rowan Williams,
Archbishop of Canterbury

This is a book about worshiping the true God and letting the true God act in us. It tells us as plainly as possible that the true God is a God who cannot stop giving and forgiving, and that our knowledge of this true God is utterly bound up with our willingness to receive from the hand of God the liberty to give and forgive.

Miroslav Volf, one of the most celebrated theologians of our day, here undertakes not just to explain the doctrines of the Christian faith but to persuade us that this God is supremely worth trusting. He offers us a unique interweaving of intense reflection, vivid and painfully personal stories, and sheer celebration of the giving God. He writes with enormous sensitivity to possible objections, to the ways in which what he says may sound hollow or insensitive, and incorporates a real element of dialogue into his argument. In that sense, this is a book that engages its readers with great force and immediacy.

I cannot remember having read a better account of what it means to say that Jesus suffered for us, "in our place". And his analysis of the challenges Christian forgiveness faces in a society that is both sentimental and profoundly unforgiving is something that ought to be required reading for anyone seeking to understand the Western world in this sour and anxious age. Some of his turns of phrase will stick like burrs in the mind: Without sin we should be like God in the way that baby bears are like mother bears; God gives and loves by nature as surely as a duck quacks by nature – God's love isn't some kind of acquired skill. And the sensitive use both of his own experience as a parent, and of his and his family's life in one of the places in Europe most haunted by diabolical violence gives a depth to his meditations that is of rare quality.

In his concluding "Conversation with a Skeptic", Miroslav's doubtful partner in the conversation admits that the God of the book is "a pretty good god as gods go, the only trouble being that I can't believe in any of them". Miroslav responds by gently inviting the skeptic to think what it means if such a picture of God is so deeply in tune with the skeptic's sense of what a healed and beautiful human life looks like, and at least to give serious time to absorbing the vision. The whole of this remarkable book constitutes an invitation to such absorption – an invitation that should be equally powerful for the believer and the unbeliever. For all its quiet depth, it is proclamation of the most urgent and moving and, I hope, converting kind.

Dr Rowan Williams
Archbishop of Canterbury

Prelude: The Rose

The first thing I saw was a tear – a huge, unforgettable tear in the big brown eye of a ten-year-old girl. Then I saw tears in her mother's eyes. And in all these tears, just enough joy was mixed with pain to underscore that pain's severity: their joy at seeing him, their three-month-old brother and son, and their intense pain that it was the first time they'd seen him since he was just two days old, when they'd kissed him good-bye. I sensed in those tears the ache that he, flesh of their flesh, was being brought to them for a brief visit by two strangers who were now his parents, and the affliction of knowing that the joy of loving him as a mother and sister would never be theirs.

The joy and the pain of those tears led me to a repentance of sorts. My image of mothers who relinquished their children for adoption, though not as bad as that of the fathers involved, was not exactly positive either. I could not shake the feeling that there was something deficient in such an act. The taint of abandonment marred it, an abandonment that could be understandable and was certainly tragic, but abandonment nonetheless. To give one's child to another, it had seemed to me, was to fail in the most proper duty of a parent: to love no matter what.

As I was reflecting on those tears, I came across a passage in Aristotle's *Nicomachean Ethics.* "Witness the pleasure that mothers take in loving their children. Some mothers put their infants out to nurse, and though knowing and loving them do not ask to be loved by them in return, if it be impossible to have this as well, but are content if they see them prospering; they retain their own love for them even though the children, not knowing them, cannot render them any part of what is due to a mother."[1] The text comes from Aristotle's discussion of friendship. He used the example of mothers to make plausible that "in its essence friendship seems to consist more in giving than receiving affection." For Aristotle, a "birth mother" would manifest the kind of love that is characteristic of a true friend, a love exercised for that friend's sake, not for benefits gained from the relationship.

"It is hard to know that you have a child in the world, far away from you," wrote Nathanael's birth mother in her first letter to us. It is hard because love passionately desires the presence of the beloved. Yet it was that same love that took deliberate and carefully planned steps that would lead to his absence. In a letter she wrote for Nathanael to read when he grows up, she told him that her decision to put him up for adoption was made for his own good. "I did it for you," she wrote repeatedly, adding, "Some day you will understand."

She loved him for his own sake, and therefore she would rather have suffered his absence if he flourished than to have enjoyed his presence if he languished; her sorrow over his avoidable languishing would overshadow her delight in his presence. For a lover, it is more blessed to give than to receive, even when giving pierces the lover's heart. My image of birth mothers has changed: "She who does not care quite enough" has become "she who selflessly gives." When we parted, a smile had replaced the tears on the face of our son's birth mother. Now it was my turn to cry. Back at home, with him in one arm and an open album she made for him in the other, I shed tears over the beauty and the tragedy of her love.

About three months earlier, the most extraordinary thing had happened on an ordinary day in an ordinary maternity ward between three ordinary human beings. After chatting with us for half an hour or so – to assure herself once again that we were the right parents for her child – Nathanael's birth mother called the nurse and asked her to bring in her two-day-old baby. There he was, wonderful to the point of tears, rolled in to us in a crib. She took him and held him for a while in her arms, in a last maternal embrace. Then she handed him over to my wife Judy. In one simple act, painfully sad for her and wonderfully joyful for us, she gave him to us, and she gave us to him.

She gave us that most incredible gift at about eleven o'clock one beautiful March morning. Just one hour earlier, a man in dark uniform wearing dark sunglasses had given us something entirely different. He had appeared at the window on the driver's side of my car. As I rolled it down, my ears were still ringing with the ominous, evenly paced sound of his boots hitting the pavement. "Driver's license and insurance card!" I still did not know what I had done to be stopped by the police. Even when I had first seen the flashing red and blue lights behind me, I had been puzzled. Then, as he paced back to his car, it dawned on me. We had stopped at a doughnut place at an intersection to get a quick bite in place of the breakfast we had missed. After finding out that a child would be given to us, we had had only twenty-four hours to get our nest ready, and we had stayed up until four o'clock in the morning trying to name our boy. From the parking lot in front of the doughnut place, I had not seen that the street to our right was one-way. After a bite and a sip of coffee – tired, excited, and a bit bewildered about what was to happen – I drove out onto that one-way street the wrong way and positioned myself to turn right toward the hospital. Directly in front of me, on the other side of the intersection, was a police car. Soon the siren was on, and I was pulled over.

Not knowing that in the U.S. you aren't supposed to get out of the car to talk to a police officer, I opened my door, took one step, and said, "Mr. Officer, we've just had this wonderful news ..." I was interrupted in mid sentence. "Get back into your car!" he barked at me. I tried one more time: "May I explain ..." Again, I was interrupted by that same bark, more irritated this time: "Get back into your car, I said!" Clad in a uniform, with his eyes – those windows of the soul – hidden behind dark shades, he was all power, all law, all business. His humanity? Locked up somewhere deep inside, underneath the shiny police belt buckle. His generosity? Hidden behind the badge of office. Within the space of one hour, I got a nasty ticket from a gruff cop, and a tender child from a loving birth mother.

I don't expect police officers to give out candy for traffic violations. But even in the old communist Yugoslavia, where I grew up,

, you could talk to traffic police like human beings. Maybe my experience on the streets of southern California was an exception. But it fits into a larger pattern of what we may call the gracelessness that is slowly spreading like a disease throughout many of our cultures. Some may suggest that we are no worse off today than we were fifty years or even two centuries ago. My sense is that we are. But my main point is not to note a decline; rather, to name a problem. We live in a culture in which, yes, extraordinary generosity does happen. But at the same time, that culture is largely stripped of grace.

It's not a gracelessness that's necessarily apparent at first glance, but it nonetheless underlies so many of our interactions. If I were to say that today everything is sold and nothing is given, that would be an exaggeration. But like any good caricature, it distorts reality in order to draw attention to what is characteristic. Mainly, we're set up to sell and buy, not to give and receive. We tend to give nothing free of charge and receive nothing free of charge. "The person who volunteers time, who helps a stranger, who agrees to work for a modest wage out of commitment to the public good, who desists from littering even when no one is looking ... begins to feel like a sucker," wrote Robert Kuttner in *Everything for Sale*.[2] To give is to lose.

It's not just that we are calculating rather than generous. In buying and selling, we are often not even fair. "You don't get what you deserve; you get what you negotiate," the saying goes. With only our own interest in mind, we try to squeeze the last drop out of those with whom we are dealing. Far too often, power – not fairness and certainly not generosity – is the name of the game. We assert ourselves and our own interests through raw physical strength, political connections, or loads of cash; through sexual prowess, sarcastic comments, lies and half-truths; through anything that can serve as a weapon in this low-grade war called life. We fight, and we often take spoils or go away defeated. Whether considering business, politics, family, or education, the big fish eat the little ones. Laws and regulations do limit excessive abuse; however, they only mark the space in which the war is waged. They don't eliminate the war.

Sex is as good a site as any to observe the slide away from generosity, through self-gratification, profit maximizing, and selling and bartering, to nasty warring. Watch any currently popular TV series – *Sex and the City* or *Desperate Housewives* for example – and it would never occur to you that sex might be a gift two people in a lifelong covenant give each other, a sacrament of their lasting love. Instead, partners randomly "hook up", each hungry to sexually satisfy some inchoate craving that has no definite object and can never find rest. They crave chocolate, they grab a chocolate bar; they crave sex, they just grab the most willing partner. Worse still, wars are waged with sex. Sex can bring status and define who belongs and who doesn't. It can serve to inflict a sweet revenge or to reward cooperation, or it can be a tool to manipulate and dominate. By having sex, we can easily do almost anything other than truly give and receive – give and receive pleasure and give and receive each other as treasured lovers.

Loss of generosity doesn't just leave us sexually unfulfilled, in search of pleasures that are ever more intense but never truly satisfying. Left unchecked, the slide away from generosity ultimately robs us of significant cultural achievements, on which our flourishing as individuals and communities depends. Let's mention just a few of the losses a lack of generosity can put into motion. Without generosity, our economic system would falter, and the exchange of goods and services could easily become unsustainable exploitation of the poor by the rich. Without generosity, our democratic political system would decay, and powerful interest groups would likely exclude much of the electorate and rule them to their detriment. Without generosity, our educational system couldn't be sustained; nothing can secure the services of good teachers who are, by definition, neither sellers nor takers, but givers who cannot be bought even if they do get paid. The list could go on.

A "rose" from Antoine de Saint-Exupéry's *Little Prince* reminds us of a more personal kind of loss that comes from a lack of generosity, an intimate loss that, at the same time, is a loss of a whole world of meaning. From the star where he tended three volcanoes and a single rose, the little prince found his way to Earth, where thousands of roses can be found in people's gardens. "People where you live," the little prince said to his pilot friend, "grow five thousand roses in one garden ... yet they don't find what they're looking for ... And yet what they're looking for could be found in a single rose..." And he added, "But eyes are blind. You have to look with the heart."[3]

To find that for which you are searching in a single rose is, however, more than just a matter of looking with the heart. For the heart to see rightly, the hand needs to give generously. That's the deeper wisdom the little prince goes on to reveal.

His mysterious affair with the rose began when he responded to the rose's simple request, "Would you be so kind as to tend to me?" The gift of care made it *his* rose, the only one in the whole world. "It's the time you spent on your rose that makes your rose so important," the wise fox told him (64). Take that gift away, and the one special rose blends into a 100,000 other roses, beautiful and interesting for a while, but in the long run, ordinary and even boring.

The gift of care didn't just transform the rose, however. When the little prince looked up to the stars above the Earth, they shone in a new way because on one of them he had left behind the rose he loved. It cast a spell over the whole heavenly firmament, like a buried treasure casts a spell on all the islands where you think it may lie hidden. That one rose changed his whole world. And what did his unfaltering loyalty to a flower do to him? It gave him a new radiance, a halo, invisible but palpable. "The image of the rose [is] shining within him like a flame within a lamp, even when he's asleep," said the pilot (69). He was a boy in love, vibrating with desire and yet strangely at rest. He had found what he was looking for.

On that cool March morning, after the rude cop let us go, we received a "rose" – and then another four years later, on a hot July midday. Each of those roses, Nathanael and Aaron, said to us, "Would you be so kind as to tend to me?" – well, not in those words, but in the piercing and relentless cries of a baby hungry for food, for touch, for tender and soothing words, for the presence that delights, for time and space to grow; in a word, cries of a baby hungry for love. So we tended them, and out of millions of little boys, they became our boys, unique and more precious to us than all others put together.

Like our sons, all of us were a gift when we were born – a peculiar yet most beautiful of gifts, a gift that at first only receives, a gift that gives back only the joy parents might feel in giving and the delight they might experience in the child's flourishing. Often enough, tiredness chokes up joy, and worry extinguishes delight. But still, most parents do their best to give, and they do so knowing well that their gifts will never be returned in full, but perhaps will be paid forward, that children will give to their own children or to others they encounter on their life's journey.

We know it is good to receive, and we have been blessed by receiving not only as children, but also as adults. Yet Jesus taught that it is *more* blessed to *give* than to receive (Acts 20:35), and part of growing up is learning the art of giving. If we fail to learn this art, we will live unfulfilled lives, and in the end, chains of bondage will replace the bonds that keep our communities together. If we just keep taking or even trading, we will squander ourselves. If we give, we will regain ourselves as fulfilled individuals and flourishing communities.

But giving is difficult. So how can we find the ability to give? Giving is also a fine art. How should we do it? And when enlightened egoism seems the most rational thing to adopt, giving can seem pointless. Can it be rendered meaningful? It is to these questions, beginning with the last, that we turn in the first part of this book.

Chapter 1

GOD THE GIVER

In *The Brothers Karamazov*, Fyodor Dostoyevsky tells a story about an old peasant woman, very wicked, who died without leaving a single good deed behind. All she did, she did for herself alone, illicitly taking what she could take and acquiring by legitimate means what she could acquire, but not giving anything to anyone, nothing useful or beautiful, no helpful deeds, not even a kind look. After she died, the devil seized her and plunged her into the lake of fire. The story continues,

> So her guardian angel stood and wondered what good deed of hers he could remember to tell to God; "She once pulled up an onion in her garden," said he, "and gave it to a beggar woman." And God answered: "You take that onion then, hold it out to her in the lake, and let her take hold and be pulled out. And if you can pull her out of the lake, let her come to Paradise, but if the onion breaks, then the woman must stay where she is." The angel ran to the woman and held out the onion to her. "Come," said he, "catch hold and I'll pull you out." He began cautiously pulling her out. He had just pulled her right out, when the other sinners in the lake, seeing how she was being drawn out, began catching hold of her so as to be pulled out with her. But she was a very wicked woman and she began kicking them. "I'm to be pulled out, not you.

It's my onion, not yours." As soon as she said that, the onion broke. And the woman fell into the lake and she is burning there to this day. So the angel wept and went away.[1]

Some may read this story naïvely, as a recipe for how to get into paradise with minimal effort. If you do just a single good deed, God will pull you on the slender thread of that generosity out of the lake of fire. But the deed must be good, given to others in true generosity. If you do it just for yourself, just to get you out of hell, the thread will break, and you'll end up licked by flames for eternity.

If this wonderful story were a recipe for getting into paradise, it would be a bad one. True, it would get one thing right. God, here personified in the guardian angel, is immensely good even to the wicked. God seeks to save them and weeps when they are desperately stuck in their sin. But it would get the main thing wrong. It's not by our generosity, however slender, that we are saved, at least not according to the Christian tradition. We are saved by *God*'s generosity.

But the story isn't about how to get into paradise as much as about how to avoid hell – not the fiery lake at the end of one's life and of the world's history, but the hell in the here and now, whose flames are made up of greed, selfishness, cold calculation, pride, indifference, exclusion, and many such things. No life worth living is possible without generosity. Indeed, it is doubtful whether the tender plant of newborn human life would even survive without generosity.

Yet from the get-go, we seem to be but one bundle of cravings that screams for satisfaction of needs that appear to go unfulfilled and for interests that feel threatened from all sides. That's the big fissure in the life of human beings, individually and collectively – a yawning gap between deep self-centeredness and true generosity.

Can we bridge the gap? We can, if we can show that in all our self-centered cravings, we are ultimately craving love – which is to say, craving both to receive love and to give it. Such recognition would be the first part of the bridge on which we could travel from the land in which even what looks like generosity is a form of self-centeredness to a land where generosity is our true self-interest. But how can we construct such a bridge? We can't construct it using secular materials – or at least, I haven't seen it happen so far, and I can't imagine how it could. It takes God to make such a bridge, a God who is love, a God who gives and forgives, a God who created human beings to find fulfillment in love. This chapter – this book as a whole – is an attempt to construct such a bridge, and it is an invitation to then walk from one side to the other, from self-centeredness to generosity.

So the first and central question is, Who is God?

Images of God, Reality of God

There is God. And there are images of God. And some people don't see any difference between the two.

A capable, good-hearted, and devout servant by the name of Félicité from Gustave Flaubert's "A Simple Heart" fell prey to this confusion between God and God's images. She was alone and unappreciated, and her parrot Loulou became "almost like a son, a lover to her", so much so that, when he died, she had him stuffed. Soon the gospel's image of the Holy Spirit as a dove began to merge with her stuffed parrot, and she fell "into the idolatrous habit of saying her prayers on her knees in front of the parrot". Finally, Flaubert wrote, as she breathed her last, "she thought she saw, as the heavens opened, a gigantic parrot hovering over her head."[2] Abandoned by others, she transferred her love to the parrot, transforming it into a god. An earthly image morphed into a divine reality.

Most people who fuse God's image and God's reality aren't nearly so naïve. Some, like great critics of religion, argue that God is simply a projection of human ideals onto a heavenly screen; that God is, as Karl Marx thought, a reflection of the human need to be consoled in misery and to cope with weakness. For them, God doesn't exist as a reality independent of human beings. "God" is the name that the foolish, the miserable, and the weak give to what is nothing more than a useful figment of human imagination.

I will leave these critics aside here, and instead focus on what is perhaps the most troubling confusion between God's reality and God's image, which falls somewhere between the naïve Félicité and the shrewd Marx. It's believers who fall prey to this confusion. We don't see them kneeling before parrots. Neither do they trumpet, "God is a human projection." They don't brazenly say, "God doesn't exist; only images of God do." To the contrary, they piously affirm, "God is a reality independent of our minds" and "God is nothing like a parrot, or any other creature."

And yet they worship idols without even knowing it. Unlike Félicité's parrot, their gods are not made of the hard matter of this world and don't sit elevated on sacred pedestals. Instead, they dwell in their worshipers' minds and are made of the soft stuff of their own cherished ideas. They simply assume that who they believe God to be and who God truly is are one and the same. God is as large (or as small) as they make the Infinite One to be, and none of the beliefs they entertain about God could possibly be wrong.

But in fact, our images of God are rather different from God's reality. We are finite beings, and God is infinitely greater than any thoughts we can contain about divine reality in our wondrous but tiny minds. We are sinful beings, and God is different from what we conceive in our selfishness and pride. Finite and self-centered as we are, we often forget God's warning through the prophet Isaiah: "For as the heavens are higher than the earth, so are my ways higher than your ways and my thoughts than your thoughts" (55:9). When we forget that, we unwittingly reduce God's ways to our ways and God's thoughts to our thoughts. Our hearts become factories of idols in which we fashion and refashion God to fit our needs and desires.

Yet the most powerful and seductive images of God are not the ones we craft in the privacy of our hearts. They are the ones that seep into our minds as we watch TV, read books, go shopping at the mall, or socialize with our neighbors. Slowly and imperceptibly, the one true God begins acquiring the features of the gods of this world. For instance, our God simply gratifies our desires rather than reshaping them in accordance with the beauty of God's own character. Our God then kills enemies rather than dying on their behalf as God did in Jesus Christ. To use Flaubert's metaphor, the dove of the Spirit becomes the parrot whose plumage bears a striking resemblance to our culture's values.

To worship *God* rather than idols of our own making, we must allow God to break apart the idols we create, through the Spirit's relentless and intimate work within our lives. First, we need to know where to look for knowledge of the true God. It would be a mistake to seek that knowledge primarily in the world around us. God is not an object in this world. There's no map that says "X marks the spot." Whatever we find in the world will be ... the world, and not God. Neither can we find God in the infinity that lies beyond the cosmos. God is not an unnamed something on the other side of the temporal and spatial edges of the universe. Rather, as Christians, we find God in Jesus Christ, God's Word incarnate as witnessed in the Scriptures, God's written word.

It's not enough, however, to know where to look for God. We also need eyes and ears that can recognize the true knowledge of God when we come across it. For it could be that even as we look at Jesus Christ and read Scripture, as the prophet Isaiah put it, we "keep listening, but do not comprehend" and "keep looking, but do not understand" (6:9). Think of people who observed Jesus teach and heal and embody the life of God – and they saw nothing but a "false prophet" or a "political rebel". Our eyes and ears need a heart ready to receive the truth of God's reality rather than one that longs for the comforts of false gods.

Finally, even when we look in the right places with a ready heart, we still might miss the one true God. We need to be willing to let our very effort to know God slide out of our hands, opening them to God's continued and unexpected self-revelation. Otherwise, like the dog from Aesop's fable, we may end up dropping the real piece of meat in order to grab its reflection in the water.

Two false images of God are particularly irresistible to many of us – mostly unconsciously. The first I'll designate as *God the negotiator* and the other, *God the Santa Claus*. Though we have fashioned both to serve our interests, they are each other's opposites. With one, we want to make advantageous deals. From the other, we want to get warm smiles and bagfuls of goodies. We run from one to the other. Some of their features are reminiscent of the God of Jesus Christ. But we've drawn these images of God mostly from two currents of the culture in which we swim – the current of hard and unforgiving economic realities, in which we exchange goods to maximize benefits, and the current of soft, even infantile, desires, in which we long to be showered with gifts simply because we exist.

God the Negotiator

There is a scene in the movie *Amadeus* in which the renowned Viennese composer Antonio Salieri, as a boy, kneels before a crucifix and tries to make a bargain with God: "Lord, make me a great composer! Let me celebrate your glory through music – and be celebrated myself. Make me famous throughout the world, dear God! Make me immortal!" What will God get for doing him the favor? "In return I vow I will give you my chastity – my industry, my deepest humility, every hour of my life. And I will help my fellow man all I can."[3] He was offering God a deal: I'll sacrifice for you, and in return you'll fulfill my desire for immortality and glory.

Why did Salieri even think that God would consider such a proposition? Because, like many of us, he must have believed that God is a negotiator. We propose to do something for God, and God in turn agrees to do something for us. Alternatively, God demands something of us, and if we do what God demands, then God gives. This is the way God is, such reasoning goes. God is basically a negotiator.

We don't think very far ahead when we embrace the image of God as negotiator, however, because if that really were the case, human beings would always end up with a raw deal. For one thing, God doesn't need anything we have to offer. God can walk away from any proposition. And as any negotiator knows, it is impossible to strike a good deal under these conditions. When Salieri offers God his chastity, industry, and humility in return for musical genius, God can tell him, "I've got something you want, but you've got nothing I need," and then proceed to give musical genius to Salieri's nemesis, a young brat by the name of Wolfgang Amadeus Mozart.

Second, even if we could entice God into making a deal with us, we would have no way of enforcing compliance. Since God doesn't need anything and divine power infinitely exceeds human, God can break any contract – give us a bit of "cash" as compensation, and leave us out in the cold.

We are at a disadvantage if *we* are the ones trying to obtain something from God – if it is we who say, "I'll give you this (devotion) in exchange for that (musical genius)." But that's not the end of our disadvantages if we basically see God as a negotiator. Before we even think of offering anything to God, God has already made demands on us, tough demands. Take, for example, the law of Moses as encapsulated in the Ten Commandments, a summary of God's will for humanity. It was a heavy burden for the people of Israel. Even though God gave it for their well-being, it proved to be too difficult for them to fulfill, and we today find it daunting as well.

If we see the God of Jesus Christ as negotiator, we'll experience the law of Christ as an even heavier burden than the law of Moses. In the Sermon on the Mount, Christ intensified the Old Testament commands and interpreted them to refer to inner states, not just outward acts: He intensified the prohibition against murder into the command not to be angry (Matthew 5:21–23); he transmuted the prohibition against adultery into the command not to lust (Matthew 5:27–30); he expanded the command to love one's neighbor to include the command to love one's enemies (Matthew 5:43–47). Even tougher than the Ten Commandments, what Jesus is urging upon us in the Sermon on the Mount is nothing less than to be "perfect ... as your heavenly Father is perfect" (Matthew 5:48). Clearly an impossibility for mere humans! And yet if we had to relate to God as a negotiator, we would have to be divinely perfect before we could fulfill our end of the bargain and receive anything from God.

But God is not a negotiator. It is true that Scripture portrays God in ways remarkably similar to that image. In the Old Testament we read, for instance, "If you will only obey the LORD your God ... all these blessings shall come upon you and overtake you, if you obey the LORD your God" (Deuteronomy 28:1–2). Yet before the commandments were given to the people of Israel, God delivered them from slavery in Egypt. But it wasn't to get something out of them.

They were delivered for the simple reason that God heard their cries of affliction, kept the promises made to their ancestor Abraham, and through deliverance and faithfulness wanted to manifest the greatness of God's love in the world.

Why did God give the commandments to a people already delivered from slavery? To get their obedience so as to be able to reward them with good things in return? The commandments themselves are in a sense "rewards", given not for God's sake, but for the sake of people's well-being (see Deuteronomy 10:13). They are not arbitrary rules. They trace the way of life as distinct from the way of death.

In *Amadeus*, Salieri ended up as a bitter old man, angry at God, angry at the world, angry at himself – to the point of attempting to take his own life. The entire course of his life rested on the deal he thought he made with God. That God proved to be, as he put it, "wicked", giving him "thirty-two years of meaningless fame" only to thrust him into permanent oblivion.[4]

In fact, however, no deal had ever been made between them. Salieri had made a proposition to God as he was kneeling under the cross. But God never took him up on it. Why? Because the God hanging on the cross for the salvation of the world is not a negotiating God! On the cross, God is not setting up the terms of a contract that humans need to fulfill in order to get what they want. Neither is God saying on the cross, "I died for you, now you've got to do what I tell you." Instead, as we will see in chapter 4, on the cross God's own self is given for the sins of humanity.

God's goods are not for sale; you can't buy them with money or good deeds. God doesn't make deals. God gives.

God the Santa Claus

We know that we are at a disadvantage in trying to make deals with God. Size and strength matter. So we run to a God who will shower us with gifts. We want God to be our heavenly Santa Claus.

A week or so before Christmas, I was walking with my two young sons toward the village green in our town of Guilford. As we turned the corner, we saw a tall and imposing Santa Claus, black boots, red suit, white beard, rosy cheeks, and all. Aaron, my two-year-old, who knew who Santa was but had never seen a live exemplar, grabbed my pants and started pulling back, terrified of this huge and unusual apparition. Nathanael, my six-year-old, exclaimed, "No, Aaron, no! Don't be afraid! This is Santa! He'll give us something!" And sure enough, for no other reason than for their showing up, Santa gave them some candy.

Santa gives. He doesn't lay down any conditions prior to giving the gifts, even if parents lamely try to warn little imps that Santa gives only to good boys and girls. After dispensing his gifts, Santa makes no demands. With a bottomless bag of goodies, he comes out of nowhere – well, almost nowhere. And after granting everybody's wishes, he returns to nowhere.

Some scholars of popular religion describe Santa as a god of consumerist materialism whose sole purpose is to give. And indeed, many people think of God in this way, as a Santa Claus conveniently enlarged to divine proportions. God is an infinitely rich, always available, and unfailingly generous giver – or at least, that's what we feel a god worthy of divinity ought to be. God gives without conditions and without demands. As the sun shines and a spring flows, so God gives – solves our problems, fulfills our desires, and makes us feel good. A Santa Claus God demands nothing from us. A divine Santa is the indiscriminately giving and inexhaustibly fertile source of everything that is, and everything that is to come our way.

God *is* an inexhaustibly fertile source of everything. But is it true that God demands nothing? If it were true, how could Jesus urge us, as he does in the Sermon on the Mount, to be perfect as God is? Here is what we do as worshipers of a Santa Claus God: We embrace the conviction that God is an infinitely generous source of all good, but conveniently forget that we were created in God's image to be in some significant sense like God – not like God in God's divinity, for we are human and not divine, but like God "in true righteousness and holiness" (Ephesians 4:24), like God in loving enemies (Matthew 5:44). To live well as a human being is to live in sync with who God is and how God acts.

If it weren't for our propensity to sin, we'd live like God lives, just as little bears live the way mother bears do. Sadly, however, in some mysterious way, it is possible for us to think, act, and exist contrary to the ways God does. In fact, without exception, all of us live contrary to God. As I will explain shortly, we betray thereby who it is we were made to be in relation to God and one another. For this reason, and in light of our God-given purpose to mirror who God is in the world, the infinitely generous God in whose image we were created becomes for us the God who demands. As a help to our frailty, God gives a law that says, "You should ..."

Unlike Santa, God doesn't just scatter gifts, smiling in blissful affirmation of who we are and what we do no matter who we happen to be and what we happen to do. God also urges us to do this or not to do that. And as we will see in chapter 4, God's face twists in the pain of disappointment and even frowns in angry condemnation when we fail to live as we ought to, bringing devastation to ourselves as well as to those around us.

God generously gives, so God is not a negotiator of absolute dimensions. God demands, so God is not an infinite Santa Claus. So what is the relation between God's giving and God's demanding? In other words, what is the difference between a Santa Claus God and a gift-giving God? The bare-bones answer is this: a Santa Claus God gives simply so we can have and enjoy things; the true God gives so we can become joyful givers and not just self-absorbed receivers. God the giver has made us to be givers and obliges us therefore to give. Let me explicate this thought.

God the Creator

"*Daaad*, where's my milk!?" says the child, peeved that the glass is not in his hand as soon as he tells his dad he's thirsty. The little boy expects food as soon as he needs it, and if he doesn't get it right away, he is miffed. To him, "May I", "Please", or "Thank you" are unnecessary. He demands because moms and dads, he thinks, are there mainly to serve him; the black hole of his childish self-absorption seems bottomless. He has yet to learn that much of what good parents do for him springs from their generosity. They don't, strictly, *owe* it to him.

But his dad, too, often makes a mistake similar to the boy's. He forgets that his own food along with everything else, including that beautiful even if demanding child, is not somehow owed to him. It's God's creation. It's God's gift. That thought occurs to him occasionally and vaguely. But then it happens. He is surprised by a stunning sunrise with which a particular new day greets him – a spectacular canvas strewn with incredible colors, golds, blues, oranges, grays, and mauves of altering shades and shapes. Or perhaps he sits, perched above the turquoise Adriatic Sea, in the pine forest by the chapel of St. Jerome on the Croatian island of Ugljan, and delights in the strange glow of the sun's evening rays caressing the ground through the trees. Such moments of almost palpable grace are, for those who have eyes to see, a window into the nature of creation itself. It's not just "there". It's *given* by God. As the apostle Paul wrote with simplicity and force at the culmination of his letter to the Romans, "from him [God] and through him and to him are all things" (Romans 11:36).

But does the Apostle really mean that *all* things are gifts from God? Even things we have plundered from others? Even our perverse pleasure in mistreating them? Is the Apostle like Agha in Nikos Kazantzakis's *The Greek Passion*, the cruel lord of Lycovrissi? Agha thought the good God has showered the world with perfect gifts. "If you are angry, He's made the whip and the *raia's* [non-Muslim subject's] buttocks. If you're depressed, He's made the *amanes* [melody]. If, lastly, you want to forget all the sorrows and worries of the world, He's made Youssouflaki [a pretty boy]."[5] No, clearly for the Apostle, the source of moral evil lies within us, and not with God.

Or does the Apostle think that all pain and suffering are God's gifts? Has he never seen an illness cripple a beautiful and fruitful life at the peak of its strength? Could he never imagine a tsunami taking a beloved child – oh, so many beloved children! When such things happen, what seems like a gift turns to poison. The Apostle was very much aware of the poison; he felt it even in his own sick and mistreated body. And he did not believe it came from God, though he was persuaded that God can redeem every situation (see Romans 8:28–39).

If, like the Apostle, we believe in a good and all-powerful God who gives, we can't see why there should be such horrendous evils as plague our world. God ought to have been able and willing to prevent them. Yet if we don't believe in a good and all-powerful God, we can't protest against those evils. That's then what the world simply is, a place in which tectonic plates shift, volcanoes erupt, immune systems break down, and big fish eat the small. We can then mourn our losses but have no reason to expect anything better. We feel caught between a rock and a hard place.

Is evil, whether humanly caused or natural, God's gift? It is not. Evil just inexplicably is. God didn't create it. It's a twisting of God's creation, a negation of its original goodness, and therefore an assault on God. In the end, God will finally and definitively overcome evil. And even now God is engaged in countering it. Just as God was mysteriously in the Crucified One, God is in the midst of humanity's suffering, listening to every sigh, collecting every tear, resonating with the trembling of every fear-stricken heart. Just as God was in the Resurrected One, God is in each helping hand, in each act of self-sacrifice, in each life laid down for another, and God occasionally even heals and protects without any human mediation. God suffers and God helps.

God works against evil and suffering. But God, in immense divine power and inscrutable divine wisdom, also works *through* evil and suffering. In Romans 5, the apostle Paul made a puzzling comment about "boasting" in his suffering (v. 3). What's there to boast about, as if suffering were a fortune he's inherited or a prize he's won? Would not bemoaning suffering be more appropriate? But he had an eye not just for the undisputable evil that suffering presents, but also for the good that God can bring about through suffering, as the death of Jesus Christ whom God has raised from the dead demonstrated. For the God who resurrects, nothing is the end.

The poison of evil and suffering cannot undo or even overwhelm the goodness of creation. To the extent that the world is unspoiled by evil and sin and remains God's good creation, to the extent that God uses even evil to create something good, things in the world are God's gifts – sunsets and swamps, calm seas and tempests, the honey and the sting.

Let me give you an example from my own life of how a sting can be a gift.

The Gift of Infertility

Can infertility be a *gift*!? Poison and a curse – that's how an unexplained infertility of ours felt to me for what seemed like an eternity. Nine years of trying to have a child of our own was like having to drink bitter waters from a poisoned well month after month. Nothing could break the sinister hold of barrenness on our lives, not strict adherence to whatever expert advice we could get, not prayer, not the latest infertility techniques, not fasting, nothing. One hundred months' worth of hopes, all dashed against the stubborn realities of bodies that just wouldn't produce offspring. At times, like Abraham, we hoped against hope, and yet the God "who gives life to the dead and calls into existence the things that do not exist" (Romans 4:17) wouldn't help our bodies give us an Isaac of our own.

Christian community wasn't much help either. Every time we would go to worship, the laughter and boisterousness of the little ones milling around in the community room would remind me of unfulfilled dreams. The season of Advent was the worst. "For unto us a child is born, unto us a son is given," I would hear read or sung in hundreds of different variations. But from me a child was withheld. The miracle of Mary's conception, the rejoicing of the heavens at her newborn child, the exultation of Elizabeth, all became signs of God's painful absence, not God's advent. "And the government shall be upon his shoulders ..." If God's Son indeed was in charge, it seemed that he didn't care to move even his royal finger in our favor. At Christmas, I felt like a child in a large family, the only one to whom parents had forgotten to give gifts. Others' joy increased my sadness. "And his name shall be called, 'wonderful, a mighty God ...'" No, not wonderful; at best, puzzling. No, not a mighty God; at best, a sympathetic but disappointing divine observer.

Then came the absolutely unforgettable moment when a nurse rolled two-day-old Nathanael into the room of Lisa, his birth mother, in a maternity ward in Chino, California. She took him into her arms for a moment, then gave him to us to be our own – the most incredible of gifts! And then Michelle, Aaron's birth mother, let my wife Judy witness the miracle of birth, the birth of Michelle's own flesh and blood whom she gave to us as our son. Nathanael was then four. Later that day, as the tender and awestruck big brother, he cradled tiny Aaron in his arms. As I watched them, my joy as a father was complete.

During those nine years of infertility, I wasn't waiting for a child who stubbornly refused to come, though that's what I thought at the time. In fact, I was waiting for the two boys I now have, Nathanael and Aaron. I love *them*, and I want *them* in their unsubstitutable particularity, not children in general, of which they happened to be exemplars.

Then it dawned on me: Fertility would have robbed me of my boys. From my present vantage point, that would have been a disaster – the disaster of not having what I so passionately love. Infertility was the condition for the possibility of these two indescribable gifts. And understanding *that* changed my attitude toward infertility. Since it gave me what I now can't imagine living without, poison was transmuted into a gift, God's strange gift. The pain of it remains, of course. But the poison is gone. Nine years of desperate trying was like one long painful childbirth, the purpose of which was to give us Nathanael and Aaron. True, had we had biological children of our own, I would have loved and wanted them, and I would have been spared the pain. But that's what *would* have happened. It didn't. I have Nathanael and Aaron. It's *them* that I love. It's *them* that I want. And it's *they* who redeem the arduous path that led to having them.

So what will happen with the poison that spoils God's good gifts? God will either turn it into medicine or remove it completely. The gifts will remain – which are we ourselves and everything that surrounds us.

Breath

Earlier I wrote that it is disadvantageous for us to treat God as a negotiator, both because God needs nothing that we have and because God asks more than we could ever give. If all things come from God, we can see that it is also *unwise* to treat God as a negotiator. Just before declaring that all things are from God, the apostle Paul asked rhetorically, "Or who has given a gift to him to receive a gift in return?" (Romans 11:35). The correct answer is no one. No one has given a gift to God first, and no one will receive a gift as a reciprocal gesture. The argument is terse but watertight: If all things come from God, then nobody can give anything to God in a way that obliges God to give in return.

In many ancient religions, sacrifices served to sustain gods. Gods would die if not nourished by humans. And if gods needed sacrifices, then sacrifices could extract things from the gods. To get what they needed, gods would give what humans desired. Not so with the one God, according to the apostle Paul. No sacrifice can extract anything from God, because everything given as sacrifice came from God in the first place. To give to God is to take from God's right hand and put that very thing back into God's left hand.

That's not always obvious. Some of us may protest, "But I've worked very hard. I've learned my multiplication tables and done my piano lessons; I've finished college and gotten a fine job; I've furnished a house, raised a family, and supported the poor. I've received a great deal, but I've achieved something too! Though I am not 'a self-made man', I've made something out of myself! Can't I give to God from what I myself have attained?" The argument is good – to a point.

Here is how the argument is good. The second story of creation in Genesis is fascinating in the role it ascribes to human beings in God's ongoing creative activity. It gives two reasons why "in the day that the LORD God made the earth and the heavens" no "plant of the field was yet in the earth and no herb of the field had yet sprung up". The first reason has to do with God: "for the LORD God had not caused it to rain upon the earth". The second reason has to do with human beings: "and there was no one to till the ground" (Genesis 2:4–6). The simple story makes a profound point: For creation to exist as a habitat for humanity, both God and human beings have to do their parts. Human beings cooperate with God in the work of creation.

It would seem then, that human beings *can* contribute something of their own, and not just receive from God. And yet that conclusion isn't quite right. The same story of creation continues, "then the Lord God formed man from the dust of the ground, and breathed into his nostrils the breath of life; and the man became a living being" (Genesis 2:7). In other words, the very existence of human beings comes from God. We live, not so much on a *borrowed*, but on a *given* breath. We work, we create, we give, but the very ability and willingness to work, along with life itself, are gifts from God.

Moreover, these are not just gifts we can take and then run with on our own. They are gifts that, like breath, must be given over and over for us even to exist, let alone accomplish anything. "What do you have that you did not receive?" asked the apostle Paul rhetorically (1 Corinthians 4:7). The answer is: nothing, absolutely nothing.

Most of us don't quite "get" the extent of God's gift giving, even if we grasp it intellectually. We live more or less like Raleigh Hays, the hero of Michael Malone's novel *Handling Sin*. He was a decent citizen and a responsible family man who "obeyed the law and tried to do the right thing" and who thought he had secured for himself the decent middle-class life he led. He was wrong. Through a series of unlikely events, he had to be shaken into awareness that some "grace had *given* him, for no earthly reason, like surprise presents, everything, absolutely everything, he'd thought he earned, and sustained by his own will, and deserved".[6] To come to believe that God has given us "absolutely everything" is to know what it means that, as creator, God is a giver.

Denying Gifts, Wronging the Giver

In addition to the story of creation, Scripture tells the story of redemption. As I have noted earlier, human beings are not just creatures of God; they are sinful creatures too. So God ends up giving not just as a creator, but also as a redeemer.

Here is roughly how sin works in relation to God the giver. All things are from God and through God, and yet we want to be independent of God, standing on our own two feet, claiming God's gifts as our own achievement. The young Karl Marx, barely twenty-six years old, put this sentiment as boldly as possible. In a text that remained unpublished during his lifetime, "Economic and Philosophical Manuscripts", he gave an expression to the heart of his rebellion against God:

> A being only counts itself as independent when it stands on its own feet and it stands on its own feet as long as it owes its existence to itself. A man who lives by grace of another considers himself a dependent being. But I live completely by grace of another when I owe him not only the maintenance of my life but when he has also created my life, when he is the source of my life. And my life necessarily has such a ground outside itself if it is not my own creation.[7]

Marx held firmly to human independence. It almost seemed to him a value that lies at the bottom of all values. Because the reality of God as creator is incompatible with human independence, he denied the existence of God.

Most of us, especially the believers among us, won't deny God's existence in order to secure our independence. Instead, we think that we can have it both ways. We believe that we can stand on our own two feet, independent of God, and still affirm that God is the creator of everything. But that doesn't make sense. We can be both dependent on God and free; dependence on God is the source of our being, and therefore, our freedom. But we can't be created by God and independent; God sustains creatures in being and in freedom.

When we assert our independence, when we ascribe to ourselves what comes from God, we *wrong* God – at least as much as I would wrong an author whose ideas I would peddle as my own. That's our main sin against God the giver. If, like Raleigh Hays, we see ourselves as more or less honest, hardworking citizens, we may believe that we deserve what we have, and even a bit more because an evil world is cheating us of our proper reward. We might not feel particularly grateful for what we have because we think that, rather than receiving it, we earned it. And we want to dispose of our hard-earned goods the way we please; they become not so much gifts given to us to enjoy and pass on, but rather our exclusive possessions.

Assertion of independence, pride of achievement, sense of entitlement, an absolute right to dispose with our goods – these are the ways in which we live in contradiction to who we actually are in relation to God. And in these ways, we, decent citizens, live as inveterate sinners. To live in sync with who we truly are means to recognize that we are dependent on God for our very breath and are graced with many good things; it means to be grateful to the giver and attentive to the purpose for which the gifts are given.

God the Redeemer

At this point, we might expect for God to step back in as a hard negotiator. After all, in treating gifts as achievements and entitlements, we have failed dismally as recipients. Shouldn't the giver *deprive us of gifts* – at least, future gifts – if we can't even recognize them as gifts and instead claim them as our own well-earned possessions? A human giver might see it that way. But God acts differently. God continues to give, refusing to make giving dependent on our receiving things rightly. Indeed, since our very existence is a result of God's grace, if God were to stop giving, we would stop existing.

Willing as God is to continue giving even after we have failed as recipients, shouldn't God at least want to recast the relationship? "You don't know what it means to receive gifts," God might say, "so from now on, I'll give only if you face up to what you've done and act responsibly. First, you've got to get yourself out of the deep hole dug by your sin, and then if you live up to my standards, you'll get the appropriate rewards."

But there is no way for us to crawl out of sin's hole. Indeed, the very attempt to crawl out on our own only sinks us in deeper. That may seem a strange claim. But if God is the source of all our good, then God must be the source of our freedom from sin. When we attempt to free ourselves on our own, we deny the true source of our goodness and *wrong* God by claiming for ourselves what is God's. We sin by trying to overcome sin on our own. In the words of the Apostle, we "nullify the grace of God" and declare that "Christ died for nothing" (Galatians 2:21).

Similarly, fulfilling God's law cannot be our own achievement for the simple reason that, in relation to God, *nothing* is our own achievement. That's why the great Protestant reformer Martin Luther wrote, "Though you were nothing but good works from the soles of your feet to the crown of your head, you would still not be righteous or worship God or fulfill the First Commandment, since God cannot be worshiped unless you ascribe to him the glory of truthfulness and all goodness which is due him."[8] Nothing we can do can either get us out of sin's hole or prevent us from falling into it. Only God can.

Then what does God do with us? We mishandle God's gifts and fall short, and God gives us more – the gift of freedom from the guilt and power of sin. "Since all have sinned and fall short of the glory of God," wrote the apostle Paul, "they are now justified by his grace as a gift, through the redemption that is in Christ Jesus, whom God put forward as a sacrifice of atonement by his blood, effective through faith" (Romans 3:23–25). God gives gifts, God cancels the debt we incur by improperly receiving them, and then God gives us the ability to receive gifts properly.

Luther's God

As both creator and redeemer, God is an infinitely rich and most generous giver who receives nothing in return. In chapter 2, we will see that there is an even more basic way in which God gives. In God's own eternal life apart from the world, gifts circulate among the Holy Three who are the Holy One. They give and they receive. In relation to the world, however, God's gifts only flow out.

No one in the whole Christian tradition has championed this thought with more force than Luther – force borne out of desperation before the negotiator God of his tormented youth. He is known for his rediscovery of God's justification of the ungodly. Instead of rightfully condemning sinners, God, rich in mercy, bestows righteousness upon sinners, justifying them irrespective of their merits or demerits. But at the heart of justification of the ungodly is God's generous love. As both creator and redeemer, God is a pure giver.

One of the more profound statements ever made by a Christian theologian is the final thesis of Luther's *Heidelberg Disputation*, written in 1518, barely six months after he had nailed his epoch-making Ninety-five Theses on the Castle Church door in Wittenberg. The Ninety-five Theses were a call to arms against church abuses. The final thesis of the *Heidelberg Disputation* summed up the "ideology" that generated the call. Luther formulated it as a contrast between two kinds of love, human and divine: "The love of God does not find, but creates, that which is pleasing to it. The love of man comes into being through that which is pleasing to it."[9]

Consider, first, what Luther calls human love, but which is better described as distorted love. It's elicited by the object of love; it's basically passive in the sense that it depends on the object of love. Its only activity, says Luther, consists in "receiving something" (57). A person sees beauty – or goodness or truth – and wants to have it. As a consequence, people who love in this way seek their "own good" in those they love; they don't bestow any good on them. A man may shower a woman with gifts, but he may be doing it so that he can ingratiate himself to her, enjoy her, keep her, or even worse, so that he can display her as a trophy. When we love in this way, we are receivers, not givers.

Contrast this kind of possessive love with divine love. First, divine love never had to come into being at all; it wasn't elicited by its object. It simply is. It doesn't depend on the truth, beauty, or goodness of the beloved. Second, as Luther stated, because God's love isn't caused by its object, it can love those who are not lovable, "sinners, evil persons, fools, and weaklings in order to make them righteous, good, wise, and strong". Luther concluded, "rather than seeking its own good, the love of God flows forth and bestows good".

Such divine love is supremely manifested on the cross on which Jesus Christ took the sin of the world upon himself. "This is the love of the cross, born of the cross, which turns in the direction where it does not find good which it may enjoy, but where it may confer good upon the bad and needy person" (57). Unlike merely human love, divine love gives and doesn't receive.

Some theologians claim that all God's desires culminate in a single desire: to assert and to maintain God's own glory. On its own, the idea of a glory-seeking God seems to say that God, far from being only a giver, is the ultimate receiver. As the great twentieth-century theologian Karl Barth disapprovingly put it, such a God would be "in holy self-seeking ... preoccupied with Himself"[10]. In creating and redeeming, such a God would give, but only in order to *get* glory; the whole creation would be a means to this end. In Luther's terms, here we would have a God demonstrating human rather than divine love.

But we don't have to give up on the idea that God seeks God's own glory. We just need to say that God's glory, which is God's very being, *is* God's love, the creative love that wants to confer good upon the beloved. Now the problem of a self-seeking God has disappeared, and the divinity of God's love is vindicated. In seeking God's own glory, God merely insists on being toward human beings the God who gives. This is exactly how Luther thought about God. So should we.

Yet, have I now come full circle, inadvertently embracing God the Santa Claus, who gives without demanding anything? No, and the difference is this: Unlike gifts received from Santa Claus, whose gifts are the end of the story, God's gifts *oblige* us to something further. To what do God's gifts oblige us? What is the nature of obligation? Let's examine the second question first.

God, Gifts, and Obligations

Some gifts come to recipients with no strings attached. I fill a Samaritan's Purse box with goodies and send it to a distribution center to be passed on to a needy child, and I expect nothing from the recipient, not even a "thank you". But many gifts oblige recipients in one way or another. There was a cartoon in the *New Yorker* a few years ago showing two couples standing in the foyer by the front door. One couple was about to leave after having been guests of the other. The caption under the cartoon read: "Since we are not into payback dinners, would $80 be acceptable for a reasonably pleasant evening?" In most cases, a gift in some sense asks the receiver for a "payback"; it requires a counter-gift.

Some people disagree. A true gift is an utterly free gift, a pure gift, they argue. If you attach an obligation to it, you undo the gift. It's no longer a gift, but a loan. But in reality, that's not how we mostly use the word "gift". In our everyday lives and in most literature, including the texts of Holy Scripture, a pure gift is one kind of a gift, not the only kind. Most gifts are not pure, given without expectations; of human gifts, possibly none are pure.

If we expect a return, no matter how subtly or hopefully, then how is gift giving different from loans and contracts? It is different not because obligations are absent but because they are neither exacted nor specified in advance. Before I give you a gift, I can't tell you what I want in return and when; if I did, I wouldn't be giving a gift but proposing a deal. But a gift that I give calls for a return gift – a different and possibly even greater gift to be given back at a later time. Is this expectation of return also true in regard to God's giving?

As we have seen, we cannot give God anything that *obliges* God to give us something in return. To oblige God to reciprocate, we'd need to give something to God before God gives to us. But everything we have is from God. As the original giver, God always gives and never returns gifts; that's why, in principle, Salieri cannot get musical genius from God in return for his chastity and industry. Our "gifts" cannot oblige God in any way. But do God's gifts oblige us in some way? They do – but not in the way a dinner invitation obliges us to have our hosts over for a "payback" dinner.

Let's first examine our obligations to human givers. When we issue an invitation to our hosts a week or so later, we are offering them a counter-gift. The initial gift has pulled us into a circle of gift exchanges. In the world of ancient Greece and Rome, this circle was imagined as a dance of three sisters called the Three Graces: one bestows gifts, another receives them, and the third returns them. "Why do the sisters hand-in-hand dance in a ring which returns upon itself?" asked the first-century Roman political leader and philosopher Seneca in his famous treatise on gifts. He replied, "For the reason that a benefit passing in its course from hand to hand returns nevertheless to the giver; the beauty of the whole is destroyed if the course is anywhere broken, and it has most beauty if it is continuous and maintains an uninterrupted succession."[11] The circle will close. Benefits will return. They will return in what is, of course, an altered form. It is in poor taste to give your friends the same bottle of wine they gave you! A different bottle or a bouquet of flowers, however, is still a return.

But the circle cannot close in regard to God. We cannot return benefits to God for the simple reason that everything we return to God was God's to begin with. "But parents give money to children so that the children can give parents gifts," someone might reason. "In this way, children acquire means of expressing their affection for parents and learn to give." The analogy between a parent and a child doesn't go very far, however, in illustrating God's giving to us. The parent has parted with money after giving it to the child; it is now the child's and at the child's complete disposal. But that's not how God gives.

Consider what Luther said about God the creator: "He is, however, not like a carpenter or architect who, after completing a house ... turns over the house to its owner for his residence ... and then goes away ... God the Father initiated and executed the creation of all things through the Word ... He remains with His handiwork until He sees fit to terminate it."[12] When God gives, it's not a transfer of goods. We receive things from God not because God takes them from here (where God happens to be) and places them there (where we happen to be), but because God is present where we are and is continually giving to us all the things and abilities we have. To return something to God would be like pushing back to the giver the hand that gives.

There is a second reason why we cannot return benefits to God. God already has everything. God enjoys unsurpassable plenitude and lacks nothing that a gift from humans would satisfy. If we cannot return anything to God, does this mean that God cannot receive anything from us? Scripture tells us that God can and wants to receive. But rather than receiving something God needs but doesn't have, what God receives is delight – the lover's delight at the sight of the beloved whose very existence is that lover's gift. What God also receives is pain – the lover's pain when love has been betrayed.

The gifts of the divine Lover move downward to humans. The image that Luther used consistently is that of flowing: "The love of God flows forth and bestows good," he wrote in the *Heidelberg Disputation*. Liquids flow in one direction only, from here to there, but not back again. The movement is unidirectional.

If we cannot return benefits to God, then how can obligations to God be attached to God's gifts to us? Right after the statement at the end of Romans 11 that all things are *from* God, *through* God, and *to* God, and that no one has given a gift to God *first* so as to oblige God to reciprocate, the apostle Paul began Romans 12 with the following injunction: "I appeal to you therefore, brothers and sisters, by the mercies of God, to present your bodies as a living sacrifice, holy and acceptable to God, which is your spiritual worship" (12:1). So the God who gives is the God who expects a sacrifice, and the expectation of a sacrifice is grounded in the gifts received: "I appeal to you *therefore* ..." In other words, "You've received; therefore you should present a sacrifice." What then is this sacrifice that is neither a gift nor a counter-gift to God? To what do God's gifts oblige us and why? Let's explore these questions step by step, starting seemingly from afar. As we proceed, a contour of a bridge between our selfishness and our God-based giving will emerge.

Faith

God's gifts oblige us, first, to a posture of receptivity. Rather than wanting to earn God's gifts (if we imagine God as a hard negotiator whose demands we have to satisfy) or receive them in return for some favor (if we imagine God as a patron on whose generosity we depend), we should see ourselves as who we truly are, namely, receivers and receivers only. We do that by relating to God in faith. The first thing to which God's gifts oblige us is faith.

It may seem strange to say that we are *obliged* to faith or to a posture of receptivity. After all, gifts should be freely received just as they should be freely given. Even when it comes to contractual relations, we are not obliged to receive any benefits. Contracts oblige one party to give specified benefits to the other party, but they don't oblige anyone to receive those benefits. A party to a contract can refuse benefits without breaking the contract. It is punishments that we are obliged to receive, not gifts. And if someone obliges us to receive gifts, they will not feel like gifts. Why is it that God's gifts oblige us to receive them, whereas human gifts have no such obligation attached to them?

To want to earn benefits from God or to receive them as payback gifts is to say three wrong things at once: (1) God is a negotiator God; (2) we can give something to God in exchange for something we want; and (3) we are agents independent of God who can relate to God any way we find to our liking. None of these things is true, however. God is not a negotiator but a pure giver. We can give nothing to God but have received everything from God. Finally, we are not independent of God but are living on a given breath. To fail to recognize these three things is to live blindly and to claim God's gifts as our own achievements. To recognize these truths is to understand ourselves as who we truly are, fundamentally receivers.

And that brings us to faith. Faith is not something we give to God. In that case, faith would be a work, and a silly kind of work because it would be work we do even though it doesn't benefit anyone. But exactly the opposite is true. To have faith in God is to be "without works" before God (Romans 4:5). Faith is the way we as receivers relate appropriately to God as the giver. It is empty hands held open for God to fill. That's why, as Luther put it, faith "honors God"; it tells the truth about God and our relation to the divine Giver and ascribes to God what is due. In contrast, good works offered to

God dishonor God; they tell a lie about God and our relation to the divine Giver, and they take away God's due.[13]

Beggars hold their hands open in a posture of expectant receptivity. The last words that a tired, sick Luther wrote at the end of a very full and influential life were, "We are beggars – that is true."[14] These words may strike many of us today as despondent and resigned. In contrast, we moderns prefer to see ourselves as achievers rather than beggars. Begging is humiliating, and we will abase ourselves to beg only when we are at the very end of our ropes. To us, it makes no difference whether we beg from neighbors or from God. But for Luther, that made all the difference. To receive *from God* in faith is the height of human dignity.

"Human dignity!?" someone may ask, raising eyebrows in puzzlement or even protest. "It feels like faith diminishes us! It seems to underscore our inability rather than our power!" But that feeling of diminishment and humiliation comes from wrongly conceiving our relationship to God. If we were independent from God the way we are independent from each other, and God expected us just to receive, God would be like an overbearing father who always knows better and will not let his daughter do anything on her own. But we are not independent in relation to God. Our power to be and to act comes from God. Faith merely recognizes this. Hence faith doesn't tell us how little we are and what we can't do. On the contrary, it celebrates what we most properly are – God's empowered creatures – and it frees us to our greatest accomplishments.

Faith tells us that we do not exist simply to live our three score and ten years without pain, with ease and enjoyment, to accumulate possessions, power, or knowledge, to receive accolades and enlarge our egos. How empty such life would be! Faith is an expression of the fact that we exist so that the infinite God can dwell in us and work through us for the well-being of the whole creation. If faith denies anything, it denies that we are tiny, self-obsessed specks of matter who are reaching for the stars but remain hopelessly nailed to the earth stuck in our own self-absorption. Faith is the first part of the bridge from self-centeredness to generosity.

Gratitude

Second, God's gifts oblige us to *gratitude*. The apostle Paul finished his long "motivational speech" to the Corinthians about giving to the poor in Jerusalem with the exclamation, "Thanks be to God for his indescribable gift" (2 Corinthians 9:15). Whenever a gift is given, gratitude is appropriate. God gives. We thank God. The Apostle did not use the word "obligation", but it is surely implied. Gratitude is *due* to the giver – whether human or divine.

But isn't gratitude a gift we give back to the giver? Don't we even speak about "returning thanks"? If gratitude were a gift, when we thank God we would be giving something back. But as we have seen, giving back to God is impossible. Since many people think of gratitude as a return gift, it pays to ask whether that's true.

What would happen if gratitude were truly a return gift? First, a grateful person would be under no obligation to reciprocate beyond giving gratitude. We would part with our hosts who have entertained us with a fine meal, thank them profusely, and that would be the end of the matter. But it's not, or it shouldn't be. We feel obligated to return the favor, to entertain them, to send flowers, or to offer some other gift.

Second, if gratitude were truly a return, those who reciprocated would be under no obligation to be grateful. We could just invite our hosts over and could dispense with saying "thank you" for having been invited to their home. But we can't. We owe gratitude to the giver, whether we reciprocate or not. Gratitude is not a return gift but is owed in addition to that gift.

When we "give" thanks, we impart nothing to givers. What is it then that we owe to the giver when we owe gratitude? When we are grateful, we *express our appreciation* of the fact that they have given to us. Of course, we may then go on to do something for them *out* of gratitude. But that's not gratitude; that's a *sign* that we are grateful.[15] It is similar with our gratitude toward God. Those who thank God tell the divine Giver that they appreciate the gifts received; they honor God for that.

Gratitude toward God is the corollary of faith in God. When I have faith, I *affirm* explicitly that I am a recipient of God's favors, and implicitly I recognize and affirm God as the giver. When I am grateful, I recognize and *honor* God explicitly as the giver, and I implicitly recognize and affirm myself as a recipient of God's gifts. In a way, faith and gratitude are two sides of the same coin. At the same time, there is a certain progression from faith to gratitude. Faith receives God's gifts *as gifts*; gratitude receives them *well*.

"Say 'thank you'!" we urge a child who has happily received a gift and then wants to run off to enjoy it. "No, you can't just run off; you have to say 'thank you'!" "No, you can't just mutter it under your breath!" "No, you can't turn away as you say it; you must look the person in the eye!" "No, you can't just get it over with quickly; you must mean it!" These are some early lessons in saying "thanks". They all work against an almost inborn reluctance to express gratitude.

Gifts can help and delight us. Gifts can also wound our pride. They can create a relationship of dependence or inferiority and an uncomfortable sense of a vague obligation. It's often humiliating to receive. Ralph Waldo Emerson exaggerated, but not much, when he wrote, "We do not quite forgive the giver. The hand that feeds us is in some danger of being bitten."[16] And if it is humiliating to receive, it is even more humiliating to express *appreciation* to the giver. Even as adults relentlessly trained in proper decorum, we often feel awkward when saying "thank you".

That's how it is between human givers and receivers, especially if the givers are rich and powerful and the recipients are poor and weak, and even more so if the rich and powerful are bad givers, seeking to humiliate and unduly oblige the beneficiaries of their largesse. Such gifts do not benefit, they lacerate.

It's different with God. True, God is infinitely richer and more powerful than humans. But God and human beings do not occupy the same space. We are not competitors for the same goods. It makes no sense to compare ourselves with God as we compare ourselves with one another and feel small if we are poor or incompetent in comparison with someone else. God is incomparably greater – on a completely different plane than we are. God's gifts do not lessen human beings. Human beings *exist* because of God's gifts – not merely in the sense that they would cease to exist if God did not give, like a starving child if it did not receive nourishment, but in the more significant sense that their very existence is a result of God's giving.

God's gifts don't diminish those who receive them. They don't come with the message, "You are small and insignificant, and I am big and important." God's gifts establish. They come with the message, "You are loved, and therefore you exist." With that message, gratitude becomes easy because it is not primarily gratitude for getting what we lacked and could have acquired ourselves if we were not so insignificant, but gratitude for the wonder of just being there as fruits of God's creativity and objects of God's blessing.

Availability

The first two obligations inscribed in God's giving – faith and gratitude – result from the *fact* that God is a giver. Faith recognizes and affirms, and gratitude appreciates that everything that we are and have comes from God. But there are two more ways in which God's gifts oblige us, and they have to do with the *purpose* for which God gives. True, God gives so that we can exist and flourish, but not only for that. God gives so that we can help others exist and flourish as well. God's gifts aim at making us into generous givers, not just fortunate receivers. God gives so that we, in human measure, can be givers too.

Toward that end, God's gifts call on us to make ourselves *available* to their Giver. Recall that the apostle Paul described gratitude as something we "give" to God. And yet nothing is given when we thank God. Similarly, when the Apostle spoke of human availability to God, he used the language of giving. He praised Macedonian Christians for having given "themselves first to the Lord and, by the will of God, to us" (2 Corinthians 8:5). Is favor transferred when we give ourselves to the Lord? It's not. We're simply living the way God created us to live. We can't give anything back to God, not even ourselves, since we were never our own in the first place. We live and breathe and have our being in God. The most we can do is to make ourselves available for God to be used as instruments.

Notice that, in making ourselves available, we are not doing God any favors. We give ourselves for God's *use* to benefit creation, not to benefit God. That's what it means to be a "living" sacrifice, which the apostle Paul urges Christians in Rome to become (Romans 12:1). A sacrifice is normally dead, given in ancient religions to benefit gods by nourishing and sustaining them. But that would be a sacrifice that a negotiator God required. God the giver requires a living sacrifice, ready to do God's work in God's world.

In this way then, does God still "get" something God would otherwise not have? The self offered to God and the work done by the self in the world? In a sense, yes. But what God gets is precisely what God created: human beings as God's instruments. We shouldn't think of God as the unfortunate parent of a spoiled child who feels that the child has done her a particular favor when he has done his homework. Even if our availability delights God, it is God's gift to us and to the world, not our gift to God.

What does this kind of availability mean for us? At one level, it means that we don't pursue our own purposes in the world but are ready to pursue God's. *God sets the purposes* and commands us to realize them; we listen to what God desires and are at hand to be at the divine Commander's service. At a deeper level, availability means that we don't live in the world as we see fit, but are willing to be and act in the world as we see God being and acting. *God provides the model*, and we are ready to observe and imitate.

But God's setting of purposes and providing the model for us are external aspects of a much more intimate relation between God and human beings. For in relation to human beings, God is primarily neither the commander-in-chief, nor the governing archetype. And in relation to God, human beings are primarily neither obedient subjects, nor faithful imitators. God is too close to us to be mainly our commander or our archetype. Even though God is radically transcendent – no, *because* God is radically transcendent – God is closer to us than we are to ourselves, to use a phrase from

Augustine, the great church father from the fifth century. God is not just outside us. God is in us. And God's main way of relating to us is to indwell us and to work through us. Francis of Assisi prayed in the prayer he himself composed: "Make me an instrument ..."[17] To have this prayer answered is to be available for God.

Today most of us want to be agents, not instruments. We want to act, not to be acted upon, not to be used by another who acts. We are afraid that as instruments, we would be reduced to mere means. Didn't the great eighteenth-century German philosopher Immanuel Kant teach us that we should always treat human beings, ourselves included, as ends and never as mere means?[18] To be available for God, to be made an instrument for God, is to be available for mistreatment – or so it might seem at first glance. But is that really the case? The answer depends on what it means for God to use us. And this brings us to the fourth obligation.

Participation

Recall that when Luther described the nature of God's love, he used the metaphor of flowing. God's love does not suck out the good it finds in others, as distorted human love does. It "flows forth and bestows good".[19] The metaphor of flowing reveals the outbound and unidirectional movement of God's gifts.

What happens to the flow when it reaches us? Does it then stop, having bestowed the gift and fulfilled its purpose? If the flow were to stop, we would be only receivers, not givers. We would then be unlike what is most divine in God. God would be a pure giver, and we would be no givers at all; we would receive from God, but instead of giving, we would only acquire through legitimate exchange or take by force. But we were created to be and to act like God. And so the flow of God's gifts shouldn't stop as soon as it reaches us. The outbound movement must continue. Indeed, in addition to making us flourish, giving to others is the very purpose for which God gave us the gifts. To pass them on, participating in God's gift giving, is the fourth thing to which God's gifts oblige us.

In his 1520 text, *The Freedom of the Christian*, in which Luther offered a summary of Christian faith, he again picked up the metaphor of flowing, applying it not just to God, but to human beneficiaries of God's favor as well.

> Good things flow from Christ and are flowing into us. He has assumed us and acted for us as if he had been what we are. These good things flow from us on to those who have need of them so that we should lay before God our faith and righteousness that they may cover and intercede for the sins of our neighbor which we take upon ourselves, and so labor and serve them as if they were our very own.[20]

We are not simply the final destinations in the flow of God's gifts. Rather, we find ourselves midstream, so to speak. The gifts flow into us, and they flow on from us. From Christ, gifts flow to us, each one of us; from us, they flow to those in need. As Christ "acted for us" as "if he had been what we were", so we cover the sins of our neighbor "as if they were our very own". We are simultaneously receivers and givers. We receive from Christ, and we give to and receive from each other.

To express this idea, Luther used the image of the conduit: We are channels of God's gifts to our neighbors. The image is good, except that a conduit merely conveys goods and does not benefit from them. We, on the other hand, benefit from the goods, as well as bestow them on others. Which is to say that we don't just receive the gifts, but we are constituted and changed by them.

Luther believed that Christ – or rather, God in Christ – is the source of gifts and the model for human giving. He made one more crucial step in describing the relation between God's giving and ours. Christ, he believed, is also the agent of our giving. Our giving is, as it were, an echo of his. That's where the idea of the "indwelling Christ" comes in.

The apostle Paul wrote, "I have been crucified with Christ; and it is no longer I who live, but it is Christ who lives in me. And the life I now live in the flesh I live by faith in the Son of God, who loved me and gave himself for me" (Galatians 2:19–20). Believers' lives are paradoxically both their own ("the life I now live") and not their own ("it is no longer I who live") but rather Christ's ("it is Christ who lives in me"). It is not just that Christ sends the goods to flow *into* us; Christ makes the goods flow *from* us as well, truly indwelling, motivating, and acting through us. That's Luther's point when he made what seems like a strange claim, namely that a Christian is a "Christ" to others. "Surely we are named after Christ, not because he is absent from us, but because he dwells in us; that is, because we believe in him and are Christs to one another and do to our neighbors as Christ does to us."[21] The flowing of God's gifts from us to others is the overflowing of those very gifts that Christ brought into us with his presence. The flow of gifts both in and out of us happens when we receive the one Gift of God: the Christ who dwells in us and works through us.

The idea of the Christ who indwells us helps us solve the potential problem with being God's instruments, namely, the possibility of being reduced to mere means. Notice that here God is not like a carpenter using a hammer – a lifeless and purposeless tool. We are also not just a hammer endowed with life and will. Even then we would be mere means, only now with our consent. That would be better than being used without our consent, but not by much.

Luther described the way God works in us in a memorable phrase: God never works in us without us. What does it mean for God to work both in us and with us? Through indwelling us, God enters the very core of our selves, the place from which we direct our will. God is in the "space" of "I" that says, "I want this" or "I don't want that." It is I who wants, thinks, and does, and at the same time it is Christ who acts in and through me. The apostle Paul expressed the idea with the metaphor of dying and rising. The old self has died and a new self is born – a self in whom the gift-giving God lives and bestows goods on others. Christ doesn't circumvent our will; we don't give apart from our will. We are no lifeless tools in Christ's hand. Christ doesn't bend our will; we don't give against our will. We are not reluctant and grumbling servants of Christ. The indwelling Christ makes us willing givers. We are cheerful participants in Christ's giving to the world.

But now hasn't our very self disappeared and been replaced by Christ? What else could the death of the self mean? In fact, however, it has not disappeared at all but has been reborn as a new self, as a self that has been returned to itself. Christ's indwelling presence has freed us from exclusive orientation to ourselves and opened us up in two directions: toward God, to receive the good things in faith, and toward our neighbor, to pass them on in love. A Christian, concluded Luther in *The Freedom of the Christian*, "lives not in himself, but in Christ and in his neighbor ... He lives in Christ through faith, and in his neighbor through love."[22]

But why shouldn't one live "in oneself"? Isn't that what the self is supposed to do? Not really. It's just what the self *likes* to do. The self will lose itself if it simply lives in and for itself. It will seek only its own benefits, and the more it seeks its own benefits, the less satisfied it will become. That's the paradox of self-love: The more you fill the self, the more it echoes with the emptiness of unfulfillment. Living in itself and for itself, the self remains mysteriously unsatisfied and insatiable. Since God creates the self to be indwelled by Christ, that self will be fulfilled only if it draws the living water from the wellspring of love's infinity and passes it on to its neighbors. The paradox of true love is exactly the opposite of the paradox of self-love: When loving truly, the self moves outside of itself to dwell with God and neighbor, and only then is it truly at home. When this happens, we have crossed over from self-centeredness to genuine and fulfilling generosity.

God's Life in the Everyday

The thought of God's life flowing through us is a lofty one. When we dare to entertain it, we often think of sacred times and spaces in which we encounter God. When we are rapt in glorious music of worship, when we are deeply immersed in prayer, or when we kneel in front of the altar to receive the Eucharist – in moments such as these we feel that God is close to us, that somehow God is in us and that we are in God.

We are right, of course, to associate God's presence with such times and places. God dwells in the praises of people (Psalm 22:3). God's Spirit prays in us when we pray, sometimes "interced[ing] with sighs too deep for words" (Romans 8:26). And Christ is truly present as we receive his body and blood. But these are not the only times and places when we experience God's life in us.

Notice what happens to the flow of God's life if we think of it as limited to such sacred events. It is streaming into us, but for the most part it is not flowing through us on to others. We may pray in the eucharistic prayer, "Deliver us from the presumption of coming to this table for solace only and not for strength; for pardon only, and not for renewal." But if we don't turn from facing God, so to speak, to face our neighbors, the flow of God's gifts will be arrested with us, and we will miss the purpose of the strength and renewal that come through the Eucharist. It is as we serve our neighbors – our family, friends, and acquaintances – that the dam holding the flow of gifts is lifted and the life of God continues its intended flow.

This service can happen during sacred times and in sacred spaces, when the community is gathered for worship. All members of the community are endowed with spiritual gifts to serve one another, whether through teaching, exhortation, works of mercy, or any other way God may see fit (1 Corinthians 12). Yet God's gifts flow to others above all when the community scatters, having been nourished in God's presence, when we are back home with our families or at work as carpenters, bankers, doctors, waiters, or teachers. Every word and every deed, every thought and every gesture, even the simple act of paying attention can be a gift and therefore an echo of God's life in us.

You sit on your couch, beer or soda in your hand and junk food by your side watching TV for hours – that's ordinary. You work around the clock not because you have to feed your family, but for no other reason than to park a better car in your garage than your neighbors have – that's ordinary. You get up from the couch to play with your kids or you give your time and energy to help educate a prisoner or lend an ear to an elderly person – that's extraordinary. Why? Because you are giving. Every gift breaks the barrier between the sacred and the mundane and floods the mundane with the sacred. When a gift is given, life becomes extraordinary because God's own gift giving flows through the giver.

Chapter 2

How Should
We Give?

There were once two brothers. One was rich and the other poor. The poor one was a peasant and toiled while tilling the land, growing turnips and other vegetables. As it happened, one of his turnips grew so enormous that it took a cart drawn by two oxen to transport it. He didn't want to eat it, and he didn't want to sell it, so he decided to give it as a present to the king. The king marveled at the extraordinary object and suggested the peasant must be very lucky. "Oh, no," said the peasant, "lucky I am certainly not. I am a poor man tilling the earth. I have nothing, and I am forgotten by all." The king pitied him and gave him plenty of gold, land, fields, and flocks.

When his wealthy brother heard what riches his poor sibling had acquired with a single turnip, he envied him and pondered how he might acquire more than his brother did. Instead of a single turnip, the brother presented the king with gold and horses, hoping for a larger gift than his brother's in return. "The king took the present," the fairytale continues, "saying that he could give him in return nothing rarer or better than the huge turnip. So the rich brother had to put his brother's turnip into a cart and have it taken home."[1]

One way to read the story would be to say that the poor brother gave a selfless gift to the king and received a fortune in return. His older and wealthy sibling wanted to enrich himself by giving a gift and ended up with a more or less worthless object. Alternatively, we could also question the purity of the poor brother's gift. With his extraordinary turnip, he may have tried to ingratiate himself to the king and succeeded. He wasn't giving to honor the king but to manipulate him into giving in return. He was giving as selfishly as his brother but was simply shrewder. Under the guise of giving, they were possibly both trying to get.

We give gifts in many situations and for many purposes, and like the gifts of one or both brothers, many of them aren't gifts at all. For instance, we want to grease the wheels of bureaucratic machinery made rusty by corruption, so we slip an envelope under the table. We want to deliver an insult disguised as kindness, so we act like the cartoon character who sees a sign in a shop window "Things no one wants" and says to a friend, "Let's get her a little something." We are exploiting a person and want to keep on doing it, so we give gifts hoping to mask the truth of the relationship. We want to harm a person and, like Judas, betray him with a kiss. We want to show our superiority, so we throw an extravagant party, the mother of all parties (as in one recent case, where an ice sculpture in the form of Michelangelo's *David* spouted vodka from its male appendage). Or the force of habit just pulls us along, as when we reluctantly exchange gifts for Christmas.

When we give like this, giving has obviously gone bad. But it need not be this way. So how should we give in order to give well? Before we try to answer this question, let's first make some distinctions.

Taking, Getting, Giving

Natalie Davies distinguishes between three basic modes in which we relate to one another: the coercive mode, the sales mode, and the gift mode.[2] The coercive mode refers to various forms of theft. In this mode, we *take* what is not ours and what is not being offered to us. Armed with insider information, we sell our stock before it tumbles down, and the hapless buyers take the loss. Or to use a more innocent example, at work we slip a pen into our pocket and take it home.

The sales mode refers to the market of buying and selling. Here we give something in order to *get* a rough equivalent in exchange. I need a bike, and I pay money to the shop owner in exchange for it. Or instead of giving money for goods, I barter: I swap the skis my son has outgrown for a pair of longer ones.

Finally, the gift mode refers to relations between donors and recipients. Here we *give* favors that we don't owe and the recipients don't deserve. If recipients return favors, they do so unforced, after a time lag, and in a different form. I give a book to a friend for his birthday out of appreciation for his friendship and maybe with the vague thought that he might remember my birthday – though hopefully not by giving me the same book I gave him! In the coercive mode, we take illicitly. In the exchange mode, we acquire legitimately. In the gift mode, we give generously.

We find the same basic categories at work in Scripture. Ephesians 4 shows us how to order our lives, how to live as new selves rather than as old. In the process of contrasting the old life and the new, the text speaks briefly to all three modes mentioned – taking, acquiring or getting, and giving. In particular, verse 28 reads: "Thieves must give up stealing; rather let them labor and work honestly with their own hands, so as to have something to share with the needy." Thieves illicitly take what is not their own. They violate those from whom they steal, robbing them of their goods and overriding their very personhood.

We sometimes take blatantly. Like Frank Abagnale, a protagonist in the film *Catch Me If You Can*, I might live a life of fraud and illicit gain by pretending to be a Pan Am pilot, a doctor, a lawyer, and a sociology professor, and in the process cash in $2,500,000 in fraudulent checks. But there are also more subtle ways of being a taker. For example, if I refuse to work while still availing myself of what I need – food, shelter, clothing, or even more – I am taking unfairly. Of course, I may be unable to work. Then others are obliged to support me. But if I am able to work and refuse to, I am taking illicitly. Hence the command "Anyone unwilling to work should not eat" (2 Thessalonians 3:10) – a bit of Holy Scripture that found its way even into the officially atheist Marxist constitution of the former Soviet Union. Takers, says Ephesians, must become getters.

Getters exchange goods. Most often they give work to their employers, who give them wages in return. That's what honest work means: You get what you put in, no more, no less. If you get less than what you put in, then either you were generous to your employer or your employer was stealing from you. If you get more than what you put in, then either you were stealing from your employer or your employer was generous to you.

Takers should become getters, but getters in turn should become givers. The point of exchanging work for goods or pay, says Ephesians, is not just to satisfy our own needs without having to steal, but to help others in need. One important purpose of work is "to have something to share with the needy". To be a getter and to be a giver are not mutually exclusive alternatives. To the contrary, unless wealth has fallen into our laps, to be givers we must also be getters. It takes work to give, whether what we give is money, useful goods, or our undivided attention.

We give away some of what we have earned, say, 10 percent of our income as the Old Testament law specifies, and hopefully a bit more. Moreover, our work itself can also be a gift. If I volunteer at a soup kitchen or answer calls for the public radio fund drive, I give "sweat equity". Finally, even when they are paid, the best workers give more than just that for which they receive pay. A piano teacher is a wise and witty expert, in love with music and her pupils. She gets paid, maybe even well, but she gives more than her pay compensates.

Why Give?

But why should we make the shift over to being givers in the first place? Aren't we wired to maximize our profits by whatever means society allows? Or why not stop at being getters, working honestly with our own hands and taking care of ourselves without burdening anyone else?

Ephesians' answer to these questions takes us back to the discussion of the old and new selves at the end of chapter 1. The old self is self-centered; the new self is indwelled by Christ, opened up toward God in faith and toward neighbors in love. Following the apostle Paul in Romans, for this topic I used the metaphor of death and resurrection: The old self has died and a new self was raised (Romans 6:1–11). Ephesians speaks of the old and the new self by using a different metaphor, that of clothing and unclothing: "Put away your former way of life, your old self, corrupt and deluded by its lusts," and "clothe yourselves with the new self, created according to the likeness of God in true righteousness and holiness" (4:22–24). The old self is the worn, frayed, and filthy clothing I want to strip off as soon as I get the chance; the new self is the smart, new outfit, fresh from the store, that I can't wait to put on.

The connection between these two rather different metaphors – the metaphor of passage to new life and the metaphor of putting on a new outfit – is this: *Because* we have died to our old selves and live as new selves indwelled by Christ, we *should* take off the old and clothe ourselves with the new. The unspoken assumption is that the old self is not quite yet dead and the new self is not yet fully alive. Taking off the old and putting on the new is an ongoing process of dying and rising.

At the heart of this ongoing process, Ephesians says, is the *imitation of God*. "Therefore be imitators of God, as beloved children, and live in love, as Christ loved us and gave himself up for us, a fragrant offering and sacrifice to God" (Ephesians 5:1–2). Indwelled by Christ, we imitate God in our own way as frail and sinful human beings.

So why does giving become part of our new selves? The first and primary reason is because the God whom we worship and the Christ who dwells in us are neither takers nor getters, but givers. The second and related reason is because God has given to us so that we would share with others. As I explained in chapter 1, we are not just the intended recipients of God's gifts; we are also their channels. Recall Aslan's gifts to the children in *The Lion, the Witch, and the Wardrobe*. Lucy's cordial, for instance, was for her and her friends: "If you or any of your friends is hurt, a few drops of this will restore them."[3] She was a channel, and so should we be.

Pull apart the idea of being the channel of God's gifts, and you'll see that it involves three intentions on God's part. One concerns us, the givers. Another concerns the gifts themselves. And the third concerns the recipients: our neighbors.

Take, first, God's intention for us. As channels, we exist not just to enjoy things but to pass them on. Our purpose is twofold: to flourish ourselves and to help others flourish. After God called Abraham, God gave him a double promise. The first was: "I will bless you"; the second was: I will make you to "be a blessing" (Genesis 12:1–3). The same double blessing is given to us. If we just enjoy good things without passing them on, if we are blessed without being a blessing, then we fail in our purpose as channels. We *are* givers because we were made that way, and if we don't give, we are at odds with ourselves.

God's second intention concerns the gifts themselves, whether they are material goods (like food or shelter) or immaterial things (like ideas), whether they are skills (like the ability to play music) or capacities (like the brute strength of muscles). To the extent that we are their intended final recipients, we should enjoy them and benefit from them. They are the stuff of God's blessing to us. These gifts are given to us to please us and, in a sense, to do with them as we please.

To the extent that we are channels of gifts, however, we can't just do with them as we please. They come to us with an ultimate name and address other than our own. Though in our hands, they are on their way elsewhere. The acts of enjoying the gifts ourselves while still passing them on often coincide, as when we play music in the company of others or discuss a fascinating issue with friends. We then enjoy what we give. But at other times, we must decide whether we should enjoy *or* give, as when locusts devastate crops in Mauritania and I can either purchase a new bike or give a donation to help relieve a dire need.

Finally, being a channel involves God's intentions for our neighbors. Things I am given are not just mine. Even if they are in my hands, some of them belong to my neighbors in need. I have an obligation to pass them on. If I block the flow of God's gifts, I haven't just failed the giving God; I've also failed the intended recipients.

They have a right to the gifts, and I have the obligation to give. Both their right and my obligation rest on God's giving these things to me to pass them on.

So why give instead of simply enjoying what we have legitimately acquired? One, because we should imitate God the giver, the source of all that we are and have. Two, because we are not just recipients, but also channels of all the gifts God has given us, including our hard-earned pennies.

Imitating God's Generosity

It's a tall order to give as God gives. Can we even do it? It seems just as impossible as giving all the time to everyone who's in need.

In Gotthold E. Lessing's *Nathan the Wise*, a play set in Jerusalem at the end of the twelfth century in the midst of the Crusades, there is a dialogue between Nathan, a wealthy and generous Jew, and Al-Hafi, a dervish and a treasurer of Sultan Saladin, the Muslim ruler of Jerusalem. Saladin hates the fact that people have to beg, so much so "that he sets out to get rid of them [the beggars], even if he has to become a beggar himself".[4] With his treasury empty on account of his prodigious generosity, Saladin sent Al-Hafi to borrow from Nathan. In the course of the conversation, the dervish complains to Nathan about the madness of Saladin's giving. He asks rhetorically, "It wouldn't be foolishness to mimic the gentleness of God, who without prejudice spreads himself over good and evil and plain and desert, in sunshine and rain, and not always to have God's full hand? Well? Wouldn't it be arrogance …?" (36). It's foolish and arrogant even for an opulent Sultan to want to give as God gives. Even he doesn't always have "God's full hand". Al-Hafi must borrow so that Saladin can gratify his proud folly of acting divinely generous.

We are not God, so it follows that when we give, we must give differently than God does. For one thing, God is the *first* giver. For centuries, Christian philosophers have spoken of God as the "unmoved mover" and "uncaused cause". We can say, by analogy, that God is a "non-receiving giver". Just as God causes without being caused, God gives without having received. In the language of those same philosophers, human beings are "moved movers" and "caused causes". Analogously, we are "receiving givers". We give only because we have first received. God gives from what is originally, exclusively, and properly God's own; we give from what is our own because God continually gives to us.

Second, God is the *infinite* giver. God exists without measure and can give without measure. God's resources are never depleted and vitality never sapped. Human beings are finite and can give only in measured ways. Like Saladin's, even the richest human hand empties, and we tire out. And though God gives without ceasing, our own giving must pause; we must rest to revive and replenish.

Third, God is the *utterly loving* giver. God doesn't just love; God *is* love. God bestows goods upon others without any concern for God's own good. True, God jealously guards divine glory. But God's glory is the divinity of God's love, and God's jealousy for God's glory is not so much about God's own good as about the good of the creation. In contrast, human beings are selfish lovers, and are so partly because their own well-being is so fragile. Even when our love is at its purest, we can't avoid somehow seeking ourselves and our own benefit in every gift we bestow.

Derivative, finite, and selfish in all our generosity – that's the kind of givers we are. It seems that we can never give as the primordial, infinite, and utterly loving God gives. And yet, echoing the whole New Testament, Ephesians insists that we "be imitators of God" and "live in love, as Christ loved us" (Ephesians 5:1–2). What can such commands mean? Do they just call attention to our inability and throw us, desperate, into the open arms of God's grace as Luther thought? Yes, but not only that. They also sketch out the way we can actually live when we have crossed the bridge from self-centeredness to generosity.

These commands call us to be similar to, not identical with, God. We are not divine and cannot give exactly the way God does. But we can and should give *similarly* to how God gives. We are created in God's image (Genesis 1:27). Our new, redeemed self is "created according to the likeness of God" (Ephesians 4:24). We can still imitate God the giver with goods we have received, to the degree that our finite resources and limited strength allow and without ever acting in total selflessness. And that's what Ephesians, along with the rest of the New Testament, urges us to do.

Of course, the dangers in imitating God are never far away. Wanting to give without measure, we can bring ruin to ourselves and those close to us. In wanting to give without recognizing our need to receive, we can become arrogant and humiliate those to whom we give. Finally, in foolish pride, we self-centered human beings can end up more like a grotesque parody of the utterly loving God than like God's imitators.

To give as God gives, but in a way that is humanly possible, is a fine art. But it's an art that can be learned because the art itself is one of the gifts God offers to humanity. We can learn to give wisely and humbly. In Ephesians, such giving is part of the task of "learn[ing] Christ" (4:20). Recall Luther's bold statement that we are Christs to one another. Christ is living his life through us because he dwells in us. Just as in Ephesians 4, the idea of Christ's indwelling has been transmuted into the injunction to "clothe" ourselves with Christ, so the idea of Christ living his life through us – the idea that we are Christs – has been transmuted into the call to "learn Christ". Through the power of Christ's Spirit, we can learn to give like God in Christ does.

But what *is* it that we need to learn? How does God give and how should we, as God's imitators, give?

God's Freedom

God gives freely. Take creation, for example. God is under no compulsion to create. Before God creates, nothing exists – nothing greater than God, nothing smaller than God, nothing equal to God, nothing at all. That's what Christian theologians mean when they say that God created the world out of nothing, *ex nihilo*, as the Latin phrase goes. It's not that at the beginning there was a strange something called "nothing" that God used when creating. It would be silly for nothing to be nonetheless something. Rather, absolutely everything that is not God owes its existence to God. As creator, God is a giver, and no person or thing from outside could possibly force the Almighty to create.

Might the compulsion to create come from inside, a critic could press further, from within God's own nature? That's what the great neo-Platonic philosopher Plotinus thought. As Étienne Gilson put it, Plotinus's highest principle, which he called the One, "is what he has to be" and "acts as he has to act on account of what he necessarily is".[5] As creator, Plotinus's God would give because God couldn't do otherwise. For Plotinus, God was more like an "It" than an "I", more like a thing than a person. For Christians, it's the other way around, and that makes all the difference. God is more like an "I" than an "It", more like a person than a thing. God wills and decides. And as God wills and decides, God is free in the narrow but important sense of being self-determined.

Being self-determined cannot be the whole story of divine freedom, however. For then God's freedom would be arbitrary. God would decide this rather than that for no other reason than the inscrutability of divine will. If God were free to create in this way, creation would be as arbitrary as if God flipped a coin to decide whether to create or not. There would be no more reason for the fact that there is something instead of nothing than there is reason for why today I chose to write with a black pen instead of a blue one, or to wear a jacket instead of a sweater.

God's giving is not a whim, however. God gives as creator when the plenitude of divine love turns away from itself toward the nothingness of non-being. Out of abundance of that same love, God the redeemer showers a world gone awry with the gifts of eternal life and deliverance from sin. To be moved by oneself in love is to be divinely free. Moved by oneself, one is not compelled; directed by love, one is not whimsical.

Voluntary Gifts

Since God gives freely, we should too. That's how the apostle Paul thought of gift giving; it should be voluntary. He praised believers from Macedonia for giving "voluntarily" to the poor of Jerusalem

(2 Corinthians 8:3). Similarly, he urged that the Corinthians' gift be ready when he came to collect it "as a voluntary gift and not as an extortion" (2 Corinthians 9:5).

Why is freedom in giving so important? Because the gift consists more in the freely undertaken choice to give than in the things given. In this regard, the Apostle might well have agreed with Seneca, the great Stoic writer on gift giving, who said: "For, since in the case of a benefit the chief pleasure of it comes from the intention of the bestower, he who by his very hesitation has shown that he made his bestowal unwillingly has not 'given', but has failed to withstand the effort to extract it."[6] As for Seneca, for the Apostle the "eagerness" of the giver matters more than the magnitude of the gift. God loves "a cheerful giver" (2 Corinthians 8:12 and 9:7).

And yet we noted earlier that we are obliged to give. God's gifts themselves oblige us, and God's commands reinforce that obligation. Now we see that we are obliged to give freely – and there's the rub. How can we give freely if we are obliged to give? Inversely, how can we be obliged to give if we give freely? Is it possible to be *obliged* to give *freely*?

Well, we're also commanded to love

The apostle Paul thought so. True, he never *commanded* the Corinthians to give, and he underscored this for them (2 Corinthians 8:8). But he exerted enormous pressure on them using some potent rhetorical weapons. He played with their sense of shame: they would humiliate themselves if they didn't give (2 Corinthians 9:4). He had them compete with other donors: the Macedonians gave, so the Corinthians should stick to their promise and give (which is also what he said to the Macedonians in 2 Corinthians 9:2). He appealed to their debt to him: he would be humiliated if they didn't give (2 Corinthians 9:4). And he did all this in order to nudge them to give, as he put it, "not reluctantly or under compulsion", but voluntarily (2 Corinthians 9:7)!

Was the Apostle twisting their arm to be free? Some strange freedom this must be! But maybe our sense that to be free is to act under no constraint whatsoever is mistaken. We tend to think that we must be autonomous and spontaneous to act freely. Behind this identification of freedom with autonomous spontaneity lies the notion of a self-defined and free-floating person. Strip down all the influences of time and place, abstract from culture and nurture, and then you'll come to your authentic core. This core is who you truly are, the thinking goes – unique, unshaped, unconstrained.

But that's more like a caricature of a divine self than an accurate description of a human self. Using the image of the beast, Luther argued that human beings are always ridden by someone, either by God or by the Devil.[7] That's a crude way of putting it, but it's basically right. The point is not that either God or the Devil *compels* us. In that case, our will would turn into, as Luther put it, "unwill". It's rather that, unlike God, we always exercise our will as beings constantly shaped by many factors – by language, parental rearing, culture, media, advertising, and peer pressure, and through all these, we are shaped either by God or by God's adversary. Often we don't perceive ourselves as shaped at all. If we are not visibly and palpably coerced, we think that we act autonomously, spontaneously, and authentically. Yet we are wrong.

Take our preferences for one soft drink over another. I am thirsty, walk into a store, reach for a Pepsi, and walk away, never doubting that I acted autonomously and spontaneously. But why did I choose Pepsi over Coke or just plain water? I may like its taste better. But most likely it's because Pepsi's ads got to me the way Coke's didn't. I don't autonomously and spontaneously choose to be a Pepsi drinker; I'm made into a Pepsi drinker. Yet I freely chose that Pepsi can that is in my hand.

Recall what I said about the old and the new selves. Our old self died, and our new self was raised. It's a self in whom Christ dwells and through whom Christ acts, a self that has put on Christ and "learned" Christ. We *are* these new selves, and that's why we give (though non-Christians can give for many other reasons). We don't give mainly because God or God's messengers command us to. If we did, we would be giving under compulsion, and therefore, reluctantly. Instead, we give because we *are* givers, because Christ living in us is a giver. Informing every seemingly small act of Christian giving is a change in our very being, a transformation of a person from being one who either illicitly takes or merely legitimately acquires, into being one who beneficently gives. As I will explain in chapter 3, even as such transformed people, we still need to grow into the joy of giving. But the command to give is not compelling us to act against ourselves, even if it often feels like this.

That feeling that the command is against us, a sense of reluctance in giving, is not unfounded. When we have failed to put away our "former way of life", the new self becomes an obligation that butts against the ingrained habits of the old self. Yet as uncomfortable as it may feel, the pressure is not to our detriment, but in our favor. It pushes us to act true to who we most properly are. That's why we can be obliged to give freely: the obligation nudges us to do what the new self would do if the old one didn't stand in the way.

Imagine your life as a piece of music, a Bach cello suite. You've heard it played by a virtuoso. You love it and would like to play it well. But try as you might, you fail – not so much because you've had a bad teacher or haven't practiced enough, but because your left hand has a defect. You make music, but it's nothing like it's supposed to sound. Then you have surgery performed by a magician with a scalpel. Your hand heals. You return to your lessons with new vigor. And then one day, you play the piece nearly perfectly. Full of joy, you exclaim, "Yes! I love it! This is the way the music of my life should sound!" Constrained by the score because you have to follow its notation? Well, yes. But loving every moment of that constraint – and not feeling it as constraint at all – because the very constraint is what makes for the beauty and delight.

Something like this is what it means to be a free giver. God obliges us to give. But it is precisely when we act in accordance with the obligation that we have a sense of unspoiled authenticity and freedom. So in our best moments, we forget the command and just give the way we are supposed to give. We are like a motor-powered sailboat when it's "running", as sailors say: With the wind at the back of a powered boat, all resistance is gone; the boat is always where the wind would push it to be. The same is true of us when we give freely. Living out of our new selves, we are always already where the command would want us to be.

The Good of Another

We can give to bribe, to insult or deceive, to pump ourselves up and deflate others, to hide abuse, or for many other similarly ignoble reasons. And when we do, we don't give as we should. Giving has turned into its very opposite, into injury. Under the pretense of wanting to delight, it manipulates. Under the pretense of helping, it wounds. Under the pretense of generosity, it shamelessly takes.

When God gives, God seeks the good of another. As we have seen in chapter 1, this is the nature of God's giving. God doesn't need anything. That's partly what it means to be God – to lack nothing. If giving were a way of getting, God would not give at all; being in possession of all things, God wouldn't need to get anything and so wouldn't give anything. God doesn't give in order to acquire. God loves without self-seeking; that's at the heart of who God is. God gives for the benefit of others.

So should we. Indeed, to give for others' benefit is what it means to give. When we buy or sell, we give money or goods in order to receive one or the other. We engage in the transaction for our own sake; our own good drives the whole process. The same is true when we lend. As a rule, we lend to benefit ourselves. Lenders usually receive more than they give; they lend for profit. Seneca put it well: "He who gives benefits imitates the gods, he who seeks a return [imitates] money-lenders."[8] Givers renounce gain for themselves and bestow it on others.

When do we rightly give? In one of three primary situations. We give when we *delight* in someone. Lovers express and nourish their love by gift giving – a smile, a rose, a caress, a ring – anything, and even the tiniest thing can become a gift. We also give when others are in *need*. A stranded stranger receives a helping hand; we aid the sick or those who were recently laid off from work get what they need. Finally, we give to *help others give*. We give to people who work for good causes in which we believe – we give to educational institutions (maybe to build and maintain a good library) and churches (perhaps to pay their ministers), to relief organizations (say, to help alleviate the global HIV/AIDS crisis) and arts foundations (maybe to help set up exhibitions for young artists). In all three types of situations, we give because we seek the good of another. In all three, we imitate God.

Eternal Gifts

Consider first delighting in another person as a reason to give. So far, in this and in the previous chapter, I have written about God as the giver in relation to the world. God gives as creator and redeemer, for instance. In the process of examining God's relation to the world, I even claimed that God is *fundamentally* a giver, which points beyond God's relation to the world.

God doesn't have to give to the world at all, I argued earlier. God is free to create or not. But once God has created the world, God will always be a giver who seeks the good of the recipient. Why? Because God isn't a giver the way I'm a biker. I bike when I need exercise, when I'm not torpid and the weather isn't bad. God gives continually and unfailingly, because God *is* essentially a giver just as God *is* love. Luther offered a very vivid "definition" of God: God is "nothing but burning love and a glowing oven full of love".[9] That's the character of God's being, not just of some of God's actions. So God is a giver more the way ducks are quackers than in the way I'm a biker.

But what, you will ask, was the essential and eternal giver doing before there *was* a world to shower with gifts? Giving has a very simple and stable structure: someone gives something to someone else. Take one of these three away and you no longer have a gift. The consequence is this: you can't give a gift to yourself. Sure, sometimes we say, "I think I'll give myself a treat!" and proceed to pamper ourselves. But the talk of "giving" in this context is just a manner of speaking. When the giver is one with the recipient, nothing is truly given or received. Before God created, God alone existed. If God is fundamentally a giver, then God must give independently of there being anybody or anything else around. But how?

Christians believe that God, who is one and yet beyond numbering, is the Holy Trinity. God is the Speaker, the Word, and the Breath, to use a formulation based on the beginning of the gospel of

John (1:1–3). The more traditional and perhaps more adequate – or rather, least inadequate – way of talking about God as Holy Trinity is based on the end of the gospel of Matthew: God is the Father, the Son, and the Holy Spirit (28:19). The common name for the three in God is "persons", and it is among the Divine Three that gifts are most originally given. God is a giver apart from creation because God is the Holy Trinity.

Some theologians think of the three divine persons in the way that some ancients thought about the Three Graces of Greco-Roman antiquity – "one for bestowing a benefit, one for receiving it, and a third for returning it".[10] According to this pattern, the Father would give, the Son would receive, and the Holy Spirit would return. It is more likely, however, that each divine person gives, each receives, and each returns. Each loves and glorifies the other two, and each receives love and glory from them. One does not give first, with the result that the others would be indebted, but all give in the eternally moving circle of exchanges. And because they give in this way, they have all things in common except that which distinguishes them from each other. Their eternal bliss is the delight of this loving gift exchange.

In the first chapter, I wrote about the outbound and unidirectional flow of God's gifts. That flow is God's love turned toward the world. It bestows benefits without receiving any back. Gifts flow out. But now we have an image of the perfect circle of God's gift giving that is the very stuff of divine eternal life. Here God bestows benefits and receives them in return. Gifts circulate.

The flow of God's gifts is not aimless spillage. It aims to create human givers and, after they have fallen into sin, to redeem them and finally, to glorify them in perfect communion with God and one another. The flow of gifts is God's arms opened to the world, enabling us to partake of the gift exchange that makes up eternal divine life and supreme divine bliss. This is our best hope for the world to come: to "enjoy God" by receiving divine gifts and to enjoy one another in God in a perfect exchange of gifts with one another.[11] The purpose of the outbound flow of God's gifts is for us to receive living water from God's eternal source, and to thereby come to mirror among ourselves the loving gift exchange of the Godhead. Throughout all eternity, God's gifts will continue to flow to humanity – not so that God will get any benefits in return, but so that we can enjoy the divine giver, and through that giver, delight in one another.

Lover's Gifts

Occasionally, the wonder of the perfect circular movement of gifts happens in the here and now, and between human beings whose lives are deeply marred by sin.

Lovers can experience this wonder in their amorous embraces. They *can*, I wrote. Often they don't. Often enough, sexual union is more like a violent robbery – illicit taking – than it is like generous giving. For the theft to occur, we need not rape someone, nor even seek to dominate and manipulate them with sex. An egotistical seduction – of the kind described in Tom Wolfe's *I am Charlotte Simmons*[12] – in which the body of another is used and then discarded, suffices. Or sex can be like an exchange of goods – each gives to the other, but the object of both is to get what they want, not to give delight to the other. Giving is there, but it exists solely for the sake of getting. In this way, the sexual act is potentially among the most selfish moments in someone's life.

And yet! Sexual union can be a sacrament of love – not just a sacrament of human love, but also a means of expressing and mediating divine love. Pleasure – pleasure of the soul no less than of the body! – given to the other and for the other's sake *is* then a pleasure received. And a pleasure received by the other is, almost paradoxically, a pleasure returned to the giver.

Family and friends, not just sexual partners, can experience among themselves the reality of the divine gift exchange. A good Christmas celebration is an example. True, Christmas gift giving can sometimes degenerate into a caricature of itself. For me, the difficulties begin with shopping. Surrounded by all the glitzy stuff, I can't figure out what I like and what might be appropriate to give, let alone what the other might enjoy. The trouble deepens when the actual gift exchange happens. It so easily turns into a protracted exercise in reciprocal dissimulation: false generosity, phony delights, fake praises, and feigned gratitude.

But most of us can also imagine Christmas gift giving at its best. Shopping is over, thoughtfully chosen gifts are strewn under the Christmas tree, and the long-awaited ritual begins. Each person gives, and each receives. No one gives first so that others feel obliged to reciprocate; all give and receive at the same time, or rather, each receives in turn so that all can rejoice with one another. Each is grateful, each generous, and all are rejoicing in each other's joy. Gifts themselves are no longer just things that people need, like, or desire. They are sacraments of love, both divine and human. By giving gifts, givers offer their very selves. And by offering themselves, they sacrifice nothing, because in giving, they receive more than they grant. The whole ritual is a feast of delight – delight in things given, delight in acts of giving and receiving, delight in persons giving and receiving, and delight in the community constituted and enacted by the whole process.

When we have engaged in such giving, we have tasted the advent of God's new world in which love reigns. What better expression of the spirit of God's advent could there be than a community of joyful givers and grateful receivers? As we will see shortly, the exchange of gifts within community is not the only kind of giving we should practice at Christmas. Gifts should also cross the boundary of the circle. But the communal feast of mutual delight is the best image we have of God's coming new world.

Yet could we make the circle even better? Consider what Ralph Waldo Emerson wrote of true gifts in his famous essay:

> The gift, to be true, must be the flowing of the giver unto me, correspondent to my flowing unto him. When the waters are at level, then my goods pass to him, and his goods to me. All his are mine, all mine his. I say to him, How can you give me this pot of oil, or this flagon of wine, when all your oil and wine is mine, which belief of mine this gift seems to deny?[13]

Here, gift giving has reached perfection only to find that it has canceled itself out. After everything has been given and received, there is nothing more to give, implied Emerson. But that can't be – except in cases in which a good (like knowledge) is one that can somehow be given without the giver losing possession of it. If after having given I still have, then I haven't given; if after having received I don't have, then I haven't received. When I give you a pot of oil, it is yours, not mine; when I receive your flagon of wine, it is mine, not yours. So we can continue to give to each other, and we can enjoy both the goods given and received.

All things are owned in common, and therefore gifts are impossible: that's Marxist utopia. Gifts are most generously given, and therefore all things are common: that's a Christian vision of the world to come. In the life of the eternal God, all things are common because gift giving is perfect. And so it will be for human beings when the living water of God's gifts fully floods their souls.

God's Gifts, Human Needs

The three divine persons delight in one another and therefore give to each other. But delight isn't only the reason why gifts circulate within the Godhead. It's also the reason why God's gifts flow to the creatures. God delights in us, and therefore God gives. Divine delight in creatures is a bit like our delight in our own children – we delight in their feats, their triumphs, or their good looks, but even more basically, we delight in the sheer "that-ness" of their existence. That they *are* delights us. That we *are* delights God. So the divine giver gives – and delights in our delight as well as in our being.

Need is another reason why God gives. Not God's need – God doesn't have any, unless you want to call the fully and eternally satisfied divine desire to love and delight in the flourishing of the beloved a "need". God lacks nothing. It's to satisfy the creatures' needs that God gives. Love spills over the rim of the Trinitarian circle of reciprocity, and gifts flow to creatures.

The creator gives because without that giving we would not even be, let alone flourish. We don't exist out of our own resources but are essentially dependent on God. We are what a philosopher might call *ontologically* needy: our very being is in need of the power to be. The redeemer gives, because without God's giving we could not mend our lives ruined by sin. And that's what a theologian might call *soteriologically* needy: Our salvation and our welfare is our need. The consummator gives, because without God's giving we would return to dust and reap eternal ruin. Again in theological terms, we are *eschatologically* needy: Eternal life is our need. The creator gives existence and grounded trust. The redeemer gives salvation and active love. The consummator gives eternal life and living hope. We need these things. God gives them.

Naked need is the occasion for God's giving, not a need adorned with the clean, elegant robes of respectability and good works. In the latter case, God would be giving on account of merit, and gifts would become rewards. But God doesn't cease giving when our need is clad with frayed and filthy rags of demerit. If we fail to let God's gifts flow to others, a trickle may replace the flow, just as if we let God's gifts flow on to others, the flow may become a gush. But God will still give even to those who don't give, sustaining them and offering even more, despite their failure. God's goodness is dishonored if we want to merit its benefits, argued Luther in *The Freedom of the Christian*.[14] Elsewhere he insisted the flip side of this claim: God's goodness "gladly loses its good deed on the unthankful".[15]

Gifts to the Needy

God "scatters abroad" and "gives to the poor" (2 Corinthians 9:9). So should we. Let's return for a moment to Christmas giving. I described it earlier as a feast of mutual delight in exchange of gifts within the circle of family or friends. But there is something very one-sided about celebrating Christmas only by ritually enacting a community of joyous giving and receiving. Though such a loving community is an earthly good on par with any other, in a world of massive and unrelenting need, it's positively sinful for such communities to remain turned inward. The gifts should not just circulate within the community to delight its members. They should also flow to outsiders to alleviate their needs.

Consider the true gift we celebrate at Christmas, God's advent into the world. Here is how the apostle Paul told the story of Christmas: "For you know the generous act of our Lord Jesus Christ, that though he was rich, yet for your sakes he became poor, so that by his poverty you might become rich" (2 Corinthians 8:9). The Son of God did not dwell among humans just to open our vista onto the circle of blissful exchanges within the Godhead. He divested himself of heavenly wealth and became an impoverished child so the fragile flesh of humanity could be taken up into God's embrace. The circle of the Eternal Intimates opened up, and gifts traversed its boundaries to reach those in need. Our gifts shouldn't just travel on a two-way street so givers and receivers can delight in one another; they should travel on a one-way street so that the needy may be helped, being imparted to those who may not be able to give in return.

At Christmas we should celebrate two kinds of gift giving, not just one. Christmas should be a feast of reciprocal giving in a circle of intimates, a provisional enactment of the advent of God's future world. But it should also be a feast of giving to those outside the circle, a small contribution helping to align the world of sin and need with the coming world of love. The advent of the light into the darkness of the world is not the goal; it is part of the *movement* toward the goal. At Christmas we celebrate this movement. Gifts should therefore chiefly flow out to the needy; they shouldn't largely circulate among friends. *but arent infinitely needy?*

Like God, we should give to the needy without any distinction – to stranger and to kin, to undeserving and deserving. Where the needy come from, what the color of their skin is, or how they behave doesn't matter. Their needs matter, as do their incapacities (though if they are able but unwilling to tend to their own needs, they are illicit takers, not legitimate recipients). It is sometimes hard to decide what exactly constitutes a need. For instance, a need in one place (a wealthy Western nation) may be opulence in another (in sub-Saharan Africa). Different givers may assess a need differently. But whatever the assessment ends up being, when the need is present, a gift should be given, irrespective of whose need it is.

You will recall that in *Nathan the Wise*, Sultan Saladin sought to enlist Al-Hafi, an ascetic and therefore a beggar, as his treasurer, because only a beggar knows how to give to beggars appropriately. To persuade Al-Hafi and to let him know what he expected of him, Saladin disparaged his predecessor: "He gave so ungraciously when he gave; first inquired so vehemently into the situation of the receiver; never satisfied that he was lacking, also wanted to know the cause of the lack, in order to measure the cause stingily against the offering".[16]

For a giver, every need is in a sense like any other need, and the mere fact of its existence is a sufficient reason for attending to it. Only ungracious and reluctant givers inspect the causes of a need and dole out the benefits in proportion to its legitimacy.

Some needy recipients may prove unworthy. They may be ungrateful, they may squander gifts irresponsibly before their genuine need is satisfied, and they may greedily refuse to pass even a crumb from their table to neighbors in more dire need. They clearly need to learn how to both receive and give – though probably not from those who give to them, lest the givers prove to be reluctant and arrogant, and therefore bad givers. Yet if recipients are in need, gifts should be given. Need is the only justification a gift requires.

Giving to All, Giving Everything?

The world's needs are larger than any one person's capacities, though they are not larger than our collective capacities! Our resources are limited, and needs cry to us from all sides. And they all need to be met. But is meeting all needs a responsibility of each person? If that were the case, our responsibility would be nearly infinite and could never be fulfilled. The choice to save one person would be a choice to sacrifice all others![17]

We are finite beings who can't even meet all the needs of a single person, let alone all the needs of all people. There is only "one man" whose gift is meant for all – Jesus Christ (see Romans 5:15–21). My gifts are meant only for some people. God is the primordial and *why that? isn't that lazy? depending on circumstance?*

really? why not love/respect to everyone.

infinite giver, and it is God's responsibility, not mine, to give to everyone. Each of us is only a single channel, one of many through which
God's gifts flow. Our responsibility is to meet needs as we encounter
them, as they come to us in the course of our lives, whether they are
close at hand, as in the case of the Good Samaritan, or far away, as
when the Corinthians helped the Jerusalem poor.

Granted, I am not obliged to give to all people in need. But to
those to whom I do give, should I not give everything I have? Or if
not everything, then how much? Some philosophers suggest that it
contradicts the character of giving to ask that question. Giving, they
suggest, should be beyond all calculation – the complete pouring out
of the giver. Then the only true gift would be "the gift of death".[18]
But God doesn't give only for us to pass it on; God gives so that
we ourselves can exist and indeed flourish – and so that we can be
flourishing rather than languishing givers.

Some of us will find that God hasn't just given us gifts to enjoy
and pass on but also a gift for giving them away. Among many gifts
in the body of Christ that "differ according to the grace given to
us" – gifts such as leadership, teaching, or prophecy – the apostle
Paul mentions the gift of being a giver (Romans 12:6–8). Such givers
may give with "generosity" that is unreachable to most of us (v. 8).
They renounce possessions and work among the poorest of the poor,
they expose themselves to infectious diseases to alleviate suffering,
or they risk their own lives, and are often enough slaughtered like
animals, to bring the Good News into places where Christ may not
yet be named. They give beyond measure, being blessed in blessing
others, but sometimes experiencing themselves as "the rubbish of
the world, the dregs of all things" (1 Corinthians 4:13).

In a fragile and sinful world, we may be required on occasion
to give a "gift of death", as Christ died for our salvation or as a lover
might literally give his life to save the beloved. But how deeply flawed
is the world in which people must give and receive such impossible
gifts! The lover should delight in the beloved, not have to sacrifice his
life so that the beloved can exist! The beloved will stand in heartbro-
ken awe of her lover's passion, for she'd rather have lost her own life

[handwritten at top: "p go why is that a gift - why isn't it a d-ty?"]

than to have gained it at the expense of her lover's life! Gifts of death can make sense only if they are surrounded by the hope of return – return of the lover and the beloved to each other in a world where such gifts have been rendered not only unnecessary, but impossible.

We don't need to give our lives to give truly. It suffices to impart to others more than we owe them without expecting return or basking in our moral rectitude. That's a gift – an ordinary gift but a perfectly good one, even with all the ambiguities of gift giving. Nobody has a right to complain when we give such ordinary gifts – not philosophers of the impossible gift and certainly not recipients. Complaint here would be ingratitude turned insolent.

It's these kinds of ordinary gifts to which the apostle Paul urged Corinthian Christians – gifts that are given "according" to one's means and maybe a bit "beyond" them (2 Corinthians 8:3), gifts that don't relieve recipients by unduly burdening givers, gifts that create "a fair balance" between their "present abundance" and the need of recipients (vv. 13 – 14). How could it be otherwise if the flow of God's gifts to us is meant both for us and for others? We give because God's gifts "flow over" (2 Corinthians 8:2) – they flow over the rim of God's eternal life and over the rim of our own needs.

Giving to Givers

In our finitude, we can't give everything, and we can't give to everybody. What's more, we often can't even deliver what we do have and want to give. We lack skill or time; we can't be in two places at once; our energies are depleted by other things. So we give to those whom we trust will give to the needy. Saladin employed Al-Hafi to do his giving; the Corinthians and the Macedonians pooled their individually insufficient gifts and gave them to Paul and Titus for the Jerusalem poor. Similarly, we employ individuals and organizations to do our giving for us. We give blood to blood banks so it can be distributed when the need arises. We give donations to the Red Cross or World Vision when a major catastrophe strikes. We endow academic chairs so educational institutions can continue their work.

Surprisingly enough, that's how God gives, too – through others, through us. We give through others because we cannot always give directly; we are limited in many ways. God is not limited in any way; God can give directly to all. Yet God does not. Why does God still choose to give through us? Because God hasn't created us to be only receivers, but to be givers as well. Nobody is only a giver, I wrote earlier. Everybody is a receiver too. The inverse is also true. Nobody is only a receiver. Everybody is also a giver.

Earlier I said that insofar as we are the intended recipients of God's gifts, our worthiness is not an issue. God gives because we are needy as well as because God delights in us and in our delight. But is our worthiness an issue insofar as we are intended to be *givers* of God's gifts? It is. If you give what you were given to give, more will be given to you. If you hold onto what you were given to give, less will be given you. Givers "will be enriched in every way for [their] great generosity" (2 Corinthians 9:11); hoarders will lose what they have by keeping for themselves what God intended them to pass on. The principle sounds harsh. It isn't. It's the good news to the needy. Only those who want to grab for themselves what God has given for the sake of others will object. Why shouldn't those who take illicitly lose their spoils?

We see the idea of "giving to givers" at work in Paul's apostolic ministry. I've already mentioned his role as a channel of gifts to the Jerusalem poor. But he was also given the gift of heralding the gospel. He traveled from place to place, to preach the gospel and establish churches where Christ had not yet been named (Romans 15:20), and he kept returning to the churches he had already established to guide them along the way. Interestingly enough, he refused to receive charitable support from the church in which he was serving at any given time. "We did not eat anyone's bread without paying for it; but with toil and labor we worked night and day, so that we might not burden any of you," he wrote to the Thessalonians (2 Thessalonians 3:8). Not that he thought he had no right to receive pay (v. 9). Instead he chose to forgo compensation.

He refused support from his flock for many reasons, most of which had to do with his understanding of gift giving. He wanted to teach his churches to be productive so that they would be able to give rather than only receive (v. 9); he quoted Christ in saying it is more blessed to give than to receive (Acts 20:35). His main reason, however, for refusing pay might have been that his message was about God's indescribable gift, and he wanted to deliver it the same way it was given – "free of charge" (1 Corinthians 9:18). That's why he would take money from one church to serve in another but wouldn't take any money from the church in which he was serving! The Philippians supported his missionary efforts elsewhere. He hoped that the Romans would send him off to Spain (Romans 15:24). The Apostle was the recipient of these gifts but not their beneficiary; rather, he received the gift of support so that he could give the gift of the gospel freely.

When gifts are given to be passed on, recipients have an obligation to be givers. Paul shouldn't have pocketed the Philippians' money and gone off to the beautiful rocky beaches of western Illyria – present-day Croatia. He even felt uneasy that he landed in prison after being given support to preach the gospel, though he was imprisoned *for* preaching the gospel (see Philippians 1:12–18). The receipt of the original gift is itself like an unwritten contract: By receiving, I promise not to keep the gift for myself or to use it as I please, but to pass it on in accordance with the wishes of the original giver. If I receive the gift but fail to fulfill the promise, I have misdirected the gift, wronging both the original giver and the intended recipient.

Christ's Equals

Givers, we are told by some anthropologists and philosophers, are seen as socially, and possibly even morally, superior to receivers. Hardly anyone puts the claim so boldly, but many maintain that the act of giving puts a person in a position of wealth and power, whereas the act of receiving puts a person in a position of poverty and weakness. The giver is full, the receiver is empty. The giver is active; the receiver is passive.

For these reasons, a rivalry can develop between givers and receivers. To climb out of the social hole into which receiving has thrust them, receivers must return more than they were given. If they fail, they lose honor.[19] When we give, we often engage in rivalries and set up hierarchies – but that's not giving as it ought to be.

When gifts circulate within the Godhead, no rivalry happens and no hierarchy is established. The One who gives is not greater than the One who receives. For all give and all receive, and they give glory to each other with each gift they give. True, Jesus said that the Father is greater than he is (John 14:28). But that's because Jesus was the Word on its earthly sojourn, clad with the finite beauty of frail human flesh. The Father is not greater than the eternal Son, and the Son is not greater than the Spirit. They are equal as divine persons. They are equal as givers.

What happens, though, to the equality of givers and receivers when God's gift giving turns toward the world? There is no equality between God and creatures. God is God, and creatures are creatures. The difference between them is so great that it can't be measured on the same scale. Pick any number you want, and you can't say, "God is x times greater than a creature." God is radically different and immeasurably greater. And yet, paradoxically, God gives so that the relation between God and human beings can be brought to greater parity.

Recall what the apostle Paul said about the purpose of Christ's generosity. "For you know the generous act of our Lord Jesus Christ, that though he was rich, yet for your sakes he became poor, so that by his poverty you might become rich" (2 Corinthians 8:9). Luther developed this idea of swapping riches for poverty in the famous passage about "wonderful exchange" in *The Freedom of the Christian*. Like bridegroom and bride, by faith Christ and the Christian are one flesh. It follows that "everything they have they hold in common ... Accordingly the believing soul can boast and glory in whatever Christ has as though it were its own, and whatever the soul has, Christ claims as his own."[20] Christ enters the poverty of self-enclosed selves, indwells us, and makes his divine life to be our own. Christ's gift makes each of us a "Christ". When God gives to us, inequality remains – radical inequality – yet we become, in a certain regard, Christ's equals.

Love Equalizes

Like gifts among divine persons, human gifts should foster and express equality. Between lovers, there is no first and last, no greater and smaller. Love equalizes as nothing else can. Given in love, gifts neither establish the superiority of the giver, nor trigger rivalry between the giver and the receiver. Lovers give because they delight and adore. When they aim to outdo each other, it is not in getting honor, whether by giving gifts or any other means, but in *bestowing* honor. "Love one another with mutual affection," wrote the apostle Paul, adding, "outdo one another in showing honor" (Romans 12:10). Lovers' gifts elevate rather than diminish the beloved – especially if love is mutual. Good givers don't give gifts to recipients but honor to themselves. They give both gifts and honor to the recipients even if they, as a result, end up bing honored as good givers. And then as the circle moves, they get both the gifts and the honor in return.

Like Christ's gifts to humanity, our gifts to one another should aim at establishing parity in the midst of drastic and pervasive inequality. When giving to those who are in need, wrote the Apostle, it ought to be like food given from heaven: "The one who had much did not have too much, and the one who had little did not have too little" (2 Corinthians 8:15). The immediate goal is not uniformity. Equality of the kind the Apostle has in mind is compatible with one party having much while the other has little, but it's incompatible with one party having "too much" while the other has "too little".

It isn't always easy to determine what "too much" means concretely. With the help of the community that holds us accountable, each of us will ultimately have to make that decision on our own, just as each of us will stand on our own before the ultimate Judge to account for what we have done with the gifts we have received. In general, the Apostle's point seems clear: Differences in wealth are legitimate even if they are destined to disappear in the world to

come; that some suffer abject poverty while others enjoy opulence is
not. Put differently, the aim is equality of satisfied needs, precisely
those needs that motivated the gift giving in the first place.

What is given may create greater equality, someone might argue,
but doesn't the very fact of giving undermine any equality that the
gifts confer? The gift made the recipient more equal to the giver, but
it was the giver who did the equalizing. Gifts have flowed from the
giver to the recipient, with the giver seemingly above and the recipient below. Yet in truth, as I will explain in chapter 3, human givers
are not above human recipients because they are not the source of
gifts, but are their channels. Here I want to note that the gift's magnitude is irrelevant in assessing the greatness of the giver. What matters is the spirit in which the gift is given. The apostle Paul called it
"eagerness" (2 Corinthians 8:12). What is the measure of eagerness?
It's the degree of a giver's joy and sacrifice, not the magnitude of the
gift.

Consider Jesus' story about the rich givers who deposited large
sums into the temple treasury and the poor widow who put in only
two copper coins. Jesus commented, "Truly I tell you, this poor
widow had put in more than all of them; for all of them have contributed out of their abundance, but she out of her poverty has put
all she had to live on" (Luke 21:3–4). She gave more because what
she gave cost her more.

Now imagine the poor widow and one of the wealthy people giving presents to each other. She gives him her two coins, and he, as
a counter-gift, hands her the title deed and the keys to one of his
palatial summer residences on the Mediterranean Sea. She has still
given more, and for exactly the same reason that she put more into
the temple treasury! He is not above and she below. It's the other
way around. Even though he has given a palace and she only two
coins, more has flowed from her to him than from him to her. In the
economy of honor before God, a friendly smile from a beggar can
easily outdo the largest of gifts.

In *Matryona's House*, Alexander Solzhenitsyn told the story of
an old woman: "She never tried to acquire things for herself. She

wouldn't struggle to buy things which would then mean more to her than life itself. All her life she never tried to dress smartly in the kind of clothes which embellish cripples and disguise evildoers." Misunderstood and abandoned even by her husband, she buried six children but continued to give. She worked without pay and had no possessions, but her gifts had immense, if unrecognized, weight. "We all lived beside her," Solzhenitsyn put in the mouth of one of her fellow villagers, "and never understood that she was the righteous one without whom, according to the proverb, no village can stand. Nor any city. Nor our whole land."[21] A very great giver of very meager means she was!

Gifts of God, Communion with God

In and of itself, no particular thing in the world is a gift. We do have so-called gift shops, full of all sorts of little things we usually give to friends and acquaintances. But things sitting on the store shelf are not gifts. Just like any other thing, an item from that store *becomes* a gift when you buy it and give it to someone else. A gift is a social relation, not an entity or an act in itself. It is an event *between* people.

As Solzhenitsyn's story underscores, gifts don't just happen between people; they also serve "to create, nourish, or re-create" social bonds.[22] Cords of concord like nothing else, good gifts bind people together. That's one thing that distinguishes the relationship between givers and receivers from that of creditors and borrowers. To the creditor, wrote Seneca, "I shall have to return the same amount that I have received, and, when I have returned it, I have paid all my debt and am free." To the giver, on the other hand, "I must make an additional payment, and, even after I have paid my debt of gratitude, the bond between us still holds; for, just when I have finished paying it, I am obliged to begin again, and friendship endures."[23] Gifts forge communities, and as many sociologists observe, communities foster gift giving.[24]

When we say that God is the Holy Trinity, we mean that the divine persons are mysteriously one and three. The oneness of the

Three and the threeness of the One make up the divine communion of love. But how is that communion achieved? Divine persons give themselves to each other, and they do so in a special and exclusively divine way. Each dwells in others and is indwelled by others. As John's gospel tells us, the Father is in the Son, and the Son is in the Father. And as the apostle Paul implies, the Holy Spirit is in the Son, and the Son is in the Holy Spirit. By such mutual indwelling, the Holy Three are the Holy One. Because the Godhead is a perfect communion of love, divine persons exchange gifts – the gift of themselves and the gift of the others' glory. The inverse is also true: Because they exchange such gifts, they are a divine communion of love. So it is in God's eternal life, apart from God's relation to the world.

As I noted earlier, when God turns toward the world, the circle of exchanges within the divine communion begins its outbound flow. God gives to creatures because God delights in them. But God's delight is part of a more encompassing divine relationship with creatures, and the name of that relationship is communion. Human beings were created for communion with God. Granted, it's a different sort of communion than communion among divine persons. Human beings are not divine and therefore cannot be *part* of God's eternal communion. A few billion human beings can't just be added to the communion of the Three with the result that it's now a communion of a few billion and three! Yet still, there is a form of communion between God and us.

Just as the Three are the One because they mutually indwell each other, so we are one with the Divine One because Christ lives in us and through us. Whereas the Three reciprocally give and receive as equals, we only receive from God; we are given our very being, are freed from sin, and will be glorified. We don't give anything back to God. As we saw in chapter 1, faith, gratitude, availability, and participation are our appropriate responses to God's gifts, our way of loving God. Through these ways of relating to God, we recognize God as God and let Christ live in us and work through us. So God's communion with creatures differs from intradivine communion. The first rests on unilateral giving; the second is thoroughly reciprocal.

One Body, Many Gifts

We were created for communion with one another, not just with God. Correspondingly, Christ came not just to live in us, or even just to live through us. He came to make us into one body – his body, the church. For the apostle Paul, the indwelling of Christ in the believer and the creation of the church as the body of Christ are intimately related. The bread and wine of the Eucharist stand for the body and blood of Christ, and the body and blood of Christ stand for his giving of himself on our behalf. By receiving bread and wine, we receive Christ, and with Christ, we receive ourselves as one body of Christ. The Apostle wrote, explicating the relation between receiving Christ and being a community, "Because there is one bread, we who are many are one body, for we all partake of the one bread" (1 Corinthians 10:17). In giving himself to us, Christ gives us a community – ourselves.

As we read the apostle Paul's epistles, especially where he instructed Christians on how to live, it is striking how frequently he used the little phrase "one another". We've looked at one excellent example already: "Love one another with mutual affection; outdo one another in showing honor" (Romans 12:10). The Apostle mentions the phrase "one another" twice in a single short verse, and close to a hundred times in his letters! That's because interdependence and mutual service *are* the life of a body. "For as in one body we have many members, and not all the members have the same function, so we, who are many, are one body in Christ, and individually we are members one of another" (Romans 12:4–5).

Significantly, each member of the body is endowed with what the Apostle called "spiritual gifts" – roles and abilities the Holy Spirit gives to each for the benefit of the others. Each one, gifted to give, now gives to others. As the one with the gift of the apostolate, Paul is part of this community of "giving and receiving", as he calls it in Philippians (4:15). It's not just that he preaches and others "sen[d] help" for his "needs" (v. 16). The Apostle strengthens the faith of churches, and his faith is strengthened in return. He wants to come to the church in Rome, for instance, "so that we may be mutually encouraged by each other's faith, both yours and mine" (Romans 1:12).

The reciprocal exchange of gifts expresses and nourishes a community of love. Take reciprocity out of gift giving, and community disintegrates into discrete individuals. Without any reciprocity, the best-case scenario would be that we all live on our individual islands and anonymously send and receive "packages" to help those who can't help themselves, or – amounting to nearly the same (though minus the willingness of gift giving!) – we all send our contributions to the government for distribution to the needy. Clearly, in the complex societies of today, the government has an important role in tending to social needs. But the government cannot replace reciprocal gift giving. Neither can our unidirectional gifts to those in need. Without reciprocal giving, we would at best inhabit a world of lonely altruists.

Or we would inhabit a world of collaborating egoists! Take gift giving out of reciprocity, and community degenerates into individuals who'll cooperate and split apart when it suits their interests. You have a good I want? I'll persuade you that I have a good you need, we'll swap our wares, and be on our merry ways. This is the exchange mode of human relations, and there is a place for it. We have the right to exchange goods for their rough equivalents. Without such exchanges, we would languish and suffer oppression in a world organized in complex systems and populated by selfish persons. And yet to transmute most reciprocal relations into self-serving exchanges would rob us of what is essential to our very humanity.

The best gift we can give to each other may be neither a thing (like a diamond ring) nor an act (like an embrace), but our own generosity. With that "indescribable gift" called Christ, God gave us a generous self and a community founded on generosity. Such a self bestows gifts freely. It gives because it delights in the beloved and can't endure the need of the needy. In giving, it subverts hierarchies and transforms rivalries into mutual exaltations. And in all of this, it forges lasting bonds of reciprocal love. At the most basic level, generosity itself is exchanged in all our gift exchanges: My generosity is reciprocated by your generosity, and the circle of mutual love keeps turning.

How should we give? By letting our generosities dance together! But how are they able to?

Chapter 3

HOW CAN WE GIVE?

How *can* we give? Why use the word *can*? That implies that we might not be able to give. But we obviously are able, someone may argue. As long as humanity has existed, we've always given gifts, and we always will. So if something is so pervasive, why ask whether it's possible? "You know *that* you should give; God has created you to give," the reasoning might go. "You know *how* you should give; God the giver is your model. So just do it!" Yet as compelling as this pragmatic advice may be, it's just too simple. To understand why, let's look at what often passes as "giving".

Generosity – A Counterfeit Coin?

In 1936, Dale Carnegie published a famous book entitled *How to Win Friends and Influence People.* Much of it is about giving. Whether it is friends or money you want, he assured that showing genuine interest in people and giving them presents will get you there. To make a lot of money, he suggested, you have to start by offering presents, then charge a lot for them later on. The interest in others must be sincere. And he insisted that it is gifts you should give, not loans or bribes. Still, the goal of both your interest in others and of your gifts is your own gain.[1]

Carnegie's advice must be effective – the book has sold more than 15,000,000 copies and is still in print. But there's something troubling about it. It harnesses the power of the gift for purposes contrary to the nature of the gift. By definition, gifts benefit others. Yet Carnegie tells us to give in order to benefit ourselves!

Carnegie's book sells in part because we like the advice he gives. If we take a closer look at our giving, we'll probably be surprised at how many of our gifts are given ... to ourselves. We need friends in high places, so we find a way to invite them for dinner or do them a favor. We want a car repaired speedily, so we bring a bottle of scotch to our local mechanic. We hope to quiet the legitimate ire of our spouse after we've committed a small transgression, so we bring flowers or jewelry. Such gifts are investments, and like all investments, we expect them to deliver returns – the bigger, the better.

True, in giving such gifts we run the risk of not getting any return at all. The recipients may prove unresponsive. If we've negotiated a deal, we can make the other party comply with its terms. But if we've given a gift, we are at the mercy of the recipients' good will. When we give in this way, however, we are betting that the return will be even greater, in part because we were willing to run the risk of not getting any at all.

Carnegie's kind of giving is openly calculating, all his talk about genuine interest in others notwithstanding. We know from the start that we give so that we can "charge a lot" later on. Mostly we reserve such a calculating attitude to the domain of buying and selling. In market exchanges, we legitimately seek to benefit ourselves. When we give gifts while exchanging goods, we tend to do the same: we hope to benefit from them. In such cases, gift giving is folded into buying and selling.

If, in the sales mode, we are dishonest, gift giving will serve to hide bad motives and perhaps help us get away with unconscionable deeds. We are then taking illicitly, though we pretend to be giving generously. If we are honest, gift giving will help show our trustworthiness, our good will, or express our gratitude for services well performed. We are then legitimate getters whose generosity signals that we won't take advantage of others and that we appreciate their fair and competent dealings. Still, when we give in the sales mode, we give for our own good, not for the good of the recipient.

It need not be that way, of course. Even in the marketplace, we can give for the benefit of others. As the earlier example of a great music teacher suggests, the best workers give more than what they are paid for. To use a pizza metaphor, the sales mode is a crust that carries the toppings of their generosity. Yet so often in the sales mode, we give … in order to get. Our generosity is a counterfeit coin.

More False Currency

Are we better givers in what I have called the gift mode, when we claim to be giving for the sake of others? We are. But even then, we are often seeking little more than our own interest. This may come to us as an unpleasant surprise. Mostly we *think* that the good of others is our concern. Yet it often isn't. We expect a gift in return, and if we don't get it, we divert the stream of our generosity to more promising prospects. We are getters, possibly even shameless takers, who pride ourselves in being generous givers. We act like a seducer whose burning desire makes him believe that he is in love with the woman – until he wakes up next to her and can't wait to leave the room.

Or, unlike the seducer, we may want nothing from the recipient of our "gifts" and nonetheless seek our own good as we give. Instead of wanting something in return, we may want public honor. People should know of our generosity and think well of us for it! The praise we receive as givers matters to us more than the benefit of others. As Jesus put it while chiding hypocritical alms givers, we "sound a trumpet" before us and give so that we "may be praised by others" (Matthew 6:2). Take away the approving and admiring gaze of neighbors, and we'd rather just enjoy what we have than pass it on to others. It no longer pays to give.

Alternatively, we may take Jesus' warning to heart and do our giving in secret, but still give mainly to get something out of it. Our conscience may be burdened by a transgression, we may have a vague sense of not being morally good enough, or we may feel uneasy about our wealth, power, and privilege, so we give in order to silence our self-doubt. By giving secretly as Jesus urged, we pay off a debt to our bad conscience or stockpile moral capital that we intend to spend later as we see fit. The coin of our generosity may be real, but it is minted out of impure metal.

Finally, untamed and inchoate passions may drive us to give. Consider an extreme example, the narrator's grandfather in Marilynne Robinson's *Gilead*. He "lacked patience for anything but the plainest interpretations of the starkest commandments, 'To him who asks, give,' in particular".[2] A compulsive giver, he never "kept anything that was worth giving away, or let us keep it, either, so my mother said. He would take laundry right off the line ... She said she could probably go to any town in the Middle West and see some pair of pants she'd patched walking by in the street." From one angle, he looked like "a saint of some kind" (31). Yet his eccentricities, including his compulsion to give, "were thwarted passion"; he "was full of anger, at us not least" (34). As if some ugly demon veiled in the fine garments of generosity drove him, he gave more to harm those who possessed than to benefit those who lacked.

Whether we give in order to extract goods from others, win praise for magnanimity, put a fig leaf over our moral nakedness, or feed some raging beast inside, in one way or another our generosity often proves either counterfeit or impure. We give to ourselves, in whole or in part.

Are we able to receive better than we are able to give? Not by much. Receivers can poison what they receive almost as much as givers can poison what they give. As Friedrich Nietzsche observed in *Thus Spoke Zarathustra*, receivers' gratitude is reluctant, often verging on a desire for vengeance: "If a little charity is not forgotten, it turns into a gnawing worm."[3] Receivers sometimes shamelessly try to extract further benefits by feigned gratitude, flattery, and false interest in the givers. Dependent as they feel on the givers, receivers can elevate givers to a position of quasi-divinity, a source of life and well-being. Receivers then become illicit takers – takers of givers' honor through ingratitude, takers of givers' goods through manipulation, and takers of givers' proper humanity through an enactment of false dependence. We poison gifts both as givers and receivers.

Is this a dark view of human nature and human giving and receiving? I'll come to the sunny side shortly. But it's important to take a closer look at the impurity of our giving. It explains why it's so difficult for us to give and to give well.

Gift and Prohibition

Why are our gifts impure? The apostle Paul's answer took the form of a contrast between Adam, the prototype of the sinful human race, and Christ, the prototype of redeemed humanity. From Christ, we receive "the free gift" of righteousness and eternal life. Through Adam, we receive sin and death, even as we receive from him life itself and all the resources we need to survive and thrive. Through Adam, the Apostle wrote, sin "came into the world" and we all were "made sinners" (Romans 5:12, 19). In addition, sin and death poison all the gifts we receive from God and pass on to others. True, from Christ we have received the gift of redemption, medicine against sin and death. Yet the stain of sin will remain until the end of our lives and the end of human history – until that day when Christ will give us yet another gift, the gift of eternal life in a world of perfect love.

How did this sin come into the world? Where did it come from? The Apostle answered only the first question and remained silent about the second. Adam and Eve are the sin's gateway, but they are not its originators. The sin came "through" them but not *from* them. Nobody is the sin's originator, not Adam or Eve, both of whom succumbed to it, not "the serpent", who was the means of the temptation to commit it, and certainly not God, who gives only good gifts. Sin is an unexpected intruder of unidentifiable origin, but one that God permitted to enter the world. It is inexplicably there at the dawn of history, just as it is inexplicably passed on to every human being.

More important than sin's origin is sin's nature and, for us here, its relation to gift giving. Recall the story of Adam, Eve, and the serpent from the first book of the Bible. God placed Adam in a lush garden to "till it and keep it" and said to him, "You may freely eat of every tree of the garden; but of the tree of the knowledge of good and evil you shall not eat, for in the day that you eat of it you shall die" (Genesis 2:15–17). The command seems to draw an arbitrary line and is buttressed by the threat of death for crossing it. You can eat this but not that, and if you do, you'll die – a seemingly impersonal threat whose clear sense is: "I'll kill you if you don't obey me." And arbitrary rules and dire threats, the tempting serpent suggested to Adam and Eve, speak of God's stingy giving and petty jealousy. God wants to keep humans away from a tree whose food is good, delightful, and desirable, to prevent them from developing their full potential of becoming God's equals (Genesis 3:5–6).

This is a serpentine surface interpretation of God's prohibition. Adam and Eve embraced that interpretation and missed the prohibition's deeper and life-giving meaning. They believed the reason God withheld the fruit was that "God's will toward man is not good",[4] as Luther put it. Adam and Eve should have concluded exactly the opposite.

God withheld the fruit of the one tree to indicate visibly and tangibly that Adam and Eve and everything around them are not just there by surd happenstance, that they don't exist out of their own power, and that they can't dissolve into lifeless chaos as inexplicably as they came to be. The world isn't just *there*. God "who calls into existence the things that do not exist" (Romans 4:17) has given and continues to give the world to Adam and Eve for their delight. The one forbidden fruit reveals not stinginess and jealousy, but God's overwhelming generosity and goodness. Paradoxically, the withheld fruit is a sacrament of a *given* world. They missed the paradox, however, and mistreated the gift.

Even common courtesy tells us not to treat gifts as if they were our own rightful possessions or to complain about not having been given more. We can claim our paychecks and complain about their insufficiency. But gifts are meant to be taken as they are given, with gratitude appropriate to the gift. To treat gifts as entitlements and to complain about not getting more is to be a poor receiver and to wrong the giver. That would neither recognize gifts as gifts nor honor the giver as a giver. Especially if you were given as much as Adam and Eve were.

As we saw in chapter 1, the proper response to God's gifts is to receive them in faith as gifts and to be grateful to the giver. Adam's most basic sin was the loss of faith and gratitude, and with that, the loss of the knowledge that everything true, good, and beautiful is God's gift. And that's our most basic sin, too. As the apostle Paul put it, we fail to "honor him [God] as God or give thanks to him" (Romans 1:21).

Cain's Ire

A story that follows closely on the heels of Adam and Eve is that of their sons. The saga of Cain and Abel tells what happens between human beings when we don't treat everything true, good, and beautiful as God's gifts, but rather as stuff we can appropriate as we are able and enjoy as we see fit. Both brothers brought offerings to God, Cain "an offering of the fruit of the ground, and Abel for his part brought of the firstlings of his flock, their fat portions" (Genesis 4:3–4). "And the LORD," reads the crucial line in the story, "had regard for Abel and his offering, but for Cain and his offering he had no regard. So Cain was very angry, and his countenance fell" (vv. 4–5).

Some interpreters suggest that it was God who spoiled everything for Cain. Just as, according to the serpent, God arbitrarily decided that Adam was not to eat the fruit of the one tree, so according to these interpreters, God arbitrarily blessed Abel rather than Cain and understandably provoked Cain's ire. However, this interpretation disregards many textual indications that Cain was a proud, wealthy, and miserly firstborn, whereas Abel was a humble, poor, and generous second son.[5]

As Adam and Eve took from God, so Cain, partly because he was born and raised by takers, claimed his expanding goods as his own achievements. He was in competition with Abel, and he was ahead, way ahead. He was first in the order of birth as well as in power, wealth, and honor. But whereas Cain was a taker who grudgingly presented a miserly offering to God, Abel was a giver who, in gratitude for what he had received, offered to God the best of his possessions.

Do we know that?

God approved of Abel's offering but not of Cain's. In a race with Abel, Cain found himself suddenly behind, way behind.

Cain's repetition of his parents' ingratitude toward God is part of the reason God approved Abel's offering but not Cain's. In Luther's view, along with fallen angels and many earthly princes and kings, Cain abused God's gifts "as though He had given them in order that [he] might despise [his] Creator and generous Giver".[6] But the other part of the answer concerns Cain's relationship to Abel. Cain was a taker rather than a giver, and for takers, all people are competitors with whom they sooner or later clash. Takers may leave competitors alone if the latter are insignificant. But they'll try to bring down those who are above them. As long as Abel was nobody, he was a good brother. As soon as Abel rose to become somebody, especially somebody in God's eyes, Cain had to strike – which just proved him to be an illicit taker of goods and, if it need be, of another's life.

Sin is a gift of sorts – it is "given" to us in an inscrutable way as someone sinister may give us secretly a dose of poison. But it's not just a terribly bad gift, the opposite of a good gift, as harm is the opposite of help. Sin is a kind of "anti-gift", which counteracts and neutralizes the goodness of all our gifts. On account of our selfishness and arrogance, every gift is already subverted, undone, and transposed however slightly into a non-gift, into an instrument of taking. Look carefully at even the most generous givers, and you'll discover in them some of the features of illicit takers. Even as the very best givers, we are sinners. As we will see shortly, as givers we are not *only* sinners, not even *mainly* sinners, but we are invariably and inescapably sinners.

Our Basic Goodness

From the warm glow of our seemingly obvious and uncontested gift giving at the beginning of this chapter, we have walked through the dark alleys of our more dubious gift exchanges and reached the "heart of darkness" – the universal sinfulness that poisons all gifts.

In *Heart of Darkness*, twentieth-century English novelist Joseph Conrad explores the hypocrisies of imperialism. The imperialists saw themselves as legitimate getters and beneficent givers. They liked to believe that they traded fairly with indigenous people and, as a bonus, brought the light of civilization into the darkness of their barbarity. Yet in reality, they were shameless takers who extracted goods and destroyed cultures in order to replace them with their own. Mr. Kurtz, an ivory hunter in southern Africa who embodied the impenetrable darkness, did the same, just openly, even if he did want to leave an impression of an "exotic Immensity ruled by an august Benevolence".[7] He bartered, swindled, and stole ivory, and he suppressed and intended even to "exterminate all the brutes" (46).

Most of us are neither self-righteous imperialists nor self-confessedly evil imitators of sinister Mr. Kurtz. Yet to the extent that we are sinners, similar impulses that governed him rule in us. We illicitly take, sometimes brazenly and often under the guise of legitimately acquiring or generously giving. Each one of us can make a journey to the heart of darkness, like Marlow, the protagonist of *Heart of Darkness*, did when he traveled up the Congo River in search of Mr. Kurtz.

In view of that darkness, then, can we really give at all? Or do we invariably act out of twisted self-love and, like Luther's sinner, "take from God and from men what belongs to them and give neither God nor men anything of that which it has, is, and is capable of"?[8] Is genuine giving then impossible? Is it just a pleasant deception indulged in by individuals and communities to mask the harsh realities of what are, in truth, merely self-interested exchanges? In gift giving, are we just playing a game in which, as Bourdieu put it, "everyone knows (and does not want to know) that everyone knows (and does not want to know) the true nature of the exchange"?[9]

According to the apostle Paul, we all sin (Romans 3:23) and are under the power of sin (Romans 7:14–24). And as Luther has argued, we sin all the time, blatantly disregarding God and neighbor when we are at our worst, slyly proud and clandestinely selfish in our own achievements when we are at our best, or falsely humble when we see ourselves as unworthy.

But even if all of us are sinners from head to toe, none of us is a sinner through and through, with nothing good remaining in us. As sinners, we are still God's good creatures. To illustrate the relationship between being a good creature and being a sinner, Reformation theologians used the analogy of water and ink. Water is the good creation, ink is sin, and the sinner is a glass of water with a few drops of ink. All the water in the glass is tainted, but it's still mostly water, not ink. Analogously, all our good deeds are marred by sin, but they are still mostly good deeds, not crimes masquerading as merits. Now apply this to gifts. We give gifts. None of them are pure. Yet with all their impurities, many of them are still genuine gifts, not just hidden ways of loving ourselves.

Selfishness, Pride, Sloth

Three aspects of sin – all three of which are facets of self-love – militate against the purity of gift giving to which our basic goodness drives us: selfishness, pride, and sloth. They form the backdrop for three ways God's presence in our lives counters sin's subversion of our gift giving.

Take, first, *selfishness*. "In all that he does or leaves undone," wrote Luther, a human being "seeks his own advantage and his own way. He seeks his own honor rather than God's and that of his neighbor."[10] We often give measly gifts or don't give at all because we selfishly want to multiply our own goods, and giving to others takes things away from us. (Large gifts selfishly given are not *gifts*; they are investments.) To give is to lose, we fear, with some justification.

More often than not, our resources are limited. When we give, we seem to diminish the possibilities of our own enjoyment. Even when our resources are plentiful, they are insecure. It's much easier to descend from riches to rags than to move up from rags to riches. If we give and then misfortune strikes – if we lose a job, the stock market tumbles, or we fall seriously ill – we ourselves might end up in need. Finally, resources give us power; they open doors that would otherwise remain closed, and they let us exert influence where we would otherwise have none. Giving things away seems to diminish our power, even if it's true that we often maintain power by pretending to give. To enjoy the good things of life, to secure our well-being in the future, and to maintain power, we hold tightly onto things instead of truly sharing them or passing them on.

Second, *pride* besmirches our gifts. "To trust in works, which one ought to do in fear," wrote Luther in the *Heidelberg Disputation*, "is equivalent to giving oneself the honor and taking it from God ... But it is completely wrong ... to enjoy oneself in one's works, and to adore oneself as an idol."[11] Notice to what Luther is objecting. It's all right to enjoy our works as we enjoy a fine meal, a lover's kiss, or a striking landscape. But it's not fine to *adore ourselves* on account of our good works. For then we take away honor that belongs to God and give not to benefit others, but to receive praise from others or ourselves.

It's understandable why we might want to adore ourselves, to repeat Luther's phrase. Others' favorable opinion of us, as well as our own positive self-esteem, often feel like scarce goods. We compete with others not just for things, but also for a reputation as upright, talented, and useful people. Even the most excellent reputation is easily lost, sometimes without any cause beyond the envy of our competitors. And except for the Narcissuses among us, we are plagued by guilt for having wronged others and shame for not having lived up to expectations. So we give – not to benefit others but to be pleased with ourselves. Our giving is marred by the desire to congratulate ourselves and to be congratulated by others.

Finally, the sin of *sloth* hinders us as givers. We rarely think of sluggishness, indolence, slowness, or inertia as sins. It's bad for your body to be a couch potato, maybe even for your mind, we reason. But what does it have to do with your soul? Yet sloth is not just bad for you; it's sinful. Twentieth-century Swiss theologian Karl Barth wrote eloquently on the topic, arguing, "sin has not merely the heroic form of pride but also, in complete antithesis yet profound correspondence, the quite unheroic and trivial form of sloth. In other words, it has the form, not only of evil action, but also of evil inaction."[12] That's why in the penitent's prayer we confess that we have sinned against God "by what we have left undone", not just by "what we have done".

It takes work to give. To pay attention when someone speaks, you must concentrate; to make a donation to a charity, you must not only earn the money but, as a wise giver, you must research the charity before writing the check; to help in the soup kitchen, you must ... well, set aside time and help. Often we are simply too comfortable to give; we'd rather play, be entertained, or just plain do nothing. Sometimes we are too despondent to give; all our efforts to alleviate need seem like drops of water on a hot stone. If gifts do so little good, we'd rather not go to the trouble of giving at all. Finally, selfishness and pride might have made us experts in fending for ourselves and cutting others down, but we are all thumbs when we try to help others or build them up. As incompetence reinforces indolence and indolence magnifies incompetence, we may find ourselves slowly sliding on a downward spiral into the netherworld of non-giving.

So can we counter the effects of selfishness, pride, and sloth and make our giving pure? Not before we land in God's perfect world of love on the other side of this world's history. Only when, in communion with God, we become the perfect image of God as individuals and communities, will our giving attain purity. We will give and receive generously, not selfishly; humbly, not proudly; and eagerly, not slothfully. And we won't quite know where giving ends and receiving begins. We will rejoice in receiving no less than giving because we'll delight in each giver's joy and rejoice over each recipient's delight.

But we live very much east of Eden and are still far from that world. Moreover, we can't get ourselves there through our own capacities, strengths, and efforts. So we can't make our gifts pure. But our gifts can be *better*. In chapters 1 and 2, we saw that our giving is participation in God's giving. It will come as no surprise then that we need God to better ourselves as givers. If we are good givers to the extent that we echo God's giving, then only God can reverse the ill effects that selfishness, pride, and sloth have on giving.

A Triangle of Giving

To understand how God counters the ill effects sin has on giving, we need to look first at how, in the Christian view of the way things are, God makes the very act of giving possible. I noted in chapter 1 that God makes giving possible in the sense that God makes everything possible. If God didn't give, we couldn't give. There would be nothing to give and nobody to either give or receive. Without God, gift giving would be what a philosopher would call ontologically impossible.

If you don't believe in a creator God, you'll reject the claim that gift giving is impossible without God. No matter how the world came to be, it's obviously there, you might reason. And once it's there, there's stuff to give and there are people to give and receive. So clearly, if the world can exist without God, giving is ontologically possible without God. But even if that were the case, would it *make sense* to give without God?

Recall the most elementary structure of giving: Somebody gives something to someone else. To have a gift, you've got to have at least two people and a tangible or intangible thing that is given from one to the other – say, a flower or a blessing. But that's just a gift's skeleton, not yet a whole gift. You'll need muscles and organs for giving to actually happen. For instance, a gift presupposes a shared understanding that makes it possible for people to recognize a gift when they see one. Think of a Martian who lands on earth and is welcomed by humans. They unroll a red carpet and a little girl hands the Martian a bouquet of flowers. Unless the Martian has studied our customs before landing, she'll have no idea she is being honored with a gift.

One of the things a gift's skeleton has to have to come alive is the willingness of givers to impart more to recipients than they expect to receive. If, to the contrary, we want to receive more than we impart, we are not giving. The recipient or some other observer, who could, like God, peek into our hearts and discern our intentions, would quickly dismiss our giving. We are slyly and gently extracting, not giving.

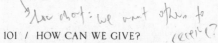

The crucial question is this: As rational beings, why would we ever want to give more than we expect to receive? When we give, we may end up with a raw deal. What we've truly given, we've potentially lost. It makes sense to give only if the world is set up in such a way that when we give – when we impart more than we expect to receive – we don't lose, but in fact end up gaining. Take somebody like Mother Teresa – a whole lifetime's worth of unheroic giving, helping the poor and the sick! It seems impossible to sustain such a steady stream of generosity unless there is an expectation that each gift is not a loss to the giver, but in some sense a gain.

Such expectation seems unreasonable without God, which is why we need God to build a bridge from self-love to generosity. As Immanuel Kant powerfully argued, it takes an omnipotent and omniscient creator, redeemer, and consummator to match our goodness with happiness.[13] It takes the same kind of God to turn our gifts into seeds out of which a bountiful harvest will grow. "He who supplies seed to the sower and bread for food," wrote the apostle Paul, "will supply and multiply your seed for sowing and increase the harvest of your righteousness" (2 Corinthians 9:10). We don't give *so that* we might receive more back; we would then selfishly calculate with our "generosity". But *as* we give for others' benefit, we know that that very unselfish act will be for our gain.

Take, as an example, a particularly radical gift. The gift we most highly value is the gift of the self, whether that entails laying down one's life for another or radical devotion and service over a period of time. Like Margarete in Søren Kierkegaard's retelling of the story of Faust, we feel that we love truly only when we achieve that state of self-giving, of which religious thinkers, philosophers, and poets so eloquently speak, where in some sense we "completely disappear" in the beloved.[14] Yet in our sober moments, we rightly hesitate, knowing well that disappointment is inevitable and that, if we give ourselves so completely, we are likely to end up squandering ourselves.

We oscillate between calculating and holding back on the one hand, and abandoning all measure to give ourselves completely, on the other. In the first case, we are left with a gaping hole of unfulfillment as we find ourselves basically alone in the world of self-centered calculations. In the second case, we risk an unbearable contradiction in our very identity, because that to which we have given ourselves completely can at any time be yanked away from us. Callous and calculating as he was, Faust abandoned Margarete. But she had given herself to him and could not give him up without "ceasing to be".[15]

Untethered from God, self-giving love cannot stand on its own for long. If it excludes God, it will destroy us, for we will then deliver ourselves to the mercy of the finite, and therefore inherently unreliable, objects of our love. The only way to ensure that we will not lose our very selves if we give ourselves to others is if our love for the other passes first through God, if we, as Augustine put it succinctly and profoundly, love and enjoy others *in God*. Those who serve the poor often express such a stance by saying that they serve Jesus in the one they help. The same is true of all Christian giving.

Kierkegaard himself explained this idea eloquently in *Works of Love*, a profound meditation on the nature and practice of love. Will not those who forget themselves in self-giving love be forgotten? he asked, zeroing in on the central question. He answered,

> No, the one who in love forgets himself, forgets his suffering, in order to think of someone else's, forgets all his misery in order to think of someone else's, forgets what he himself loses in order lovingly to bear in mind someone else's loss, forgets his advantage in order lovingly to think of someone else's – truly, such a person is not forgotten. There is one who is thinking about him: God in heaven. Or love is thinking about him. God is Love, and when a person out of love forgets himself, how then would God forget him! No, while the one who loves forgets himself and thinks of the other person, God is thinking of the one who loves. The self-lover is busy; he shouts and makes a big noise and stands on his rights in order to make sure he is not forgotten – and yet he is forgotten. But the one who loves, who forgets himself, is recollected by love. There is One who is thinking of him ...[16]

Kierkegaard concluded: "That is why the one who loves receives what he gives" (281). The gift will return to the giver one way or another and, in all cases, from God. Recipients may return a gift, and then the willingness of givers to impart more than they expect in return has reached its fulfillment. Recipients might not return a gift, however, because they are either unable or unwilling. If they don't return the gift, the planted seed will die, but God will make it bear fruit in a bountiful harvest.

If gift giving involves only givers and recipients, givers run a risk of coming up short and, in light of ineradicable human selfishness, mostly do come up short. Hardly any good deed then goes unpunished. If, on the other hand, God is the third party in the relationship between givers and recipients, givers cannot lose. They always receive what they give, and more. That's the "law" of the *flow*: Those who pass gifts on receive more abundantly from the source of all gifts. The apostle Paul makes the same point when he talks about God's rewards to givers (2 Corinthians 9:6–11).

But are the givers still givers if they get from God more than they give to others? Hasn't gift giving turned into selfishness, with the help of God's generosity? Not if we don't give *in order* to receive more in return, as I have suggested earlier. Notice, moreover, that according to the apostle Paul, givers receive from the one to whom they cannot give at all and may receive nothing from those to whom they do give. If I give you more than I expect to receive from you, I still give even if somebody else gives me more every time I give to you. But the crucial thing is that they must *give* me more, rather than pay me for giving to you. If I *earn* twelve dollars with every ten dollars I give, I am ... well, earning and not giving. But if I am *given* twelve dollars for every ten dollars I give, I am giving and not earning, even if I end up benefiting just as much as if I had been paid. For what I receive is a gift on which I have no claim, supplied by the generosity of the giver. The line between giving and acquiring is fine. It takes vigilance not to cross it.

We can't earn anything from God, I've argued. God needs nothing, and all things, including all the work we could ever do for God, are God's gifts to us in the first place. So God doesn't pay givers; God *gives* to givers. The fact that God gives to them in response to their giving and that God gives them more than they give to others – that God gives them, as Jesus says, "a good measure, pressed down, shaken together, running over" (Luke 6:38) – doesn't turn their giving into earning. True, we often treat God's gifts as payment for services rendered. But when we do, we fundamentally misconstrue God's relationship to us and mistreat God's gifts. God is not an employer, not even a very generous employer. God is a *giver*.

God of Abundance

Limited resources are one of the reasons we don't give. No matter how much we have, our resources are finite, and we ourselves, fragile. Take our amenities away and we feel diminished. Take food and shelter away, and we languish and even die. To care well for ourselves and those entrusted to us, we seek to acquire and keep rather than to give away. To give, we must overcome a hard-wired selfishness born partly of our inescapable finitude. And that's where the God who gives abundantly comes in. Such a God makes giving possible. But how?

God doesn't just give; God "scatters abroad", writes the apostle Paul, echoing the psalmist (2 Corinthians 9:9). The image of the God who strews liberally may mislead us to conclude that God has given to the Corinthians in profuse abundance, so they could give to those less fortunate. After all, didn't the Apostle write about their receiving "every blessing in abundance," about "always having enough of everything", of being "enriched in every way" (vv. 8–11)?

But that's all about what God is *able* to do for them, not what God has already done. The Corinthian believers were poor, and the Apostle knew it. The Macedonian believers who also contributed to his collection for the Jerusalem poor were even worse off. When they gave, they were in the midst of "a severe ordeal of affliction" and plagued by "extreme poverty" (2 Corinthians 8:2). God seems to give measly gifts, but the Apostle and the psalmist wrote about God "scattering abroad"!? A cynic may conclude that the talk about

God's abundant giving is just a piece of religious ideology designed to suck the blood of the poor.

Most of us are concerned primarily with the *things* that God gives – with necessities that millions of people lack or with luxuries in which a few wallow. Such gift items are important for the simple reason that so many people in our world don't have sufficient food, water, clothing, and shelter. And they are important because they are part of God's blessing, intended for our good and our enjoyment. So if God's resources are inexhaustible, why doesn't God give more?

The relationship between God as giver and the growing poverty in the world is a complicated one that lies beyond the scope of this book. We should keep two things in mind, however. First, God doesn't just give so that we can have and enjoy but so that we can pass gifts along to others. As we have seen in previous chapters, we are given to so we can be givers, not just recipients. Second, what's primarily at issue is not why God doesn't give more, but why *we* don't pass on to the needy what we already have. At the current levels of economic productivity, there is enough "stuff" around that no one need go hungry and everyone's basic needs can be met. Yet they are not. We pass too little on. If Christians in the United States alone gave 10 percent of their income, the problem of world hunger could be solved.[17] But those of us who have tend to squander or hoard, and what we do pass on is often misappropriated by middlemen. No, it's not clear that increasing the amount of things given by God would actually help.

We want God to multiply the loaves and fish to feed the multitudes, as Jesus did in the Gospels. But the Apostle suggested that we'll be able to feed the multitudes if we'd let God change how we think about the loaves and fish we already have. Consider the extraordinary claim he made about Macedonian believers: Their "extreme poverty ... overflowed in a wealth of generosity on their part" (2 Corinthians 8:2). The Apostle knew, of course, that you can't give what you don't have. They gave "according to their means, and even beyond their means" (v. 3), no more than that. But he also believed that we don't have to have an excess of goods in order to give.

We can be poor and afflicted – indeed, we can be extremely poor and severely afflicted – and still give. We can be affluent and secure – indeed, we can be opulent and bursting with power – and still not give. Wealth doesn't make us givers; poverty can't prevent us from being givers. The poor can give a kind word, a sympathetic ear, or a helping hand. But they can also share food, clothing, shelter, and money – and they generally do it in greater proportion to their means than the wealthy do.[18]

Transformed Attitudes

Giving depends on the proper attitude toward three things: toward things we possess, toward others, and toward ourselves. Take, first, the attitude toward *goods*. Our relation to things changes once we truly understand that everything has been given to us by God. If we believe that what we have is ours because we've earned it, we'll have a hard time giving. We'll expect everybody to earn their possessions, just as we think we've earned ours. "Earning is hard. Life can be tough. But if you persevere, you'll succeed." We may give in individual cases because we may feel compassion for people stricken by misfortune or we may want to be particularly nice to someone. But earning and possessing will be our way of living. Giving will be an occasional diversion.

On the other hand, if we believe that God has given us everything, then giving will be our way of living. We'll still work to earn, because the gift of work is the primary means by which God gives what we have. But earning and possessing will become folded into giving. God gives us life, powers, and abilities, and so we earn and possess. We'll earn and possess so we can give, as when we share our food with the hungry; we'll give even while earning, as when we create goods and offer services with dedication, care, and wisdom; and we'll give even by possessing, as when we open our home for others to enjoy. Earning and possessing are not just a bridge between our desires and their satisfaction. They are a *midpoint* in the flow of gifts: from God to us, and through us to others. We give because we have been given to; we don't let others simply fend for themselves because we haven't been left to fend for ourselves.

Consider, second, our attitude toward *others*. We can think of others as competitors for the possession of goods. We won't give then – unless the difference is so great that the competition is no longer a contest, in which case we'll be able to afford to give, just as a team that's way ahead can afford to let the other team score. But if the game is close, we won't give the other team an inch. To give would be to risk suffering defeat.

Alternatively, we can consider others as the intended beneficiaries of God's gifts. God gives to them – and gives to them through us! – and so we give too. Then giving is like playing a noncompetitive game. On Mediterranean beaches, a circle of players sometimes forms, and they kick a ball to each other. The point of the game is to keep the ball in the air. If one player mis-kicks the ball, another may take extreme effort to prevent it from touching the ground and to get it back into the circle. She is giving a gift to the person who made the mistake, but she is not thereby contributing to her own defeat. To the contrary, everybody gains from the effort.

Since God gives to all, and gives through each, cooperation can replace competition, and the gifts can circulate. As the apostle Paul put it, the present abundance of one party will satisfy the need of the other, and at some later point, the abundance of that other party may help satisfy the need of the first one (2 Corinthians 8:14). The goal of each is not just protection and enhancement of what's his or her own, but a "fair balance" for all.

Finally, what makes giving possible is a new attitude toward the *self*. "Our Lord Jesus Christ," wrote the Apostle to a congregation of reluctant givers, "became poor, so that by his poverty you might become rich" (2 Corinthians 8:9). What does "rich" mean here? Often we take it to refer to spiritual riches. But the whole passage of which the verse is part is about helping the poor. So clearly, the riches that Christ gives have something to do with possessions. The Apostle mentioned God providing the Corinthians "with every blessing in abundance", including the bountiful harvest grown from the seed of their giving (2 Corinthians 9:6–9). But for the Apostle, wealth is not primarily a matter of "having" but of "being", terms that twentieth-century psychoanalyst Erich Fromm used to designate two basic modes of human existence.[19]

In the sense of having, we can become rich, for instance, by hard work, shrewd investment strategy, and a great deal of good luck. But how do we become rich in the sense of *being*? It is possible to have a fortune and as many talents as any Renaissance man and still *be* poor. The bottomless pit of our hollow core will never be satiated. No matter how much we have, we remain "not-enough" people. The gratification of our desires will then know only outer obstacles but no inner restraint. No matter how much we have, we will still hunger and thirst, railing against the obstacles others place in the path of the satisfaction of our insatiable desires. As to the gifts that we may give to others, our hollow core will suck in everything and leave us with empty hands, all our wealth notwithstanding.

Inversely, we can be paupers and still *be* rich. How? The Apostle's answer was this: If we are indwelled by the Christ who became poor so that we can become rich, we will be rich. No matter how little we have, we will be "more-than-enough" people. To have little and yet to have more than enough may be a strange thought for many today. We work in an economy that runs on the principle that to have more cake tomorrow we must eat our cake today, and we are conditioned by ubiquitous advertisements urging us to want more, no matter how much we already have. And yet without being "more-than-enough" people, our wanting will always outpace our having, and we'll end up perpetually exhausted and forever dissatisfied.

If the presence of the gift-giving Christ makes us rich, rest will replace weariness, and peace will banish unending restlessness. Like the apostle Paul, we will then know the secret of being content whatever the circumstance, "of being well-fed and of going hungry, of having plenty and of being in need" (Philippians 4:12). And like the Apostle, we will then give, even if we must work hard to do so and sacrifice what's rightfully ours (see 1 Corinthians 9:1–24).

but what about the urgent need to give, giving gift?

A rich self has a distinct attitude toward the past, the present, and the future. It surveys the past with *gratitude* for what it has received, not with annoyance about what it hasn't achieved or about how little it has been given. A rich self lives in the present with *contentment*. Rather than never having enough of anything except for the burdens others place on it, it is "always having enough of everything" (2 Corinthians 9:8). It still strives, but it strives out of satisfied fullness, not out of the emptiness of craving. A rich self looks toward the future with *trust*. It gives rather than holding things back in fear of coming out too short, because it believes God's promise that God will take care of it. Finite and endangered, a rich self still gives, because its life is "hidden with Christ" in the infinite, unassailable, and utterly generous God, the Lord of the present, the past, and the future (see Colossians 3:3).

Christ, the Giver of Our Gifts

Pride leaves a stain on our giving, I suggested earlier. We give – and exude the self-righteousness of the morally upright. We give – and wield power over recipients in order to subdue them or extract their goods. We give – and flood recipients with a sense of our human and spiritual superiority. To give well, we need to leave arrogance behind. But how can we, when every act of giving seems to underscore our moral rectitude and power? Here too, God comes to the aid of our weakness.

One way God counters our pride is by driving our giving underground, by enveloping it in the shroud of secrecy. "Whenever you give," said Jesus, "do not sound a trumpet before you." Rather, "do not let your left hand know what your right hand is doing" so that your almsgiving "may be done in secret" (Matthew 6:2–4) – no two-handed, demonstrative, and self-promoting gifts allowed! Only one-handed, clandestine, and self-effacing gifts permitted![20] The rule is calculated to deflate pride, to deprive it of the air of praise from others that pride so desperately needs.

The second way God counters our pride is by teaching us how to value gifts. Mostly, we are mesmerized by a gift's size. The greater the gift, the more in awe of the giver we stand. But size doesn't matter, Jesus said. As I suggested of Jesus' teaching about the poor widow's gift, in reality the largest gift can be smaller than the smallest one, and the smallest gift can be greater than the largest one. The sacrifice of the givers and the purity of their intention, not the magnitude of the gift itself, constitute the gift's measure. Rejecting size as the gauge of a gift's greatness unsettles the giver's pride. Favorable comparisons nourish pride, but it's harder to gauge the greatness of people's sacrifice or the purity of their intention than it is to gauge the size of the gift. If we accept Jesus' standard of a gift's greatness, the givers' sense of moral superiority and power will languish.

Yet the main way God removes pride's stain from our giving is not by teaching us either how to give (secretly, not conspicuously) or how to measure gifts (by sacrifice and intention, not by size). For even when we've learned these two lessons, they counter pride but do not come close to removing it. Just as we can be proud of our humility, so we can be proud of giving modestly; we can be a "publican" or "a poor widow" and still put ourselves on display like any Pharisee or flamboyant giver. And the belief that sacrifice is the measure of a gift's greatness may just democratize pride rather than remove it – it may turn it from the prerogative of the wealthy and powerful into a possibility for everyone. Indeed, pride cannot be removed by teaching at all. We can be proud of anything we have learned.

It's not primarily God's teaching but God's presence and activity in us that can effectively heal our pride. We've seen that God is the giver of all gifts, even those we give to one another. Christ dwells in us, and the life we lead is Christ's life in us. The gifts we give to one another are Christ's gifts, not our own. Or rather, gifts are our own by being Christ's. For Christ is not a puppeteer and we the puppets. Christ is present at the core of our selves and therefore doesn't leave us behind, so to speak, when he works through us.

It's not just that all we have is from God – and then in our own good will, strength, and effort, we take from the storehouse of God's gifts to us and pass some on to others. That's true, but that's the point about the origin of gifts made in the previous section: God gives, so we have something to give. But there is more. Our passing on the gifts to others – our good will, strength, and effort – is God's. In Luther's terms, because the gift-giving Christ acts in us, when we give we are gift-bearing Christs to others. When we give, it's Christ who gives. As we think about ourselves as givers, there's something to rejoice about. We are instruments in God's hand, and we give to delight others and to alleviate their needs. But there's nothing to be proud of. God is doing the giving, and it is God, not us, who deserves honor and gratitude.

Strange Gratitude

Consider the apostle Paul's view of gratitude. To those of us used to thinking of ourselves as agents of our own giving, his comments on gratitude will seem strange, even unfair. As he mentioned gratitude in what amounts to a fundraising letter to the Corinthian believers, we might expect him to speak of the gratitude of the Jerusalem poor to *them*. But he doesn't. Somebody else gets the gratitude. "Your great generosity," he wrote, "will produce thanksgiving to *God* through us"; the gift "not only supplies the needs of the saints but also overflows with many thanksgivings to *God*" (2 Corinthians 9:11–13). The Corinthians do the giving, but God gets the thanks! Does that make sense? Only if it's true that when the Corinthians give, it's God who gives.

Human givers do receive thanks of sorts, but only indirectly. The Apostle's letter to the Philippians is one long thank-you note. They have financially supported his missionary efforts, and now he is writing to thank them – except that he never actually thanks them! Many of the epistle's readers are puzzled as to why. If he thanked them, would it look as if he were soliciting another gift (see Philippians 4:17)? Would he thereby acknowledge himself as their inferior? Whatever the reason, does the Apostle act like those who are greedy enough to accept gifts but too proud to acknowledge the debt?

Most likely he doesn't thank them directly because he believes that he hasn't received gifts *from* them but *through* them. The giver is God. They are the channels. In writing the letter, the apostle Paul did what Resha, in Gotthold Lessing's play *Nathan the Wise*, says she wants to do in regard to the young knight Templar, who saved her from the fire: "I want to thank God at the feet of this proud man."[21] Similarly, the Philippians received indirect thanks from the Apostle: In a letter addressed to *them*, he *thanked God for them* as supporters of his ministry (Philippians 1:3–11). And this is exactly as it should be – provided that it's God who gives when the Philippians give.

Contrast Seneca's view on gifts and gratitude with the Apostle's. In the treatise *On Benefits*, Seneca wrote, "In the case of the benefit, this is a binding rule for the two who are concerned – the one should straightaway forget that it was given, the other should never forget that it was received".[22] Modest givers forget that they have given; indeed, they forget while they are giving, claims Seneca.[23] Hence they resist the recipients' gratitude. Grateful receivers, on the other hand, never forget what they've received. Ingratitude is their worst vice.

Seneca's advice was wise. But can it work? Givers' forgetfulness and receivers' memory seem at odds with one another. The modesty of givers requires ingratitude from receivers; and the gratitude of receivers feeds the arrogance of givers. Seneca had trouble holding the modesty of givers and the gratitude of receivers together. The apostle Paul, on the other hand, held onto both the forgetfulness of givers and the memory of receivers without contradiction. He did that by making givers the instruments of God's giving. It's God who gives through human givers; human givers can forget their own giving. It's from God that recipients receive; recipients can remember the gift and give thanks to God. The vice of the giver's pride is banished, but the virtue of the recipient's gratitude retained. Givers are not superior to recipients on account of giving, and recipients are not diminished on account of receiving. Both are God's creatures, and both are recipients of God's gifts, even if one receives to pass on and the other receives to enjoy.

Imagine you are invited to a palatial home for a weekend getaway. Your hosts fly you there in a private jet. They wine you, dine you, and treat you royally. A chef prepares all your meals, and a waiter serves you. You ski through beautiful countryside toward a lakeside, and there chairs are arranged around a raging fire. A waiter greets you, wanting to know which of the five items on the menu you want served. And then the weekend draws to a close. As you are ready to step into the jet to be taken home – as you are about to wake up from your dream and face harsh reality – you thank your hosts. If they replied, "You are welcome. Glad to do what we can for the poor," or something to that effect, as much as you'd enjoyed your weekend you'd feel diminished in the process. But if instead they tell you, "We've done nothing for you; others – chefs, waiters, pilots – have done all the work." "But it's your home," you protest, "and it's your hard work that made all this possible." They look up and say, "It's all from God." You've enjoyed a wonderful gift, and there's no bitter aftertaste of being diminished by it.

Recipients' ingratitude may be one of the most difficult obstacles for givers to overcome. It wounds a giver's pride. "Look what I've done for him," says the giver, "and he can't even bring himself to say 'Thank you'!" True, the cause of a recipient's ingratitude may lie in the giver. A giver may be reluctant, for instance. A giver may exaggerate his sacrifice, act "with the air of the one who was robbing himself".[24] Or a giver may insult the recipient by "haughtily flinging" him a gift; the injury outstrips the benefit, and the recipient "shows gratitude enough" by pardoning "such a man for giving a benefit".[25] Sometimes, however, even a gift well given is received ungratefully.

In *The Brothers Karamazov*, Fyodor Dostoyevsky recounted the meeting between the saintly Father Zosima and a "lady of little faith". She wanted to become a sister of mercy, and as she thought about it, she was "full of strength to overcome all obstacles. No wounds, no festering sores" could frighten her. "I would bind them up," she said, "and wash them with my own hands. I would nurse the afflicted. I would be ready to kiss such wounds." But what if the patient didn't meet her with gratitude? she asked herself. What if he began abusing and rudely commanding her, "which often happens when people are in great suffering"? Here is how she responded to her own question:

"I came with horror to the conclusion that, if anything could dissipate my love to humanity, it would be ingratitude."[26] How can we continue to give when the cold winds of ingratitude blow in the face of our giving?

It will not help much if we simply remind ourselves: God gives to the ungrateful, and so should we. But it will help if we remember that it's God who gives when we give. For then we need to deflect gratitude that comes to us anyway. We are not its proper addressees. God is. And if we are convinced that gratitude doesn't properly belong to us, then ingratitude doesn't touch us. We are not disrespected by ingratitude; our pride is not injured. The ingratitude of recipients wrongs not us but the gift-giving God – the God whose goodness "gladly loses its good deed on the unthankful".[27] And so we too continue to give, even to the ungrateful.

The self in whom Christ is active is modest. It doesn't give in order to aggrandize itself, prove its moral worth, or demonstrate its power. It can forget itself in the act of giving and reach out to neighbors in love – it gives in order to delight in others and to help them in their needs.

Spirit of Generosity

Our giving is not just stained by selfishness and arrogance, however slight these stains may be. Often we are slothful givers, sometimes to the point of failing to be givers at all. We leave undone what we know we ought to do. We may lack energy or ability; we may feel that giving makes no difference and little sense. We withdraw a giving hand from others. We attend to our own needs and reward ourselves with luxuries both small and large. We are energetic and skilled in working for ourselves, but we are sluggish and clumsy in giving to others. What then makes it possible to give? God's Spirit counters our indolence.

So far, we've looked at God's twofold relation to us. First, we are God's creatures. Everything we have and are comes from God, and not just at the beginning of our lives to get us going, so to speak, but all along the way. Second, we are God's redeemed creatures. We are indwelled by Christ. Christ lives in us. When we give, it's Christ who gives through us. There is yet a third aspect of God's relationship to us. As God's redeemed creatures, we are endowed by God's Spirit. But why? What does the Spirit add?

First, the Spirit opens the doors of our hearts for Christ's indwelling. We must say "yes" for Christ to dwell in us, receiving him in faith and gratitude as God's gift. But how can we? Our eyes are blinded by sin, our will held captive by its power, so how do we even recognize Christ as God's gift, let alone desire him to make us into new creatures by dwelling in us? The apostle Paul's answer: the Spirit. Christ is in us, and we belong to Christ if the Spirit of God dwells in us (Romans 8:9–11). By the power of the Spirit, we make ourselves available for Christ to be born in us and to set us on an unsettling and yet deeply fulfilling journey of faith. By the Spirit, the Christ who is for all becomes the Christ for each and in each. The Spirit is the gift that gives Christ.

Second, the Spirit puts the talents of each person at Christ's disposal. In Mary, Christ's activity refracts itself through her character; in Peter, Christ's activity refracts itself through his propensities and talents. The same Christ works in each; but in each, Christ works differently because each is different. The Spirit connects the one activity of Christ with the different capacities and characteristics of each person Christ indwells. When that connection between Christ and our specific talents happens, spiritual gifts are imparted. The Spirit is the gift that gives spiritual gifts.

Think of the Spirit as the arms of our hearts that embrace Christ and as the open doors of our energies and skills that welcome Christ in. In these two ways, the Spirit enables each of us in our specific way to be a Christ to others — and thereby heals our indolence. Earlier, when discussing the stain of pride, I said: As we give, it's Christ who gives; the gifts are Christ's, and our pride is banished. Now, in discussing the stain of sloth, we can say: We give because, enabled by the Spirit, we have embraced the gift-giving Christ. The Spirit comes. Christ dwells and acts in us. Our inertia is overcome.

Gift, Fruit, and Future

The Spirit connects us with Christ and overcomes our indolence in four significant ways. The first has to do with our *talents*. We may be talented, but our talents can remain idle and undeveloped. Or we may employ them for our own benefit only – to legitimately acquire or to illicitly take. In that case, we do with our talents as we please and please ourselves as we do. But God gives us talents the way God gives us all other gifts: for ourselves as well as for others.

For the apostle Paul, spiritual gifts are "functions" of Christ's *body* (Romans 12:4–5), not simply each person's possession. Eyes don't see for themselves alone; they see for the body. Feet don't walk for themselves alone; they walk for the body, implied the Apostle (1 Corinthians 12:14–17). Spiritual gifts are deficient if they serve only their bearers, especially if their main purpose is to feed the bearers' vanity. They are for the community's benefit, for its "upbuilding", to use the Apostle's term (1 Corinthians 14:1–19).

Consider, second, what the Apostle called "the *fruit* of the Spirit" (Galatians 5:22–23). We may call it a Christ-like character, consisting in virtues of "love, joy, peace, patience, kindness, generosity, faithfulness, gentleness, and self-control". Notice whose fruit these qualities are: the Spirit's. We might think that if they are the Spirit's fruit then they can't be ours as well. But that's not how the Apostle thought of it. The link between the Spirit and us is so intimate that the fruit *is* ours by being the fruit of the Spirit who indwells us.

The organic metaphor of fruit is significant. Fruit is neither made nor squeezed out of a plant; it grows on its own. So do Christ-like virtues. And so does giving, when it's at its best. It then becomes second nature.

During the Nazi occupation of France, citizens of the small Huguenot community of Le Chambon saved the lives of many Jews by hiding them from their persecutors. When pressed to say why they courageously risked their own lives for others or when praised for their moral greatness, they were genuinely puzzled. "How can you call us 'good'?" they responded to the author of *Lest Innocent Blood Be Shed*, a book that offers an account of their extraordinary generosity.

"We were doing what had to be done ... You must understand that it was the most natural thing in the world to help these people."[28]

The most natural thing in the world is to risk one's life for another!? It is the most natural thing for a good tree to bear good fruit. But how is it possible to be a good tree growing in a forest of bad ones, as the Huguenots of Le Chambon certainly were? The answer to this question has many components. I have explored some of them in this chapter. But they all ultimately come down to this: We are good trees who bear good fruit, wrote the apostle Paul, because "we live by the Spirit", whose fruit our gift giving is (Galatians 5:25).

The Spirit counters our indolence as givers by molding our character to conform to Christ's and employing our talents for others' benefit. The Spirit also gives us *hope*. Often we experience a sense of futility in giving. We give, and recipients seem none the better for it. Unscrupulous people insert themselves between our gifts and the recipient's benefits, and gifts seem to disappear together with their intended benefits. Or recipients seem to receive gifts like a black hole sucks in light. Giving doesn't make sense, not so much because we lose by giving but because the world doesn't gain much. We give, but it seems to us that we aren't mending the world.

What is the relationship between our gifts and others' benefits? We tend to think of it in terms of cause and effect. The gift is the cause; the benefit is the effect. As causes produce effects, giving should produce benefits. Often that's not what happens, so we despair of giving.

But in fact, our gifts and others' benefits are not related as causes and effects. They are related as the cross and the resurrection. Christ gave his life on the cross – and it seemed as though he died in vain. His disciples quickly deserted him, his cause was as dead as he was, and even his God seemed to have abandoned him. But then he was resurrected from the dead by the power of the Spirit. He was seated at the right hand of God and raised in the community of believers, his social body alive and growing on earth. Did Christ's "gift of death" cause his own resurrection and its benefits for the world? It didn't. The Spirit did. So it is with every true gift of our own, however small or large.

Like Christ's healings or feedings of multitudes, often our gifts offer immediate help. We give, and the hungry are fed, the sorrowful comforted, and loved ones delighted. We are like a tree, laden with fruit that only waits to be picked. At other times, we give, and the gift seems less like a ripe fruit than like a seed planted in the ground. For a while, nothing happens. Dark earth covered with cold winter holds the seed captive. Then spring comes, and we see new life sprouting, maybe even growing beyond our wildest imagination.

Sometimes it seems as if a fate worse than lying in the dark earth befalls our gifts. It is almost as if some evil bird takes away the seed we planted before it can sprout and bear fruit. We labor in vain. We give – and it seems that no one benefits. Yet we can still hope. The Spirit who makes a tree heavy with fruit and who gives life to the seed that has died will ultimately claim every good gift that the evil one has snatched away. Just as the Spirit resurrected the crucified one and made his sacrifice bear abundant fruit, so the Spirit will raise us in the spring of everlasting life to see the harvest of our own giving. Our giving is borne by the wings of the Spirit's hope.

Community

Finally, the Spirit counters our indolence by placing us within the *community* of Christ's body. Community helps craft us into good givers. It's in the community that the Spirit suffuses our giving with hope; we hope because we are part of a community of hope. It's in the community that the Spirit molds our character; we display a life of virtue because we live in a community that values and fosters virtue. And how does the Spirit energize and direct our talents? We allow the community's needs to lay claim on us, and we seek the community's wisdom to help us discern what we are good at. Finally, it is by the Spirit and through the waters of baptism that we die with Christ and rise to new life in him. We don't receive the Spirit's hope, the Spirit's fruit, the Spirit's gifts, and Christ's life on our own as isolated individuals. They are ours as we are members of a community of giving, whether that community is a family, a circle of close friends, or a church.

If we live with good givers – if we watch them succeed, fail, and persevere, if we are challenged by them or called to account by them – then we too become good givers. "Be imitators of me, as I am of Christ," wrote the apostle Paul in his first letter to the Corinthians (11:1). As he had foregone the right to payment for his service as an apostle, so the enlightened believers in Corinth should forego their rights and not do what offends others (8:1 – 11:1). Good practices are not quite contagious, at least not in most cases. Otherwise no instruction or admonition would be needed. But without good practices, no instruction or admonition would be effective. To be good givers, we must be apprentices to good givers.

Earlier I wrote that community *helps* craft us into good givers. Why *helps*? Why not just *crafts* us? Of what does that help consist? Disciplining us into being givers? Employing technologies for shaping our indolent selves into active and skillful givers? No, bad communities do that; they have molds and the means to squeeze people into them. And that's also how hypocrites are made, as Luther rightly observed in *The Freedom of the Christian*.[29] The relation between the life of the community and the gift giving of its members is not a direct one. Communities don't make givers. Givers are not made by humans at all. They are born – born *of* the Spirit *through* the good practices of communities. God's Spirit is the agent; people are the instruments. That's how it is in regard to giving gifts. And that's how it is in regard to crafting givers.

INTERLUDE: DANIEL'S DEATH

"You never even hinted at blaming her," I said to my mother as we were driving together recently.

Forty-seven years after the accident, I was finally piecing together one part of the puzzle I thought I already knew. My most beloved nanny, Aunt Milica as I called her, the angel of my early childhood whom I adored until her death at the age of ninety-one, was in charge of us kids when it happened. I was one then, and my five-year-old brother, Daniel, had slipped through the large gate in the courtyard where we had an apartment. He went to the nearby small military base – just two blocks away – to play with "his" soldiers. On earlier walks through the neighborhood, he had found some friends there – soldiers in training, bored and in a need of diversion even if it came from an energetic five-year-old.

On that fateful day in 1957, one of them put him on a horse-drawn bread wagon. As they were passing through the gate on a bumpy cobblestone road, Daniel leaned sideways and his head got stuck between the door post and the wagon. The horses kept going. He died on the way to hospital – a son lost to parents who adored him, and an older brother that I would never know.

Aunt Milica should have watched him. But she didn't. She let him slip out, she didn't look for him, and he was killed. But my parents never told me that she was partly responsible.

"Should I have told you?" my mother replied to me, half unsure whether she did the right thing.

"Most people would," I thought. When terrible things happen, people find someone to blame even when there's no one to blame. Somebody must be at fault, they think, and they go on to make the first plausible candidate into a culprit. Aunt Milica *was* to be blamed. Yet neither of my parents blamed her in front of their own children. Aunt Milica, the guilty one, remained my untainted angel.

"No," I told my mother slowly. "By keeping silent, you did something very, very beautiful. I admire you so much for it. Love hides a multitude of sins, says the apostle Peter …"

She is a saint, I thought, this mother of mine who had buried four of her six children – three died in her own womb, and the fourth was killed because those in charge were irresponsible and stupidly careless. My mother's pain was immeasurable, and it did not go away even half a century later. She would talk of Daniel's death on occasions, always mentioning with deep sadness that the night before he was killed, Daniel had asked to sleep in her bed. He slept restlessly, and she slept lightly even when she was exhausted by factory work, so she denied him what was to be his last wish.

The pain of that terrible loss still lingers on, but bitterness and resentment against those who were responsible are gone. It was healed at the foot of the cross as my mother gazed on the Son who was killed and reflected about the God who forgave. Aunt Milica was forgiven, and there was no more talk of her guilt, not even talk of her having *been* guilty. As far as I was concerned, she was innocent.

But my parents did speak often of forgiveness in relation to Daniel's death. In fact, the first lesson in forgiveness I remember lay in the story of how they forgave the soldier who was the main culprit. "The Word of God tells us to forgive as God in Christ has forgiven us," said my parents, "and so we decided to forgive." The soldier felt terrible, so terrible in fact that he had to be admitted to the hospital. My father, with a wound in his heart that would never quite heal, went to visit him, to comfort the one whose carelessness had caused him so much grief, and tell him that my mother and he forgave him.

In the courtroom too, my father insisted that he and my mother, who was too brokenhearted to take part in the hearing, had forgiven. They wouldn't press charges, he said. Why should one more mother be plunged into grief, this time because the life of her son, a good boy but careless in a crucial moment, was ruined by the hands of justice. After the soldier was discharged from the army and went home unpunished, my father visited him even though it took him two days to make the trip. He was concerned for the soldier and wanted to talk to him once more of God's love, which is greater than our accusing hearts, and of my parents' forgiveness.

The reason why my parents forgave was simple. God forgave them, and so they forgave the soldier. But the forgiveness itself was difficult, and for my mother, excruciatingly painful. I will revisit the pain of my mother's forgiveness in chapter 6. My father never talked about how it felt forgiving a person who killed his boy; he never talked much about how anything felt, though he was a deeply sensitive man. But that forgiveness must have cost him a great deal too, possibly no less than it cost my mother. A *soldier* was responsible for Daniel's death even if it was an accident. And the army he served was set up to defend the communist regime that had mistreated my father outrageously just a decade earlier, and that even then considered him, a Christian minister, its enemy.

Close to the end of World War II, my father was a nineteen-year-old soldier, drafted into the regular army of the Croatian puppet regime that collaborated with the Nazis. He was a baker by trade. As a soldier, he trained for a few months without ever firing a single shot and then baked bread for his military unit. He was also a socialist who marched on the streets of Zagreb protesting the unjust treatment of workers.

While in the army, one day, together with another soldier and an officer, he tried to defect to Tito's partisans who were fighting against the Nazis and for the socialist revolution. If they were caught, they would be killed on the spot for deserting. To protect them, the officer told the two young soldiers that, in case their mission failed, they should pretend that they didn't know where they were going; they were just obeying his orders. They were caught – and my father owed his life only to the fact that the officer, who was killed shortly afterward, kept quiet to save at least the lives of the two soldiers if he could not save his own.

The war was soon over, Nazis and their collaborators were routed out, and the socialist revolution was underway, led by the Communist Party. All the soldiers of the Croatian regular army were summoned to report to authorities. They were to be given passes so they could return to their homes. They had nothing to fear, they were assured, if they had committed no crimes. My father's biggest crime was that he baked bread for the non-combatant units of the defeated enemy. And his ideological sympathies were with communists, so much so that he was willing to risk his life to join them. So he confidently strode to the address given. As soon as he arrived, the door closed behind him without anyone even asking for his name. He was trapped in a communist concentration camp.

Soon he became just one shadowy figure in the long lines of camp inmates who were forced to march for months from one village to the next, apparently for no other purpose than to die along the way. They existed on hardly more than a daily ration of a bit of bread and watery soup. To eat a few beans somebody gave him along the way, he had to cook them in a dirty paint can. Just a few weeks earlier, a hungry fellow prisoner stopped for a moment to pick a ripe fruit from a tree they were passing. He was shot on the spot. Anybody who could not keep up was killed. Your life depended on a good pair of shoes. My father had such a pair – and had enough sense to cut the leather on their tips so they would not be stolen. After months of suffering without knowing whether he would be dead or alive the next moment, that flash of ingenuity seemed just a postponement of the inevitable; he had come to feel like an animal, fatally wounded but still running. He was in hell, and the dark figure of menacing death seemed like an angel of redemption. He cursed the communists, he cursed his own life. But he saved his choicest curses for the God of his Baptist upbringing.

Eventually, he whose anger was burning against God did find a God of mercy in the hell of that concentration camp. Or rather God found him. But that's a story for another occasion. It's because of God that my father could later muster the strength to forgive that soldier who had killed his son, to forgive a servant of the brutal regime that enacted on him the very opposite of forgiveness, something even worse than vengeance. He was innocent, he was a socialist who had risked his life to join the cause – but his guards didn't even want to know his name, let alone hear his story. They tortured him without mercy as if he were the worst enemy. He received indiscriminate brutality directed against the innocent. But he gave forgiveness born out of compassion for the guilty.

In recent decades, there has been much talk about forgiveness and reconciliation. "There is no future without forgiveness," we heard from leaders of the new South Africa, for instance, as that country was trying to rebuild itself after the ravages of apartheid. And quite apart from evils perpetrated by oppressive regimes, in counseling sessions with priests and psychiatrists, millions of individuals all over the world explore ways to forgive those who have wounded them so that they can find release from crippling bitterness and resentment, and mend relationships with their coworkers, families, friends, and lovers.

According to a Croatian saying, people talk about what they don't have. We talk about forgiveness because we live in a sentimental but unforgiving culture. Consider the mushrooming litigiousness in the United States. Children are suing parents for rights, lovers are suing for unfulfilled romance, conservative Christians are suing as a means to advance their political agenda, coffee drinkers are suing restaurants for serving drinks too hot for their sensitive tongues, and pedestrians who have slipped and fallen are suing homeowners for having left a pebble or two on their sidewalk. If we could, we'd sue God, it seems, for having created a world in which bad things happen.

Some such suits are understandable. If a person has been incapacitated by the malpractice of unscrupulous doctors, she ought not to have to worry how she will survive because she cannot work. Yet many suits seem frivolous. Instead of forgiving and restoring relationship, litigants seek to punish and to extract maximal compensation. More than just insisting on their rights, they seek to maximize their profits at the other's expense. Far from being concerned with justice, they are often driven by vengeance and greed.

The world of interactive entertainment may be the most disconcerting indicator of the looming gracelessness. *Grand Theft Auto: Vice City*, an insanely popular video game, places the player into the role of Tommy Vercetti, a drug dealer who has been double-crossed and is on a vendetta to get his money back. The video "places virtually no restrictions to the player's actions in the game," a commentator writes. "For example, the player can steal automobiles for transportation (hence the title of the series); rob convenience stores for a little extra cash; run over innocent pedestrians; engage in drive-by shootings; kill just about anyone; pick up and be 'serviced' by prostitutes (which temporarily increases the player's health above the normal maximum); and the list goes on and on."[1] For the duration of the game, you can let your imagination slip into the netherworld of limitless vengeance pursued with indiscriminate violence. This is a "kickass" culture, a world of brute destructive force, unbound by any moral constraints and unmoored from any hope of redemption.

Generosity? Forgiveness? What happened with these jewels of our humanity? They have fallen victim to the same dark urges that make people in the United States alone spend 7,300,000,000 dollars a year on such video games. The blood and gore of those same video games indicate where that culture is likely to end up, in a place where people abandon justice in favor of revenge and scoff at the redeeming power of forgiveness. If that happens, common life will then be possible only if some mighty Leviathan imposes its will on us and robs us of our freedom. To keep liberty we need grace. To live humanely we must learn to forgive.

But forgiveness is difficult, even painful, and sometimes it feels utterly impossible. Why should we give a gift of forgiveness when every atom of our wounded bodies screams for justice or even revenge? What would it mean for us to forgive and forgive wisely? And maybe above all, how do we muster enough strength to overcome resistance to forgiving? These are the questions I will explore in the following three chapters. What follows is, in a sense, nothing more than the unfolding of that most generous act with which my parents forgave that soldier and my saintly nanny for causing Daniel's death.

Chapter 4

GOD THE FORGIVER

Ernest Hemingway began one of his memorable short stories entitled "The Capital of the World" with the following lines:

> Madrid is full of boys named Paco, which is diminutive of the name Francisco, and there is a Madrid joke about a father who came to Madrid and inserted an advertisement in the personal columns of *El Liberal* which said: PACO MEET ME AT HOTEL MONTANA NOON TUESDAY ALL IS FORGIVEN PAPA and how a squadron of Guardia Civil had to be called out to disperse the eight hundred young men who answered the advertisement.[1]

The joke is about the ubiquity of the name "Paco" in Spain. But it works only because of the underlying longing of many to be forgiven, whether they are sons or daughters, mothers or fathers, friends or colleagues. We desire forgiveness because we value relationships, and we know that relationships cannot be mended without forgiveness.

Why does it take forgiveness to mend a relationship? First, we have to answer an even more fundamental, underlying question: How should we handle a situation when someone wrongs someone else? Wrongdoing rattles and possibly even undoes a relationship. A friend has betrayed us, and we have suffered disappointment, loss, possibly even serious harm. A father has abused us, and we carry the scars for the rest of our lives. We've been caught in a whirlwind of ethnic violence and have done to our neighbors things that no decent human being thought she could ever do. Forgiveness is one uniquely important way we deal with wrongdoing. That's why we value forgiveness.

But it's hard to carry out. Often we don't see why we should forgive. Or we want to forgive but don't seem able to. And other times, we forgive, but our forgiveness is rejected as an insult, and the relationship ends up in even greater disrepair. If we could somehow neutralize the wrongdoing, our reasoning goes, we would be able to restore the relationship without having to do the hard work of forgiving.

There are two major ways to neutralize wrongdoing. First, if we could somehow undo the done deed, wrongdoing would be gone, and forgiveness would be unnecessary. But we can't. In the heat of an argument, we say an unkind word or make an exaggerated accusation, and our opponent challenges us, "Take that back!" Even if we consent and say, "All right, I didn't mean what I said," we still haven't really taken it back. Our words remain forever uttered, even when they are long forgotten. Or in a moment of inattention, we hit a cyclist with a car, and she dies. At night or in a quiet moment of the day, we play the scene over and over again, wishing desperately to undo the tragedy and to somehow make it not have happened. But our deed remains forever done. Our life isn't a motion picture in which we can, like a discerning editor, run a bad scene backward, cut it out, and keep replacing it with better ones until we are pleased with the result and are ready to show it to a critical audience.

The reason a done deed cannot be undone is simple. Unlike movie projectors, our lives don't have a "reverse" button. Time, in which we inescapably live, is irreversible. We can't take its arrow and, when it suits us, point it backward for a while. Utterly implacable to all our pleas, time runs, and runs only forward. Until our time is up, we can do new deeds, but we can't undo the old ones. And that's why we need forgiveness.

There is another possibility for neutralizing wrongdoing and relieving us of the need to do the hard work of forgiving. If our wrongful acts did not "stick" to us as our fault and our guilt, if they were not imputable to us, forgiveness would be dispensable. A shark sees a surfer on a surfboard, mistakes her for a seal, and takes a terrifying bite. The surfer has lost a leg and owes her life only to the shark's preference for rich blubber over hard bone and lean muscle. But there is nothing here for the surfer to forgive. In attacking her, the shark did what sharks do. It cannot be blamed for its deed. Its actions are not imputable to it. The shark has seriously injured the surfer, but it hasn't wronged her.

If the victim's friend knew, however, that the place was infested by sharks but took her to surf there anyhow without warning her, then there would be something for the injured surfer to forgive. Her friend should have warned her. And the fact that he didn't is rightly considered as his wrongdoing and his guilt. He is partly responsible for the injury. The surfer was wronged by her friend, and something needs to be done with the wrongdoing if the relationship between them is to be restored. We need forgiveness because human beings are not like sharks. We are rightly faulted for our misdeeds.

So there are two important reasons we can't just dispense with wrongdoing and therefore need to do the hard work of forgiving. One has to do with the metaphysical structure of the world: Time doesn't run backward, and a done deed cannot be undone. The other has to do with our deep intuitions about human beings. Harm suffered by the negligence or the intentional act of another is imputable to the one who has done it. The wrongdoing sits like a burden on the shoulders of the one who has committed it.

What Is Forgiveness?

What does forgiveness do with the wrongdoing? A bare-bones description of how forgiveness works reveals at least two important actions.

First, to forgive is to name the wrongdoing and to condemn it. After he had spotted his own Paco among the 800 gathered in front of Hotel Montana, we can imagine the father taking his son up to his room and telling him, "Paco, your mother cried her eyes out after you disappeared without a word and with all our money. You stole what we've saved for our old age – we are not young anymore, you know! – and it looks like you squandered every penny of it on sex and gambling. You've done a very bad thing, my son."

A condemnation of the wrongdoing is one element of forgiveness, its indispensable negative presupposition. Had the father stopped with the condemnation, however, Paco would have just stood accused and would have remained unforgiven. But there is a second element to forgiveness, its positive content. To forgive is to give wrongdoers the gift of not counting the wrongdoing against them. After telling him what a bad thing he had done, a forgiving father might continue: "But Paco, my dear boy, have you looked in the mirror lately? You don't look well. Your mother and I have decided to forgive you. You are our son; we won't count it against you. Come, give your old man a big hug, and let's get ourselves a good meal and go home." The condemned wrongdoing has been lifted from the wrongdoer's shoulders. The generous release of a genuine debt is the heart of forgiveness.

Forgiveness is a special kind of gift. When we give, we seek the good of another, not our own good, or at least we don't primarily seek our own good. The same is true of forgiveness. We forgive for another's sake, though we too may benefit from the result. But there is also an important difference between giving and forgiving. We give when we delight in others or others are in need; by giving, we enhance their joy or make up for their lack. We forgive when others have wronged us; by forgiving, we release them from the burden of their wrongdoing. The difference lies in the violation suffered, in the burden of wrongdoing, offense, transgression, debt. And that's what makes it more difficult to forgive than to give.

When we are immersed in intimate relationships with deep emotional attachments, like those between fathers and sons, for instance, it makes sense to forgive even if it is difficult. But if we step back and survey human interaction more objectively, even that between family members and close friends, a worm of doubt starts to gnaw away at our happy embrace of forgiveness. Does forgiveness simply let the wrongdoer off the hook, and if so, isn't that an affront to our sense of dues-paying justice? Does a wronged person even have the right to forgive the wrongdoer? Is it wise for a wronged person to forgive? By not letting the offense count against the offender, forgiveness seems to remove a major incentive for a wrongdoer to change.

The problems with forgiveness don't stop there. Even after we forgive, the offender still seems to remain guilty, before God and before humans. Forgiveness, one could argue, removes the anger and blame we direct against offenders and lets them go free, but it can't possibly remove the guilt of the offenders' wrongdoing. Except for securing the wronged person's peace of heart, isn't forgiveness nearly superfluous, on top of being possibly unwise and certainly unjust?

If forgiveness involved only two parties, the one who forgives (the wronged person) and the one who receives forgiveness (the wrong-doer), it would not be easy to defend it against the objections contained in such probing questions. But it doesn't. For Christians, forgiving, like giving in general, always takes place in a triangle, involving the wrongdoer, the wronged person, and God. Take God away, and the foundations of forgiveness become unsteady and may even crumble.

What is God's relationship to forgiveness? It's similar to God's relationship to giving in general. Briefly, God is the God who for-gives. We forgive because God forgives. We forgive as God forgives. We forgive by echoing God's forgiveness. So to understand our own forgiving, we need to start with God's, which brings us to two com-mon misconceptions of God that concern God's relation to wrong-doing: that God is an implacable judge and that God is a doting grandparent. These echo the two misconceptions of God explored in chapter 1, that of God as either a tough divine negotiator or as a soft, heavenly Santa.

The Judge

Recall what I wrote in chapter 1 about God the negotiator. If that image governs how we think of God, we will relate to God in the mode of buying and selling. We'll try to make deals with God. If we want something from God, we'll offer God something in return.

Antonio Salieri wanted musical genius and offered God his industry, devotion, and chastity. But it's unwise to treat God as a negotiator, because God can dispense with whatever we have to offer. Moreover, given that God is infinitely rich, the divine giver can give even to those who offer nothing in return. We also dishonor God, we have seen, if we try to make deals with God. God is not a negotiator, but a generous giver who has given us everything that we have and could possibly offer. But let's leave the dishonoring of God aside for a moment and dwell a bit longer on the thoughtlessness of treating God as negotiator.

If God is a negotiator, what happens if we break the deal we've made? What happens if Salieri finds himself unable to resist the charms of the young, pretty soprano Katherina Cavalieri and slips up on the chastity part of his bargain with God? God the negotiator inescapably turns into God the judge. Salieri broke the deal, and he must bear the consequences. Salieri might want to plead for mercy. But he'd be inconsistent to make deals with God when it suited him and to receive gifts from God when it didn't. If God is a negotiator, then there's no room for gifts. You break the deal, you pay.

Just as we are at a disadvantage when negotiating a deal with God, so we are at a disadvantage when we break it. Salieri's deal didn't work. God gave young Mozart gifts Salieri couldn't even dream of. But let's imagine for a moment that God accepted the deal and Salieri broke it. Salieri would be in trouble. He wouldn't be able to hide his infraction from God; God sees everything. He couldn't run away from God when summoned to account for himself; God is everywhere. He couldn't talk God into being lenient with him. God sees through rhetorical ploys, and no moment of weakness would make God, if God were simply a divine judge, bend justice a bit in Salieri's favor. Salieri couldn't run from the hand of punishing justice; God is all-powerful and God can make him pay. If Salieri protested, as he might, God could well tell him, "A deal is a deal; and a broken deal is a broken deal." Harsh? It is. The implacable judge is what we get, however, if we relate to God as negotiator.

Luther's Scruples

Martin Luther knew what it meant for God to be an implacable judge. Thinking back about his time at the monastery before he discovered the God of pure love and started the Protestant Reformation, he wrote: "In the monastery I did not think about women, money, or possessions; instead my heart trembled and fidgeted about whether God would bestow His grace on me."[2] Why did Luther's poor heart tremble and fidget before God? Why did "a monk without reproach" still feel that he "was a sinner before God with an extremely disturbed conscience", as Luther described himself toward the end of his life?[3]

We may be tempted to dismiss Luther's troubled conscience as a case of severe religious neurosis. Indeed, a small academic industry is devoted to explaining Luther's sense of guilt psychologically. A good deal of it traces Luther's moral hypersensitivity and fear of God to his stern and excessively demanding parents, especially to his father, Hans. But Luther's keen awareness of his own sinfulness and his corresponding terror of the divine judge were not primarily psychological. They were the expected psychological consequences of prior theological judgments about God and the right way to live. If Hans had anything to do with Luther's troubled conscience, it might have been to keep the young Luther's sense of moral excellence awake and to nudge him to be honest in assessing his own failures.

Let's try to think about the matter the way Luther did. The sum of God's law is this: "You shall love the Lord your God with all your heart, and with all your soul, and with all your strength, and with all your mind; and your neighbor as yourself" (Luke 10:27). Interpret this injunction as what it is – God's command – and not as a friend's suggestion. Then take seriously two little words: *all* ("all your heart") and *as* ("as yourself"). Now imagine God as an implacable judge, and you'll begin to tremble and fidget yourself! As he examined himself carefully, Luther couldn't find a moment in his life in which he fulfilled *that* law. He loved God, but only with a portion of his heart. He loved his neighbor, but he loved himself more.

Consequently, he wrote, I could "not but imagine that I had angered God, whom I in turn had to appease by doing good works".[4] Why did he need to appease God? Because he saw God as a condemning judge.

It doesn't take Luther's kind of spiritual scrupulousness, inflamed by God's command, to discover the pervasiveness of evil in the world and in our own souls. In the novel *The Human Stain*, Philip Roth used "stain" as a metaphor for evil. "It's in everyone. Indwelling. Inherent. Defining. The stain that is there before its mark ... The stain that precedes disobedience, that *encompasses* disobedience and perplexes all explanation and understanding." As we live in the world, we leave a stained trail; "there is no other way to be here". [5] If, like Roth himself, we consider this "elemental imperfection" simply the way things are, we will have to put up with it, trying to maximize enjoyment and minimize suffering. If we believe in a gift-giving God who created the world out of love, we will hope for redemption and consummation – for the righting of everything that has gone wrong with the world at the end of time. But if we imagine God as an implacable judge, then terror of God will be the most understandable reaction. There would be nothing neurotic about it.

Luther's existential problem was not psychological but theological. He resolved it by coming to believe that there was something terribly wrong with the image of God as an implacable judge.

Failure of Punishment

If God were an implacable judge, then God would deal with wrongdoing by punishment. The demand for the wrongdoer to be punished is understandable. Having committed a wrongdoing, he receives a just penalty for what he's done. The wronged person will be satisfied. For the blow she received, the wrongdoer will get a rough equivalent, and a bit more to account for the fact that the original injury was unprovoked. There is nothing vengeful about the expectation of a punishment equivalent to the injury. The expectation is as elemental as the expectation that if I borrow fifty dollars from you, I should give you fifty dollars back.

If the wrongdoer is governed by a sense of justice rather than simply his own self-interest, he will understand the rationale for punishment. He has incurred a debt by his misdeed. By suffering punishment, he'll pay what he owes. He'll then be free, and nothing will stand in the way of his integration back into the community.

The idea of punishment seems compelling, however, only if we consider what we might call midlevel offenses – like stealing a car or robbing a bank. Magnify the crime sufficiently, and punishment leaves us unsatisfied. What would be an adequate punishment for Joseph Stalin, Lenin's evil and dictatorial successor in the old Soviet Union between the two World Wars? He not only ruined his own country and invaded many neighboring ones, but in the process exterminated some 20,000,000 people. If we are after justice, his crime will have outstripped by far any punishment we could devise for him. How many deaths would he have to die to compensate for all the lives he took? How many lives would he need to have to suffer all the pain he inflicted? Punishment alone falters before the enormity of such crime.

Go to the opposite end of the scale of wrongdoing and punishment still seems unworkable. Imagine what would happen if each of us was punished for *every* transgression we committed – for every sarcastic remark, for every unkind thought, for every intentionally misleading comment! We wrong others all the time, even if only slightly. When that fierce nineteenth-century philosopher and pitiless enemy of all sentimentality, Friedrich Nietzsche, argued that to live is to be unjust, he didn't exaggerate. In his own way, he was just echoing Luther's assessment of the human condition, who was in turn echoing the apostle Paul's belief that all human beings are "under the power of sin" (Romans 3:9) and live unjust lives before the eyes of a just God.

I explored the pervasiveness of sin in chapter 2. Here I want to draw an important conclusion from it: If to live is to be unjust, then to live is also to be punished – provided we believe punishment is the way to deal with wrongdoing. The consequences of this thought are dark. As our wrongdoings multiply, punishment would pile upon punishment, and life itself would be beaten to the ground, destroyed. Punishment is a very rough and wholly inadequate tool for dealing with wrongdoing.

A story claiming to be rabbinic appeared in a newspaper some time ago: Before setting out to create the world, the Almighty took a moment to look into the future of creation. God saw beauty, truth, goodness, and the joy of creatures, but the All-Knowing One also saw a never-ending stream of human misdeeds, small, large, and horrendous, a trail of sighs, tears, and blood. "If I give sinners their due," thought the Just One, "I'll have to destroy the world that I am about to create. Should I create just to destroy?" And so God decided to forgive the world in advance so that the world could be brought into being. Creation owes its very existence to God's forgiveness.

I don't know whether this story is authentically rabbinic or not. A similar idea can be found in the New Testament. The apostle Peter wrote that Christ was destined as God's Lamb "before the foundation of the world" (1 Peter 1:20). Building on statements like these, some theologians have suggested that the world was created so that it would be redeemed and finally glorified. Redemption, they maintained, was not a solution God thought up after human beings botched up God's first attempt. Instead it was the purpose of creation. This view may or may not be right. But it does seem that God decided to redeem the world of sin before the Creator could lay down its foundations. Each of us exists because the gift of life rests on the gift of forgiveness.

The Doting Grandparent

Recall the other prevalent way we think about God, God as the Santa Claus. We make deals with the negotiator; we expect gifts, lots of them, from Santa. Such a God gives indiscriminately and abundantly, for no other reason than for being God and with no other condition than our very existence. When we do wrong – well, we can't do any wrong in the eyes of such a God. "His parents ne'er agreed except in doting / Upon the most inquiet imp on earth," wrote Lord Byron of the young Don Juan, "a little curly-haired and good for-nothing, and mischief making monkey from his birth."[6] Something similar could be said of "Santa God's" relation to humanity. Faced with human wrongdoing, such a God becomes a doting grandparent who, for the most part, sees and hears no evil.

Most of us love the idea of being God's favorites who can do no wrong. We also live in a culture that pushes us into the arms of such a doting grandparent God. First, we see ourselves as good. Unlike Luther, as we peel back the layers of our souls in self-examination, we don't expect to find a self tainted by sin. Instead, many of us are confident that, after we have undertaken the impossible task of removing cultural influences, we will reach our own true core, which is uncompromisingly good.

We don't deny that we are self-interested, even self-centered. But that's what a self is, by definition. Luther thought it was a problem – a big problem – if we didn't love God completely and our neighbor as ourselves, as Jesus commands. We are more inclined to think that it would be a problem if we *did* what such an excessively demanding law requires. Today, a God who wants all our love strikes many as monomaniacal. And for the self to love its neighbor as itself, many of us think that it would need to cease to be itself. Our standards of moral excellence are much lower than Luther's. We think that as long as we don't harm others, we are basically fine. In contrast, Luther thought that if we don't attend to others as much as to ourselves, we're in trouble.

Second, many of us think that what we do in our own private spheres, especially what we think, feel, and desire, is nobody else's business, not even God's. If we act out what we think or desire – if we speak a word that cuts someone down or if we act out a fantasy that harms someone else – only then is there a reason for legitimate concern.

In contrast, Luther looked inside himself to examine whether he loved God as he should – with all that was in him. He examined not just his deeds but his intentions, feelings, and desires to see whether he loved his neighbor as himself. Like the apostle Paul, he believed that God is interested in the "secret thoughts of all" (Romans 2:16).

His interior life was God's affair and the affair of his religious community. Many of us consider our interior lives to be our own exclusive domain. "Bad men do what good men dream about," goes the saying. You could take it to mean that even good men prove to be bad if you examine their dreams. But many of us take the saying to mean that as long as we only *fantasize* about bad things, we're fine.

Third, we believe that we should be affirmed, no matter what. Affirmation is, of course, what a self that thinks well of itself expects. Anything else can feel like a misreading of who we are, even an insult. We've also come to believe that, for the most part, we don't need to use condemnation to pluck out the weeds of evil deeds from our gardens. Rather, by receiving abundant affirmation, we feel we can water our noble plants, our fair dealings with others, our generosity toward those around us, and the weeds will take care of themselves. Affirmation, not condemnation, is the cure for misbehavior. A God who condemned our deeds would be a bad God, or at least a psychologically unsophisticated God. An acceptable God is the one who leaves our wrongdoing alone and takes care of our well-being. A good God is the one who gives us all we need and affirms us and all our deeds. Such a God is basically a divine version of a doting grandparent.

God's Wrath

The apostle Paul ascribed to God actions and attitudes that stand in sharp contrast with how such a doting grandparent behaves. He spoke rather freely of God's "judgment", "condemnation", even of God's "wrath" (see Romans 1:18–3:20). Setting aside the litany of things that the Apostle believed merit God's condemnation, let's focus on the fact of it. In particular, let's examine the appropriateness of God's wrath, the strongest form of God's censure. We'll return to the nature of God's wrath in the next chapter.

I used to think that wrath was unworthy of God. Isn't God love? Shouldn't divine love be beyond wrath? God is love, and God loves every person and every creature. That's exactly why God is wrathful against some of them. My last resistance to the idea of God's wrath was a casualty of the war in the former Yugoslavia, the region from which I come. According to some estimates, 200,000 people were killed and over 3,000,000 were displaced. *My* villages and cities were destroyed, *my* people shelled day in and day out, some of them brutalized beyond imagination, and I could not imagine God not being angry. Or think of Rwanda in the last decade of the past century, where 800,000 people were hacked to death in one hundred days! How did God react to the carnage? By doting on the perpetrators in a grandparently fashion? By refusing to condemn the bloodbath but instead affirming the perpetrators' basic goodness? Wasn't God fiercely angry with them? Though I used to complain about the indecency of the idea of God's wrath, I came to think that I would have to rebel against a God who *wasn't* wrathful at the sight of the world's evil. God isn't wrathful in spite of being love. God is wrathful *because* God is love.

Once we accept the appropriateness of God's wrath, condemnation, and judgment, there is no way of keeping it out there, reserved for others. We have to bring it home as well. I originally resisted the notion of a wrathful God because I dreaded being that wrath's target; I still do. I knew I couldn't just direct God's wrath against others, as if it were a weapon I could aim at targets I particularly detested. It's *God's* wrath, not mine, the wrath of the one and impartial God, lover of all humanity. If I want it to fall on evildoers, I must let it fall on myself – when I deserve it.

Also, once we affirm that God's condemnation of wrongdoing is appropriate, we cannot reserve God's condemnation for heinous crimes. Where would the line be drawn? On what grounds could it be drawn? Everything that deserves to be condemned should be condemned in proportion to its weight as an offense – from a single slight to a murder, from indolence to idolatry, from lust to rape. To condemn heinous offenses but not light ones would be manifestly unfair. An offense is an offense and deserves condemnation.

Consider the pervasiveness of the human offenses that merit God's censure, particularly as Roth explored the theme of evil in *The Human Stain*. Coleman Silk, the protagonist of the book, a black man who was passing himself as a Jew, was falsely accused of racism by the academic community of the college at which he worked and driven from his teaching post. Shortly after his forced retirement, Coleman was killed by a jealous ex-husband of his lover, a criminally crazed Vietnam veteran. As Roth put it, he was "excommunicated by the saved, the elect, the ever-present evangelists of the mores of the moment" and then "polished off by a demon of ruthlessness". Having suffered under the hand of both "the pure and impure", he was "whipsawed by the inimical teeth of this world". Then Roth added, making his main point, that he was whipsawed "by the antagonism that *is* the world".[7]

The idea that the world is shot through with "antagonism" is not just Roth's, of course. It is also Luther's and Paul's. And its consequence is momentous if, unlike Roth, we grant that the whole world is "accountable to God" (Romans 3:19). If wrongdoing is so pervasive, then "no human being will be justified in his [God's] sight' by deeds prescribed by the law" (Romans 3:20). All stand condemned. God condemns, and nobody's innocent!

Are we back at the image of God as an implacable judge? God is not a doting grandparent, I've argued. Grandparents can afford to be doting; parents, if they are any good, will make sure that the little imps are raised into responsible men and women. But God would be more like a sentimental fool than a divine lover of creation, if God acted like a doting grandparent. So God condemns everything that is condemnable. But I've also argued that God is *not* an implacable judge. If God were, the divine judge would not only condemn and punish but utterly destroy a world of such all-encompassing and persistent evil. If God were an implacable judge, God would be a destroyer of creation, not its lover. So are we not back full circle? We're not.

You can sum up where we've landed in four simple sentences. The world is sinful. That's why God doesn't affirm it indiscriminately. God loves the world. That's why God doesn't punish it in justice.

What does God do with this double bind? God forgives.

God Who Forgives

Recall our discussion from chapters 1 and 2. God is love, eternal and unalterable love among the Holy Three who are the Holy One. When the plenitude of that love spills over the boundary of the divine circle, the world comes to be. The gifts that eternally circulate within the Godhead now flow outward toward creation. And were it not for the mystery of human sin, that's all God would do. God would shower creation with gifts, and creatures would delight in God, each other, and in their mutual exchange of gifts.

But as I have noted, the inexplicable intruder, sin, came into the world, harming creation and dishonoring God. And the God who gives became the God who forgives. Or rather, in view of the fact that before creating the world God knew that humans would sin, the God who gives by creating was from the start also the God who forgives. The same love that propelled God to create by giving propelled God to mend creation by forgiving.

What does it mean for God to forgive? What does the forgiving God do? In William Shakespeare's comedy *Measure for Measure*, the stern judge Antonio has condemned Claudio to die for making Claudio's lover pregnant. In scene two of the second act, Isabella, Claudio's sister, comes before the judge to plead for her brother's life. She tells him,

> "I have a brother is condemn'd to die.
> I do beseech you let it be his fault,
> And not my brother."

Antonio responds as an implacable judge would:

> "Condemn the fault, and not the actor of it?
> Why, every fault's condemn'd ere it be done."[8]

To be just is to condemn the fault and, because of the fault, to condemn the doer as well. To forgive is to condemn the fault but to spare the doer. That's what the forgiving God does.

Notice what the forgiving God *doesn't* do with a wrongdoing. God doesn't say: "Oh, it was just an accident." "Your wrongdoing was like the cracking of an overstressed beam; that's what too much stress will do to the best of us." "Your parents so badly neglected you when you were a child; your offense was just the fruit of that bad seed." One or another, and maybe even all three of these explanations may be true about a particular deed. And in that case, there would be nothing to forgive. A shark has attacked a surfer, to return to the earlier metaphor. The deed should not be imputed to the doer. There is something to mourn but nothing to condemn and nothing to forgive. What was exculpated, God doesn't condemn and doesn't need to forgive. In such cases, God at most enlightens, comforts, and rescues.

Let's assume, though, that a person has committed an offense that needs forgiving, an assumption that, given the pervasiveness of human sin, is true of everyone, as we have seen. What does God do when forgiving? Consider the various metaphors Scripture uses.

God doesn't "reckon sin", wrote the apostle Paul echoing the psalmist (Romans 4:8; Psalm 32:1–2). We incur debt, but God puts nothing in the debit column of our life's account. We owe, but we don't have to pay.

God "covers" sin (Psalm 32:1; Romans 4:7). We've sinned in plain sight of all, but God hides our sin under the cover of impenetrable obscurity. We've committed it, but it's nowhere to be found.

God puts our wrongdoing "behind [God's] back" (Isaiah 38:17). God looks at us, the wrongdoers, and doesn't see our wrongdoing because one can't see what's behind one's back, as Søren Kierkegaard says of God's hiding of our sin.[9]

God removes our transgression from us as far as the east is from the west (Psalm 103:12). Our transgression seems permanently stuck to us, but God gently removes it without harming us and takes it to a place that neither we nor anybody else could ever reach.

God "blots out" our sin (Isaiah 43:25). We have spilled ink on our new white outfit, but God makes it disappear as if it were a drop of water on a hot stone in the middle of a sunny summer day.

God "[sweeps] away" our sins "like mist" (Isaiah 44:22). At the dawn of a new day, the landscape of our soul is enveloped in the cold, thick, wet mists of our nightly failings. But then the sun of God's forgiveness comes up, the mists are gone, and all we see is the spectacular beauty of a wintry day, with surfaces of snow and water dancing at the touch of the sun's countless rays.

And then, miracle of miracles, God doesn't even remember our sins (Isaiah 43:25; Jeremiah 31:34; Hebrews 8:12; 10:17). They are just gone, gone from reality and gone from memory.

Satisfaction

But what about God's justice? Does the miracle of God's forgiveness cancel justice? Does God forgive by suspending its demands? That would be one way to think about justice. God has set up moral norms, the argument could go. They are God's law. God is above the law God has set up and can suspend it. Justice is the law. By forgiving, God suspends justice – or, more precisely, suspends one part of it. The part of justice that serves to identify an act as an offense remains in operation. The part that demands that the doer be pronounced guilty and punished is suspended, or so we could argue.

True, God did establish moral law for creation. But God is not above moral law. If God were, God could morally do anything God wanted – destroy, lie, humiliate, oppress, whatever. Then what would be the difference between God and the Devil? Only that God is stronger than the Devil and can define what is good or evil?

Moral law is also not above God. If it were, God would have to submit to the law, and the law would regulate God's behavior. The law would then be God's God, and God would be the law's servant. But that would undo God, rob God of divinity.

God is neither above moral law nor below it. Rather, moral law is an expression of God's very being. And when we look at justice through this lens, we see that God *is* just and therefore acts justly. God can't suspend justice any more than God can cease being God.

In forgiving, God doesn't suspend justice. God remains just and yet justifies the ungodly as the apostle Paul famously said (see Romans 3:26). Here is how he described the process by which God both condemns the wrongdoing and sets the wrongdoer free. He didn't use the language of forgiveness here, but the idea of forgiveness was very much at the center of his attention: "All have sinned and fall short of the glory of God; they are now justified by his grace as a gift, through the redemption that is in Christ Jesus, whom God put forward as a sacrifice of atonement by his blood, effective through faith" (Romans 3:23–25). God didn't just say, "I forgive you." Fundamentally, forgiveness is not about *saying* something, not even about putting something into effect by speaking. It's about *doing* something. When God forgave, he "put forward" Jesus Christ as a sacrifice of atonement. Further on in Romans, the Apostle expressed a similar thought with different imagery: "While we were enemies, we were reconciled to God through the death of his Son" (5:10). Forgiveness takes place through Christ's death.

There is a long tradition of interpreting the sacrifice and death of Jesus Christ as "satisfaction": God doesn't forgive until the demands of justice have been satisfied. Martin Luther thought very much along these lines, at least most of the time. How is it that God doesn't impute our sins to us, doesn't count them against us? Luther explained, "Now although God purely out of grace does not impute our sins to us, still he did not want to do this unless his law and his righteousness had received a more than adequate satisfaction. This gracious imputation must first be purchased and won from his righteousness for us."[10] How is God's justice "satisfied"? How is the forgiveness of sins "purchased"? That satisfaction, that purchase, occurred when Jesus Christ took our place, insisted Luther: "Christ, the Son of God, stands in our place and has taken all our sins on his shoulders ... He is the eternal satisfaction for our sin and reconciles us with God, the Father."[11] God forgives because Christ paid what we owed. To shift the metaphor from marketplace to courtroom, Christ was condemned in our place. That's what theologians call *substitution*.

God loves us and wants to spare us the burden of our sin, but Christ suffers because of it!? Is this fair? By "putting forward" the Son, as the apostle Paul wrote, isn't the Father abusing the Son? Doesn't substitution constitute another wrongdoing, this time against the innocent Christ? How can one wrongdoing heal another? Doesn't

Christ's death on our behalf compound sins rather than take them away?

The Father would be abusing the Son and committing a divine wrongdoing – rather than taking away human wrongdoing if Christ were a third party, beyond God who was wronged and humanity who wronged God. But he isn't. He stands firmly on the side of the forgiving God, not between the forgiving God and forgiven humanity. "In Christ," wrote the apostle Paul, "God was reconciling the world to himself, not counting their trespasses against them" (2 Corinthians 5:19). Not: Christ was reconciling an angry God to a sinful world. Not: Christ was reconciling a sinful world to a loving God. Rather: God in Christ was "reconciling the world to himself".

What happened then when God "made him [Christ] to be sin who knew no sin, so that in him we might become the righteousness of God" (2 Corinthians 5:21)? The answer is simple: God placed human sin upon God! One God placed human sin upon another God? No, there are not two Gods. The God who is One beyond numbering and yet mysteriously Three reconciled us by shouldering our sin in the person of Christ who is one of the Three. That's the mystery of human redemption made possible by the mystery of God's Trinity: The One who was offended bears the burden of the offense.

Union with Christ

Christ is not a third party inserted between God and humanity to take care of human sin. He is the God who was wronged. But if the God who was wronged also carries the burden of the offense, isn't God acting like an indulgent grandparent? No, God would be acting as an indulgent grandparent if God simply treated sin as if it were not sin. But God doesn't. God condemns the offense – and bears the burden of it, rather than simply disregarding it or placing it back on our shoulders.

And God does more. If God only spared sinners of a just penalty for sin, that wouldn't change the truth of sinners' guilt. Granted, it would spare sinners the consequences of sin. No ill would befall them because they had sinned. But they'd still be offenders, though offenders whom God, in an act of divine pretense, for some reason doesn't treat as offenders. To be truly forgiven, offenses cannot be just covered, not reckoned to the offenders. They must also be removed from the sinners, blotted out, dispersed. The evil deeds must be separated from the doers. As long as offenses stick to those who have committed them, the offenders remain offenders, even if they are viewed as if they were not.

God doesn't just spare sinners the penalty for sin. God *separates* their sin from them. How does this happen? We've seen so far that it is God, not some third party, who bears our sin. Christ who died for our sins is one with God. But Christ who died for our sins is also *one with humanity*. It is because of Christ's union with humanity that God can separate sinners from their sin.

Let's take a closer look at the effect of union with Christ. As the agent of God's forgiveness, Christ is not just one human being among many, albeit a special and unique human being on account of also being truly divine. If he were just an individual human being, he would again be a third party, a now human third party, inserted between the God who was wronged and humanity who wronged God. That would be a problem.

Let's say that Aaron, my younger son who is not yet three, incurs a major debt by breaking a valuable antique vase of his friend's parents. I can pay for it and compensate for the loss. But I can do very little about the offense he caused if he broke it maliciously, though, given his age, without full awareness of what he was doing. I can apologize, of course. If I did, I'd be doing two things. First, I'd do something on my own behalf. I'd signal that I might have contributed to the incident, maybe by not being as good at raising him or watching him as I should have been. Second, I'd do something on his behalf. Since he is too young to properly admit to the wrongdoing and show remorse for it, I'd have to do this for him.

What would my relation be to his offense and to people he had offended if in his twenties he committed a violent crime? My apology could still fulfill the first function. I could recognize my share of responsibility for the incident, though it might be smaller now than it was when he was a toddler.

But my apology could not fulfill the second function; I couldn't admit the wrongdoing for him, and I certainly couldn't bear its consequences in his place. His was the deed, his must be the apology, his must be the consequences of the wrongdoing. I cannot assume his moral liability, as I can assume a loan he might be unable to pay. Even if I wanted to, I couldn't. It is uniquely his. Moral liability cannot be transferred.[12] Even in my apology for him as a toddler, it was not so much that I was apologizing *instead* of him. Properly speaking, it was *he* who was apologizing *through me*. I was needed to express something he should have felt and expressed, were he capable of it.

Now apply to Christ's death the claim that moral liability cannot be transferred. Earlier we saw that Christ is our substitute. But how can that be if only the culprit can bear the liability for sin and not the innocent? Writing to the church in Corinth, the apostle Paul made a puzzling statement about Christ's death: "One has died for all," he wrote, "therefore all have died" (2 Corinthians 5:14). Since Christ is our substitute, after reading, "one has died for all," we'd expect him to continue, "therefore none of them needs to die." Had he written that, he would have expressed the idea that theologians call *exclusive* substitution. According to this view, Christ's death makes ours unnecessary. As a third party, he is our substitute, and his death is his alone and no one else's.

But that's not how the Apostle thought. Christ's death doesn't replace our death. It *enacts* it, he suggested. That's what theologians call *inclusive* substitution. *Because* one has died, all have died. As a substitute, he is not a third party. His death is inclusive of all. Earlier we saw that God was in Christ "reconciling the world to himself" (2 Corinthians 5:19). Now we see that *we* were also in Christ. What happened to him happened to us. When he was condemned, we were condemned. When he died, we died. We were included in his death. John Donne put it this way in his "Hymn to God, My God, in My Sickness": "We think that Paradise and Calvary, / Christ's cross and Adam's tree, stood in one place". To be in Christ means that the tree from which Adam took forbidden fruit and the cross on which Christ died stood in one place, that the old self – the old Adam – died when Christ died.

Christ Our Righteousness

The significance of union with Christ for our topic is immense. How does God separate sinners from their sin? The answer is as simple as it is profound: The sinner has died with Christ. "We know that our old self was crucified with him so that the body of sin might be destroyed, and we might no longer be enslaved to sin. For whoever has died is freed from sin" (Romans 6:6–7). Death separates the doer from the deed.

That would be dubious good news had Christ's death been the end of the story. What good could forgiveness do for a person robbed of life? What would a dead person do with freedom from sin? But the apostle Paul believed that Easter Sunday follows Good Friday. The Christ who died is the Christ who rose again. And the one who died as sinner with Christ was raised with Christ to new life. That's enacted in baptism: as the waters cover the person baptized, so the old self dies with Christ; as the person baptized emerges from the waters, so the new self is raised with Christ. "So if anyone is in Christ," wrote the apostle Paul, "there is a new creation: everything old has passed away; see, everything has become new" (2 Corinthians 5:17).

What does it mean to be a new creature? The person is a new self because she lives in Christ and Christ lives in her. The Apostle wrote, "I have been crucified with Christ; and it is no longer I who live, but it is Christ who lives in me. And the life I now live in the flesh I live by faith in the Son of God, who loved me and gave himself for me" (Galatians 2:19–20). Commenting on this passage, Luther wrote,

> But who is this "I" of whom he [the Apostle] says, "Yet not I" [or "no longer I"]? It is the one that has the Law and is obliged to do works, the one that is a person separate from Christ. This "I" Paul rejects; for "I," as a person distinct from Christ, belongs to death and hell. This is why he says: "Not I, but Christ lives in me ... The life that I now live, He lives in me. Indeed, Christ Himself is the life that I now live."[13]

Everything depends on not dividing Christ's person from our own, Luther insisted. As soon as you "live in yourself", you're subject to law and find yourself always a transgressor worthy of condemnation. If you live in Christ or if Christ lives in you, you are freed from law and sin.

In chapters 1 and 2, we saw how we can be truly ourselves and free if God lives in us. This is what it means to be God's creature – not to be a self-made, self-standing individual over against God, but to exist from God and through God. We are creatures precisely in that we live in God and God lives in us. We are sinful creatures when we fail to recognize this and live as if we were self-made, self-standing individuals. Being a new creature, redeemed from sin, is in this regard similar to being a creature as God originally created us to be. It's to live in Christ and to have Christ live in us. United with Christ, we live in God, and God lives in us.

If in relation to God we see ourselves as fully in charge of our own independent lives, Christ's life in us will seem like an alien life, imposed on us from outside and possessing and controlling us from within. We would seem to ourselves like a Mickey Mouse figure that waves at kids at the entrance of Disneyland – a mere costume in which someone else does everything. But if we see ourselves as having our true identity only in relation to God, then Christ "speaking, acting, and performing all actions" in us[14] will very much be our own proper life. To say that Christ lives in us, and yet that it's we who live our lives, as the apostle Paul said in Galatians, would then not be a contradiction. *We* know, *we* will, *we* suffer, *we* rejoice, *we* desire, *we* feel fulfilled – and we do all that and more, not despite the fact that Christ lives in us, but *because* Christ lives in us.

Transformation and Imputation

What's the effect of union with Christ? Luther thought of it in two ways. One concerns transformation of the self indwelled by Christ. Without Christ living in us, we are in the power of sin. We fail to live out the fact that everything we are and do comes from God. When Christ indwells us, we are freed from the power of sin, and the life we live is God's life in us. On account of Christ, we can walk over the chasm from our sinful self-love to a life of genuine generosity and forgiveness.

Luther used a metaphor from the world of inanimate objects to describe the transformation of the self in union with Christ. When fire heats an iron, the iron glows like fire. But though the iron glows, it's not the iron's heat but the fire's, or rather, it's the iron's heat because it's the fire's heat. Remove the iron from the fire, and the iron will grow cold; keep the fire on, and the iron will remain hot.[15] So it is with the self whom Christ indwells. It takes on Christ's qualities and becomes Christ-like. It doesn't start being and living on its own as Christ was and as Christ lived, as the "What Would Jesus Do?" bracelet suggests, for instance. Rather, the soul is and acts like Christ because Christ is present in it and lives through it. Take Christ away, and the soul falls under the power of sin; keep Christ in, and the soul is freely thinking, speaking, and acting as Christ would.

There is a second effect of union with Christ. God doesn't count our sins to us but instead counts to us Christ's righteousness. Why is this second effect needed if Christ lives in us and through us? How is it that we still sin when we are transformed by Christ's presence? A person's transformation will be complete only in the life to come. During this life, sin besets us in two ways. We fail to live trusting in God, which is our root sin, and on account of that failure, we also fall into many and varied sins.[16] When we are united with Christ, both the great sin of unbelief and the individual sins that grow out of it "are covered". God "does not want to hold us accountable for them".[17] Instead, God counts to us Christ's righteousness. This is the second effect of the union with Christ.

To describe the imputation of Christ's righteousness, Luther used metaphor from the world of personal relations. Following the apostle Paul, he likened the soul's union with Christ to marriage. Christ is the bridegroom, and the soul is the "poor, wicked harlot" who becomes his bride. Since they are one flesh, he takes from her all her failings and incapacities and gives her all his uprightness and power. He "suffered, died, and descended into hell that he might overcome" all her sins. "Her sins cannot now destroy her, since they are laid upon Christ and swallowed up by him. And she has that righteousness in Christ, her husband, of which she may boast of as her own and confidently display alongside her sins in the face of death and hell."[18]

Both our transformation and the imputation of Christ's righteousness depend on union with Christ. And so does forgiveness, the fact that God doesn't count our sin against us. Because we are one, Christ's life is our life. Because we are one, Christ's qualities are our qualities. Because we are one, we have died in Christ's death, and our sins are no longer ours but are "swallowed up" by Christ.

The title of this chapter is "God the Forgiver". But now, close to the end of our exploration of God's forgiveness, it has become clear that forgiveness is part of something much larger. What does God do with sinners and their sin? God doesn't just forgive sin; he transforms sinners into Christ-like figures and clothes them with Christ's righteousness. And even these benefits are the effects of something much more basic – the presence and activity of Christ in human beings. Such intimate communion with God has been God's goal with humanity from the beginning. We are made for God to live in us and for us to live in God. Forgiveness is one step toward the restoration of that communion, midway between our being sinners and our being new creatures.

Faith

As I have described God's forgiveness so far, it seems to happen outside of us, apart from our own activity. Back in the eternity before the world's creation, God decided to forgive so that the world could be created. Back in history, when Christ died on the tree of shame outside the gates of Jerusalem, God bore our sin, and we were both condemned as sinners and separated from our sin. And in our own lives, God lives somewhere unfathomably deep within us – behind our faculties of knowing and willing – and swallows up our sin and transforms our lives. Where are *we* in all this? Just objects of God's work? Just spectators? Where is our activity? Frozen in a stance of letting God do things to us?

It's important to remember that God's forgiveness is a gift. In chapter 1, we saw that everything that comes to us from God is a gift. Try as we might, we can't earn anything from God; God is not an employer. And God isn't an employee either; God doesn't do services for advance payment. God doesn't need anything we might want to give. More importantly, God has already given us anything we possibly could give to God. As the apostle Paul said in Romans, to oblige God to give us something, we'd have to give God something first (Romans 11:35) – a clear impossibility.

We do try the impossible, all the time. We fail, of course. But when it comes to our relationship with God, there is something more troubling than failure to earn God's favor. Strange as it might sound, it's the attempt itself. When we try, we claim as originally our own something we received as a gift from God. We give God what is God's while pretending that it's our own. In a sense, we do a foolish thing of stealing from God, hoping to pay God to do us a favor. In addition, we profoundly misread who God is. "For God is He who dispenses His gifts freely to all, and this is the praise of his deity," wrote Luther in his *Commentary on Galatians*.[19] We pretend that we aren't receiving things as gifts from God, and that pretense is our most basic sin. Whatever we receive from God is a gift, and nothing but a gift. That's true of forgiveness as well.

How do we receive forgiveness? How do we receive Christ who brings with him new life and forgiveness? The way we receive anything from God: by faith. The apostle Paul wrote, "For we hold that a person is justified by faith apart from works prescribed by the law" (Romans 3:28). What does faith do? It embraces Christ. "Faith takes hold of Christ and has Him present, enclosing him as the ring encloses the gem," wrote Luther.[20]

Notice what faith doesn't do. It doesn't wrest Christ from a God who is unwilling to give. It doesn't earn Christ from a God who wants something in return. Faith isn't some strange, empty work we do for God so that God will give us Christ. As we saw in chapter 1, faith is our hands open to receive Christ whom God has given. If I am giving you a present, all you need to do is open your hands, and it will be yours. God gives, faith receives. And because God gives even before the hands of faith open to receive, faith never goes away empty-handed. To have faith *is* to have Christ and, with Christ, a new life and forgiveness of sins.

Repentance

Add gratitude to faith, and so far, we receive forgiveness roughly the way we properly receive any other of God's gifts – whether that gift is a child, musical genius, or our very breath. By faith we affirm ourselves as recipients, and through gratitude we affirm God as the giver.

But there are also important differences between the way we receive forgiveness and the way we receive other gifts. One of them is rooted in the nature of forgiveness. It is a gift, but a peculiar kind of gift. As I have explained earlier, we forgive when someone has wronged us. And when we do, we do two main things: We claim that the offender has offended us, and we don't count the offense against the offender. Both are essential. Drop not counting the offense against the offender, and all you're left with is the accusation. Drop the claim that an offense was committed, and all you have is disregard of the offense, not its forgiveness.

To forgive means to accuse the offenders in the larger act of not counting their offenses against them. What does it mean to *receive* forgiveness, then? It means to receive *both* the accusation and the release from the debt. How do we receive release from debt? We simply believe and rejoice in gratitude for the generous gift. But how do we receive the accusation? By confessing our offense and repenting of it. By confessing, I recognize myself as the one who needs forgiveness and who can appropriately receive it. By failing to confess, I declare that I am in no need of forgiveness. To me, in that case, forgiveness isn't a gift; it's an insult, a declaration that I've done the wrong I claim not to have done.

In his talks of the Sermon on the Mount, Luther wrote, "There are two kinds of sin: one is confessed, and this no one should leave unforgiven; the other kind is defended, and this no one can forgive, for it refuses either to be counted as sin or to accept forgiveness."[21] Often I am not aware of my sins; they are hidden. Then I ask God to free me from sins "known and unknown". But when I am aware of my sin, I should confess it. Without confession I will remain unforgiven – not because God doesn't forgive, but because a refusal to confess is a rejection of forgiveness. Refusing to confess, I refuse to make forgiveness my own through confession of wrongdoing and joyful gratitude over it not being counted against me.

Confession is hard. When I confess that I've committed an offense, I stand exposed, pointing an accusing finger at myself and at the guilt of my offense. Almost instinctively, I want to clothe myself with denials and exculpatory explanations. Yet we know that confession is wonderfully freeing. After we confess, we have nothing to hide, nothing to run away from. But how do we summon the courage to walk into the land of freedom through the gate of shame?

Amazingly, God doesn't wait until we've confessed to offer and even enact forgiveness; God forgives before we confess. We know from the start that whatever it might be that we confess it will not count against us. We are loved notwithstanding our offense. We are forgiven so we can be freed from the burden of our offense and return into the arms of the loving God.

God's Forgiveness and Ours

Finally, in addition to faith and repentance, we respond to God's forgiveness by "passing on" forgiveness to others. In the Lord's Prayer we say, "And forgive us our debts, as we also have forgiven our debtors" (Matthew 6:12). The intimate link between God's forgiveness and ours is reinforced in the verses immediately following the prayer. "For if you forgive others their trespasses, your heavenly Father will also forgive you; but if you do not forgive others, neither will your Father forgive your trespasses" (vv. 14–15). In the next chapters we will explore the difficulty of forgiving and how to overcome it. Here we need to look more carefully at the nature of the link between God's forgiveness and ours. I'll discard two ways of understanding that link before advocating a third.

At least on the surface, the link seems to be this: Because you forgive your debtors, God will forgive you. Our forgiving others seems to cause God's forgiving us. If that were the case, however, God's forgiveness would not be a gift but a payment. Or if it were a gift, it would be the kind of gift only God can give – a gift that hasn't been elicited by a prior gift. In either case, we would not receive forgiveness by faith; we would earn it or draw it out by our own forgiveness of others. But that can't be right. It undercuts the idea that God is a giver.

The other way to regard the link between God's forgiveness and ours is to say that God forgives without prior payment or gift, but then takes forgiveness away when we fail to forgive our debtors, those who sin against us. That's what the parable of the unforgiving servant in Matthew's gospel suggests. After a king forgave his slave a debt that amounted to an enormous fortune, the slave turned around and threw into prison a fellow slave who could not repay him a measly hundred denarii, a day's wage. Then his lord summoned him and said, "You wicked slave! I forgave you all that debt because you pleaded with me. Should you not have had mercy on your fellow slave, as I had mercy on you?" (Matthew 18:32–33). The king then reversed his decision to forgive and threw him in prison "until he would pay his entire debt" (v. 34). The point of the story, concluded Jesus with a grim warning, was this: "So my heavenly Father will also do to every one of you, if you do not forgive your brother or sister from your heart" (v. 35).

Here our failure to forgive undoes God's forgiveness. God takes back that which was given if we don't give as God gives. God's forgiveness is here conditional on our performance. Though we couldn't earn God's forgiveness, we could, so to speak, un-earn it. The key to God's forgiveness of our sins would be placed into our own hands, based on our will and strength to forgive. The gift itself would turn into a law that demands, and one that demands more than the law written on tablets of stone ever did.

But maybe to think this way is to take an illustration too literally. All the aspects of the king's and servant's relationship need not have one-to-one correspondence in the relationship between God and humans. The point of the story may be simply that God's forgiveness and our forgiveness go hand in hand as do God's unforgiveness and our unforgiveness. Jesus may not have been suggesting that our unforgiveness *causes* God's unforgiveness. Rather than triggering a loss of God's forgiveness, our unforgiveness may just *make manifest* that in fact we haven't allowed ourselves to receive God's pardon.

That's what Luther took the petition about forgiveness in the Lord's Prayer to mean. "The outward forgiveness that I show in my deeds is a sure sign that I have the forgiveness of sin in the sight of God. On the other hand, if I do not show this in my relations with my neighbor, I have a sure sign that I do not have the forgiveness of sin in the sight of God and am still stuck in my unbelief."[22] If I am united with Christ in faith, I'll have forgiveness and Christ will live in me, forgiving through me those who offend me as he has forgiven me. If, rather than being troubled by my inability to forgive, I don't want to forgive, there is a good chance that I haven't in fact received forgiveness from God, even if I believe that I have.

How is it that we have the faith to receive Christ and, with Christ, forgiveness of our own sins and the power to forgive our debtors? How is it that we can recognize our sin and repent so as to receive the gift of forgiveness? If all things are from God, through God, and to God (Romans 11:36), then this faith and this repentance of ours must also come from that same Source.

Chapter 5

HOW SHOULD
WE FORGIVE?

"Let him burn in hell forever!" she wrote to me. It was a note from a Croatian woman who, in the political turmoil following World War II, had lost everything she and her family possessed. Josip Broz, or Marshall Tito, as he liked to be called, came to power and established a "new Yugoslavia" based on three pillars: his moral capital as a victor in the struggle against the Nazis, the military might of his victorious partisan soldiers, and the communist ideology. The family of the woman who wrote to me had suffered the fate of many of Tito's "enemies of the people". When she wrote to me, she had just seen a TV special on my work, done by the PBS program *Religion and Ethics Newsweekly*. In it, reconciliation and forgiveness – the main themes of my book *Exclusion and Embrace* – were featured prominently.[1] She liked none of what she had seen and heard. Not forgiveness but vengeance was what she wanted, even fifty years after the crime. Tito had ruined her life; she had had to rebuild it from scratch in the New World. Now Tito's life ought to be ruined, she felt – irredeemably and forever.

In discussing giving in chapter 2, I distinguished between three basic modes in which we conduct our lives. I called them taking, getting, and giving. In the first, we illicitly take what isn't ours. In the second, we legitimately acquire what we need or desire. In the third, we generously give to help and to delight others. Now in discussing forgiveness, we can distinguish between three corresponding modes in which we relate to offenders and their offenses. Revenge corresponds to illicit taking, the demand for justice corresponds to legitimate acquiring, and forgiving roughly corresponds to generous giving.

Revenge versus Justice

In general, we have little tolerance for those who illicitly take. Unless someone is in dire need, taking seems unacceptably to violate the rights of another. Often takers try to justify their misdeeds, as Tito tried to justify not only taking the property but also the lives of many innocent civilians. "Those who are well-off are capitalists," the thinking went. "They've gained their property illicitly, at the expense of the sweat and toil of common people. It's right for their property to be taken away and administered by the state of the 'workers'." Without some such attempt to rationalize their illicit taking as legitimate acquiring, the act of taking would have remained nakedly reprehensible.

For the most part, we don't approve of revenge either. But at least we understand the sentiment behind it, whereas we simply condemn the illicit taking that constitutes the original offense. Consider the experience of my colleague at Yale, Carlos Eire. His *Waiting for Snow in Havana* is a memoir of a privileged boy who, at the age of eleven, was one of 14,000 children airlifted from Cuba, separated from his parents and, with only a small suitcase in hand, dropped off in a land where he didn't know a soul. His book gives voice to a boy's yearning for what he could have had as much as it laments what he actually lost. Eire's rage is expressed graphically when he writes of his occasional desire to see his perpetrators condemned to "lick Satan's razor-studded butt forever and ever, with their tongues".[2]

Eire's dreams of revenge may seem extreme, but if we've ever been violated, they will resonate with us. As he was imprisoned and tortured by the Khmer Rouge regime, Kassie Neou, for instance, sustained himself by thoughts of revenge. "I told myself that when my time comes, I will take revenge five times worse than what they are doing to me," he later said. "As a human being, you have that kind of anger."[3]

We acknowledge deep human fury like Eire's and Neou's. At the same time, we may affirm that the retaliation born of that fury clearly is morally wrong. Revenge doesn't say, "An eye for an eye." It says, "You take my eye, and I'll blow out your brains." It doesn't say, "An insult for an insult." It says, "You cross me once, you cross me twice, and I'll destroy your character and your career." It doesn't say, "You organize an act of terror, and we'll punish you." It says, "You organize an act of terror, and we'll use the overwhelming military force of a superpower to recast the political landscape of the entire region from which you came." Revenge abandons the principle of "measure for measure" and, acting out of injured pride and untamed fear, gives itself to punitive excess. That's why revenge is morally wrong. In its zeal to punish, it overindulgently takes from the offender more than is due.

To the church in Rome, the apostle Paul wrote, "Beloved, never avenge yourselves" (Romans 12:19). Even more, they should not even curse those who mistreat them, should not engage in the vengeance of the powerless. What should they do instead? They should "bless those who persecute" them (Romans 12:14). The Apostle continued, "If your enemies are hungry, feed them; if they are thirsty, give them something to drink" (v. 20). Instead of retaliating with vengeance, they should give gifts to those who have offended them; they should help them flourish! Excess in punishment should give way not simply to justice, but to generous assistance.

Eire's book, saturated as it is by his Christian faith, is not just an account of a catastrophic loss and the rage it produced. It's also the record of a journey from vengeful imagination toward redemption. Torment of the evildoers is the temptation he is resisting. He yearns to acquire the ability to "kiss the lizard", even to kiss Fidel Castro, that "lizard of lizards", who destroyed everything Eire knew as a boy, wrecking it "in the name of fairness … progress … the oppressed, and of love for the gods Marx and Lenin".[4]

Forgiveness versus Justice

But why kiss the lizard? Why feed the enemy? Why bless the persecutor? Why not forgo vengeance, which is immoral, but insist on retributive justice instead? We might respond with Luther and say it's because "the continual forgiveness of the neighbor [is] the primary and foremost duty of Christians, second only to faith and the reception of forgiveness".[5] But why is forgiveness, rather than retributive justice, a Christian duty? In chapter 4, I suggested one reason: Consistent enforcement of justice would wreak havoc in a world shot through with transgression. It may rid the world of evil, but at the cost of the world's destruction.

In Romans 12, the apostle Paul added another, more practical reason. The line between vengeance and justice is often hard to draw. In most cases, it is difficult to assess the extent of an offense rightly and to apportion blame appropriately. What seems like justice to one person will look like vengeance to another. In trying to overcome evil by enforcing justice, there is always the danger that we may be "overcome by evil" ourselves (Romans 12:21). Wreaking destruction upon the world while potentially succumbing to the power of evil ourselves are two reasons we should not repay the evildoer in kind, with "evil for evil" (Romans 12:17).

These two reasons why we should go beyond the principle "measure for measure" are nestled in a more fundamental one: God was gracious to sinful humanity. Consider one very practical piece of apostolic instruction. In the Apostle's letter to the church of Corinth, he objected to believers' pursuing justice in a court of law. His Corinthian flock did the sensible thing and took their grievances before a judge, yet the Apostle was not pleased. He was disturbed that they weren't wise enough to settle their disputes by themselves within the community. But he was troubled by something more basic than their incompetence. "In fact," he wrote, "to have lawsuits at all with one another is already a defeat for you" (1 Corinthians 6:7). To be defeated in a dispute involving injustice, we normally think, is to lose the case, to be pronounced guilty. For the apostle Paul, to be defeated was to bring the case before the court in the first place, to even *attempt* to deal with it according to the principle "measure for measure"!

What should the Corinthians have done instead? The Apostle answered with rhetorical questions: "Why not rather be wronged? Why not rather be defrauded?" If he were to write that to us, we'd certainly tell him why: "We have rights! We've suffered injustice! You can't let people just walk all over you! You've got to draw the line! You've got to fight back!" Notice that the Apostle didn't deny that an injustice had occurred. He just didn't think insisting on retributive justice was the best way, or the Christian way, of dealing with it.

So what is? Should we simply absorb the suffered injury? That's part of it – the passive part of a larger and active strategy of conquering evil "with good" (Romans 12:21). At the sight of our sin, God did not give way to uncontrolled rage and measureless vengeance; neither did God insist on just retribution. Instead, God bore our sin and condemned it in Jesus Christ. But God did so not out of impotence or cowardice, but in order to free us from sin's guilt and power. That's how we should treat those who transgress against us. We should absorb the wrongdoing in order to transform the wrongdoers.

Revenge multiplies evil. Retributive justice contains evil – and threatens the world with destruction. Forgiveness overcomes evil with good. Forgiveness mirrors the generosity of God whose ultimate goal is neither to satisfy injured pride nor to justly apportion reward and punishment, but to free sinful humanity from evil and thereby reestablish communion with us. This is the gospel in its stark simplicity – as radically countercultural and at the same time as beautifully human as anything one can imagine.

The example of Christ, along with the Apostle's urging in Romans 12 and 1 Corinthians 6, found an extraordinary echo in a profound passage by young Martin Luther. It bears a careful reading. Those who follow Christ, he wrote,

> grieve more over the sin of their offenders than over the loss or offense to themselves. And they do this that they may recall those offenders from their sin rather than avenge the wrongs they themselves have suffered. Therefore they put off

the form of their own righteousness and put on the form of those others, praying for their persecutors, blessing those who curse, doing good to the evil-doers, preparing to pay the penalty and make satisfaction for their very enemies that they may be saved. This is the gospel and the example of Christ.[6]

Why do we forgive instead of giving in to vengeance or pursuing retributive justice which is what, in many situations, every atom of our violated bodies and our humiliated soul scream after? Because in Christ, God overcame our sin and reestablished communion with us by forgiving sin. We do as God did. We forgive because "recalling" the offenders from sin matters more to us than "avenging" wrongs we have suffered. We forgive because "saving" our enemies and making friends out of them matters more to us than punishing them.

But I Am Not God!

How should we forgive? The simple answer is that we should forgive as God forgave in Jesus Christ. But before exploring many facets of that simple answer, I need to address a serious objection. How can we forgive *as* God forgives when we are obviously not God? We are human – wonderfully, finitely, and ... sinfully human. We are not divine. How can we do *anything* as God does, let alone forgive?

We encountered a similar question in discussing giving in chapter 2, where I argued that we should give as God gives. That we are not God results in a threefold difficulty with regard to giving. First, God is an absolutely original giver who hasn't received anything; we can be givers only if we receive gifts from God. God's gifts are original; ours are derivative. Second, God is an infinite giver who can give without measure and without ceasing; we are finite givers who can give only in measure and intermittently. Third, God is the utterly loving giver who can give without concern for God's own good; we are selfish givers who seek our own good in the gifts we give. We obviously can't give exactly as God gives.

The arguments against the claim that we should forgive as God forgives are just as powerful. First, it could be said, a transgression affects us as fragile human beings differently than it affects the absolutely inviolable God. In sinning, we act in some way against God. Indeed, "acting against God" is part of the core definition of "sin". Take God out of the picture, and sin disappears. Left are evil, wrongful, or unpleasant acts and nasty, brutish people, but not sins and sinners.[7]

Though it's directed against God, however, sin in no way diminishes or disorients God. God may feel sorrow over human sin or longing for sinners to return. But sin doesn't break, invade, or ravage God, not even on the cross where God bore the full horror of human sin. If it were otherwise, God wouldn't be God. Under the assault of sin, God remains God, and that's partly why God can forgive.

It's different with humans, and that's why it's sometimes almost impossible for us to forgive. True, often an offense doesn't injure deeply. To save a few dollars, I lie to my gardener about the amount of mulch I am asking him to spread; the less he needs to spread, the less I need to pay. I've wronged him by being untruthful and, if he believed me, by cheating him of his proper pay. But I haven't seriously injured him. It's his passion for justice or his wounded pride – but not significant damage to the self – that may hinder his willingness to forgive.

Take, however, the true case of a man who seduces a woman with false promises of love, pulls her into his prostitution ring, holds her captive for months, beats and rapes her repeatedly, and forces her to provide pleasure to other men without paying her a cent – such a despicably evil pimp has deeply injured the woman. With a life shattered by brutality, can she even contemplate forgiveness? If she said to the offender, "Burn in hell!" we'd understand. And if by some miracle she did forgive, surely she wouldn't do it as God does, in the sovereign freedom of a magnanimous giver. She'd likely engage in a Sisyphean struggle to forgive. So we *can't* forgive exactly as God does.

We also *shouldn't* forgive exactly as God forgives. God doesn't just say "I forgive you!" to express divine attitude and intended action toward transgressors. God does say that too, but only because prior to that God *did* something in Christ. God condemned sin, and the sinner died in order to be raised as a new person freed from sin. Christ "was handed over to death for our trespasses and was raised for our justification", writes the apostle Paul (Romans 4:25).

We saw in chapter 4 that Christ's death was inclusive of humanity. In a mysterious way, those who are united with Christ died with him in his death. But in an important sense, however, Christ's death was also exclusive of humanity. Christ died so that no human being has to die in order to be freed from sin. That was the point of his dying: He was our substitute. Luther pulled together both exclusive and inclusive aspects of Christ's death when he wrote in his *Lectures on Galatians* that by Christ's crucifixion "sin, the devil, and death are crucified in Christ, not me. Here Christ does everything alone. But I, as a believer, am crucified with Christ through faith, so that all these things are dead and crucified to me as well."[8]

Christ died to remove the stain of sin that sticks to me as long as I live. Christ died in my place. I don't need to die to be freed from sin. And because Christ died, I also don't need to die when I forgive, when I unbind a sinful deed from the person who committed it against me. Indeed, it would be preposterous for me to think that I ever could do such a thing – die as a substitute for my neighbor's sin. When Christ died, we all died in him. But my death is only my own, and it can never be another's. In regard to the sin of another, as in regard to my own sin, Christ does everything alone. When I forgive an offense directed against me, I don't die, and therefore I don't forgive exactly *as* God does.

Does this bring us to an impasse? We should forgive as God forgives, but we can't forgive as God forgives! Earlier, in discussing giving, I suggested that the adverb "as" in the phrase "as God gives" doesn't designate identity but *similarity*. Because we are human, we cannot give exactly as God does. But because we are created to be like the God who gives, we should give similarly to how God gives. The same applies to forgiveness. We cannot and should not forgive exactly as God does. But because we were created to be like the God who forgives, we should forgive similarly to how God forgives. We don't replicate what God does. We imitate it in our own way, mindful that, as the great church father Augustine said, the dissimilarity between God and us is greater than the similarity.

Important as it is, however, imitation is not the primary way in which we relate to God. We don't just watch and learn from God, as a toddler watches and learns from his mother. A toddler and his mother are two separate people, acting independently of one another. They have two distinct bodies that occupy different spaces, and they have two intellects and wills operating independently from one another. But as we have seen throughout this book, we are not independent of God in that way. God is not absent from the space we inhabit, and our intellects and wills are carried on the wings of God's presence and activity. When we give, it is God's gifts that we pass on and it is God who gives through us. By giving, we are instruments of God's giving. The same is true of forgiveness.

But we *do* imitate God, too. We give *as* God gives and forgive *as* God forgives. But how, given this intimate relationship between God and us? A toddler may participate as his mom sweeps the garage by taking his own small broom and copying her. They are working together. The son does what he sees his mother do. He participates in his mom's work by imitating it. It's different in our relationship to God. We do imitate God, but not just by observing at a distance. God is not only above us. Jesus Christ is not just a figure from the past. God is in us. Christ lives through us. We imitate God as instruments of God: God gives and forgives, and we make God's giving and God's forgiving our own.

How does God forgive? What does it mean for us, different as we are from God, to forgive as God forgives? In short, how should we forgive? In the next chapter we will explore how it is possible for us to do the hard work of forgiving as we should.

To Forgive Is to Condemn

It could seem that, when we forgive, we trample justice underfoot. An offense has occurred, but the injured person doesn't count the offense against the offender. The offender goes unpunished, even free of guilt. Where is justice in all this? That's how things look when we consider only the *result* of forgiveness. Things get more complicated, however, when we turn to the *process* of forgiving.

What does God do when forgiving? There's one thing God *doesn't* do. God doesn't disregard the offense. God doesn't pretend it didn't happen. As we saw in chapter 4, God's wrath burns on account of the human sin that brings ruin upon creation.

Does God then forgive by calming anger against sin? No, that's not right either. God's forgiveness has little to do with God's emotional states, with a shift from burning anger, to cool indifference or even warm affection. God's wrath is not primarily an emotional state but a forceful censure of sin. In the face of an offense, God doesn't say, "I am so furious at what has happened; I better take a walk to calm down." Instead, God turns to the offender and says, "You've done something terribly wrong." Someone was wronged, and God names the act for what it is and condemns the doer. That's God's wrath. When God forgives, God doesn't condemn anymore. That's what it means for God to avert anger.

Does God *first* condemn and *then* forgive? With this question, we've almost gotten the relationship between God's condemnation and forgiveness right, but we are not quite yet there. Imagine you go on a blind date with someone you've never met before. After exchanging pleasantries, you want to show your generosity, and you give her a book, hot off the press, on a subject you've found out she is very interested in. She'd be delighted and would say something like, "Thank you! That was very thoughtful of you!"

Now imagine that instead of giving her that book, you wanted to show your generosity by giving her a different kind of gift, a gift of forgiveness. "I forgive you!" you tell her. She would be appalled: "Wait a second! What audacity! I've never seen you before in my life. What could you possibly forgive me for!? I've done you no wrong!" In the very act of forgiveness, you've accused her of a transgression. To forgive is to name and condemn the misdeed. The same is true of God. God doesn't just condemn and *then* forgive. God also condemns in the very act of forgiving.

But implicating condemnation in the act of forgiving creates difficulties. As we will see in chapter 6, it's difficult to forgive well, partly because it's hard to know exactly the extent to which someone has acted wrongfully. It's also difficult to receive forgiveness, because we don't like to be blamed and might not agree with the forgiver's condemnation. Yet condemnation and blame are intrinsic to the process of forgiveness.

To Forgive Isn't to Shrug Off

Contrast the view that condemnation is part and parcel of forgiveness with Friedrich Nietzsche's way of dealing with offenses. Explaining one central pillar of his "noble morality" (which he proposed in opposition to Christian "slave morality"), he wrote:

> To be unable to take his enemies, his misfortunes and even his *misdeeds* seriously for long – that is the sign of strong, rounded natures with superabundance of power which is flexible, formative, healing and can make one forget. (A good example from the modern world is Mirabeau, who had no recall for the insult and slights directed at him and who would not forgive, simply because he – forgot.) A man like this shakes from him, with one shrug, many worms which would have burrowed into another man; here and here alone is it possible, assuming that this is possible at all on earth – truly to 'love your neighbor'.[9]

Nietzsche suggested that we accept injury – and, more comfortingly, accept even our own misdeeds! – and simply go on as if nothing happened. This is not forgiveness, however. Censure of the deed and accusation of the doer are missing. And that's exactly Nietzsche's point: Since he didn't think that there was such a thing as valid claims of justice, he abandoned forgiveness in favor of disregarding, shrugging off, and forgetting injuries.

Often we quite understandably act as Nietzsche suggested we should. We're standing in a full bus, and somebody pushes us more aggressively than necessary as he is trying to get on. We are irritated but don't think much about the violation. We don't expect apology, and we are not thinking about forgiveness. We just disregard the act; it doesn't matter. We similarly treat many low-grade offenses that we experience daily for the simple reason that life would have to stop if we did not. That's just the way life is – and the rougher the circumstances in which we live, the more tolerant of such offenses we become (which is why many Westerners, and particularly Americans, find riding buses in places like Croatia or India so difficult).

But there are offenses that rise above the everyday buzz of transgressions and slights and that cry out for attention. An insult was delivered. Marital vows were broken. Property was plundered. We were swindled out of a position of honor. Blood was spilled. Should we just disregard such offenses? We should not – if the distinction between right and wrong matters to us. It is *morally wrong* to treat an adulterer and a murderer as if they had not committed adultery and murder – more precisely, it is wrong to treat them that way until the offenses have been named as offenses. That's why such offenses should not be disregarded. Instead, they should be forgiven.

In much of popular culture, to forgive means to overcome feelings of anger and resentment. "Forgiveness," says the immensely popular Dr Phil on Oprah's website, "is a choice you make to release yourself from anger, hatred and resentment."[10] Often people take a two-track approach. On one track, they condemn the deed and pursue the rightful claims of retributive justice. On the other track, they try to free themselves from the feeling of being diminished by the offense, from anger, bitterness, and resentment. This second track they call forgiveness. By forgiving, they hope to do themselves a favor, to be freed from negative emotions in which the offense they've suffered entangled them.

We do benefit from forgiving – just as we benefit from giving. When we give, we experience that it's more blessed to give than to receive. When we forgive, we find inner peace and freedom. But just as we *give* for others' sake, which is part of the definition of giving, we should also *forgive* primarily for others' sake, not our own.

Emotional healing is a good thing and there are many paths that may lead to it, but emotional healing is not the main purpose of forgiveness. To forgive means to forgo a rightful claim against someone who has wronged us. That's a gift we give not so much to ourselves but to the one who has wronged us, whether we are emotionally healed as a result or not. And there's no way to give the gift of forgiveness without the sting of condemnation. We accuse when we forgive, and in doing that, we affirm the rightful claims of justice. That's how it should be. It's just not all it should be.

Release of Debt

Condemnation is not the heart of forgiveness. It's the indispensable presupposition of it. The heart of forgiveness is a generous release of a genuine debt. When it comes to financial transactions, we know what it means to release a debt. I borrowed ten dollars from you, and you say, "No need to pay me back!" After I thank you, that's the end of the matter. We speak of "forgiveness" in such cases; you have "forgiven" my debt. Most properly, however, we forgive when someone has wronged us. Imagine that instead of borrowing, I *stole* ten dollars from you. When I borrow, I don't wrong you, unless I refuse to repay you at the set time. When I steal from you, I wrong you. What does it mean to release a debt when we have been wronged?

To forgive means, first, *not to press charges* against the wrong-doer. That's what God has done for sinful humanity. The story of Christ's death tells us that God doesn't press charges against humanity. Instead, on account of Christ's unity with God, Jesus Christ bears human sin. No punishment will fall on us. The divine Judge was judged in our place. We are free of the charge.

That's also what we do when we forgive: We forgo the demand for retribution. Retributive justice ties our treatment of offenders to the character of their deeds. "An eye for an eye" or a "blow for a blow" is one way of dealing with the offenses about which we read in the Old Testament. Other cultures from roughly the same period in history thought similarly. "What's the rite of purification? How shall it be done?" asked Oedipus, in Sophocles' play *Oedipus the King*. Creon responded, "... expiation of blood by blood".[11] Today it's no different. A young man watching the first executions of the perpetrators of the Rwandan genocide thinks: "This is justice. They killed, and they have to be killed."[12] He is right. That *is* justice, not vengeance as we are sometimes inclined to think. What's missing in his attitude from the perspective of Christian faith is a sense that we should not treat perpetrators according to the principle of retributive justice.

Justice requires equivalent repayment, to be sure, but repayment need not be in kind. A man who spilled blood could be banished, said Creon in the same play by Sophocles, not just killed. For rape, someone may get a prison sentence rather than being raped himself. For hitting a sibling, a child may be barred from watching her favorite TV show for a day rather than being hit herself. Some such rough equivalent is what retributive justice demands.

Forgiveness cuts the tie of equivalence between the offense and the way we treat the offender. I don't demand that the one who has taken my eye lose his eye or that the one who has killed my child by negligence be killed. In fact, I don't demand that he lose anything. I forgo all retribution. In forgiving, I absorb the injury – the way I may absorb, say, the financial impact of a bad business transaction. As the great nineteenth-century Russian novelist, Leo Tolstoy, put it in relation to non-resistance in general, by forgiving a person one "swallows" evil up into oneself and thereby prevents it from going further.[13]

To forgive is to blame, not to punish. But those who forgive need not abandon all disciplinary measures against offenders. A child may need a time-out, not as a retributive punishment but as a space to reflect on her actions. A violent offender may need to be restrained if there is any danger he may harm others. Discipline for the sake of a wrongdoer's reform and the protection of the public is compatible with forgiveness. Discipline even for the sake of upholding the moral good assaulted by the offense is compatible with forgiveness. Retribution is not. Those who forgive will have a system of discipline, but retribution will not be part of it. They ought to forgive rather than punish because God in Christ forgave. Christ is the end of retribution.

A state may have a judicial system in place whose aim is not just to reform or restrain criminals but to punish them as well. Yet as private citizens, we can forgive even when the state pursues retribution which we condemn. In May 1981, the late Pope John Paul II was shot when Mohammed Agca attempted to take his life. The pope survived. Some two years later, reported Lance Morrow,

> in a bare, white-walled cell in Rome's Rebibba prison, John Paul tenderly held the hand that held the gun that was meant to kill him. For 21 minutes, the Pope sat with his would-be assassin … The two talked softly. Once or twice, Agca laughed. The Pope forgave him for the shooting. At the end of the meeting, Agca either kissed the Pope's ring or pressed the Pope's hand to his forehead in a Muslim gesture of respect.[14]

The pope's forgiveness was a public gesture but a private act. Agca remained in prison. An individual's forgiveness and the state's punishment are compatible. One forgives, the other punishes. But a person cannot forgive while at the same time *wanting* the state to punish the offender, rather than incarcerate him for the sake of reform or restraint. In that case, one and the same agent would both forgive and want punishment exacted, and that's a contradiction. That's why those who forgive will advocate for a penal system not based on retribution.

Many Christians would disagree that there's any contradiction inherent in both forgiving and punishing – indeed John Paul II himself would likely have disagreed with it. They don't think that punishment in any way undermines forgiveness; by being punished, they feel, those who are forgiven expiate their misdeeds, they bear penalties and extinguish their guilt. But, standing as I do in the tradition of Martin Luther, I think Christ took all the punishment upon himself. None of it can be justly doled out to anyone anymore. Expiation on the part of an offender *replaces* forgiveness and removes the reason for it. It cannot supplement forgiveness. The heart of forgiveness is relinquishing retribution.

Release of Guilt

We crave forgiveness in part because we naturally dislike the pain of punishment. But we also crave it because we find it hard to bear the burden of guilt. Guilt can eat away at us like a deadly cancer. If punishment were a rite of purification, sometimes we'd gladly endure the captivity of our bodies to gain freedom for our souls; the pain of punishment is sometimes preferable to the pangs of conscience. But punishment cannot release us of guilt. Only forgiveness can. Release of guilt is the third aspect of forgiveness, after release from punishment, to which we now turn.

In the first scene of the movie *Amadeus*, we hear, behind a closed door, the distressed voice of the now aged and forgotten composer Antonio Salieri: "Mozart! Mozart! Mozart! Forgive me! Forgive your assassin! Mozart!" After a brief pause, the voice goes on, rising in volume, "Show some mercy! I beg you! I beg you! Show mercy to a guilty man!" Then it grows louder, "Mozart! Mozart! I confess it! Listen! I confess!" But Mozart is dead. He can't respond to the desperate pleas of a man plagued by unbearable guilt. Despondent and forlorn, Salieri opens the window and laments into the sky, "Mozart! Mozart! I cannot bear it any longer! I confess! I confess what I did! I killed you! Sir, I confess! I killed you!"[15] But the heavens are closed. Mozart is deaf to his pleas. Unable to either live with his terrible deed or obtain forgiveness, Salieri cuts his throat with a razor. The pain of guilt was greater than his love of life.

To forgive means to release the condemned wrongdoer not just from punishment but from *guilt*. That's what God did with human sin. As we saw in chapter 4, Christ didn't only bear our punishment on account of his oneness with God; Christ also separated us, the doers, from our evil deeds and released us from guilt on account of his oneness with humanity. In him, we died to our old and sinful selves, and with him, we were raised to new life. Our death in Christ has separated us from our guilt. Its burden no longer rests on our shoulders. We are free. And even when our conscience stubbornly refuses to stop accusing our forgiven souls, we know that God is greater than our conscience.

It was not God to whom Salieri turned to lift the burden of his guilt. He was angry at God. He thought he had made a deal with God and that God had failed him. Salieri had held to his part of the bargain, but God had betrayed him and given greater musical talent to Mozart. God had wronged him, Salieri mistakenly believed. And he would never forgive God, not even the God who might forgive him. He wanted to unburden his soul to Mozart, his victim. He wanted Mozart to take away the guilt of his transgression. But Mozart was dead, and Salieri remained unforgiven.

But let's imagine for a moment that Salieri's wrongdoing against Mozart was of a different kind and Mozart was alive to forgive the old man plagued by guilt. In that case, what should Mozart have done? What do we do when we forgive? We don't press charges against offenders, I said earlier. But more than that, we also release them from their guilt. The offenders incur guilt by their wrongdoing; that's why they confess. Those who forgive them recognize and affirm their guilt. Yet at the same time, they lift its burden from the shoulders of the offenders. After receiving forgiveness, the offenders are free from it. When those who forgive see the forgiven offenders, they see innocence, not guilt. The offenders *were* guilty. *Now* they are innocent.

Forgiver's Memory

Finally, when we forgive, we let the offense slip into oblivion – not right away, but eventually, not as a matter of course, but when the time is ripe. To many today this seems a strange idea. But it was part of Christian faith from the beginning, and it builds most significantly on Jewish tradition, the teaching of the Old Testament.

Not remember the offense!? Surprisingly, that's what God does with our sins. It's not just that God doesn't reckon them to us, forgoing both punishment and imputation of guilt, or that God removes sin from us like a heavy burden, dispersing it like morning mist. Scripture explicitly states that God doesn't even remember our sins. They don't come to God's mind (Jeremiah 31:34; Hebrews 8:12; 10:17). So it's not just that we're innocent at the moment we are forgiven. In

God's memory, we've been made innocent across the entire span of our lives. God looks at us and doesn't superimpose on us our former transgressions. Our transgressions don't exist anywhere anymore. They don't stick to us as guilt, and they don't stick to God's memory of us. We were sinners, but we are no longer sinners – in a sense, not even sinners past!

Of course, it's difficult to imagine God not remembering something. Isn't God supposed to know everything all the time? Isn't that what God's omniscience means? Still, in some strange way, God doesn't remember sin. It is beyond my scope here to examine the nature of God's knowledge of forgiven sin. It suffices to note that, throughout the 2000-year history of Christianity, spiritual writers and theologians have echoed the scriptural claim that God doesn't remember our sin and urged fellow Christians to do likewise. When we forgive, we should ultimately forget sin. The pithy phrase "forgive and forget" is commonly used to express this idea. Martin Luther, for instance, repeatedly chided those who would forgive but not forget: "Not so, dear Christian! You must forgive and forget, as you would that God should not only forgive you and forget."[16]

What does it mean to "forget" wrongs we've suffered? You will recall that Nietzsche advocated forgetting insults, injuries, and wrongs. For him, forgetting replaced forgiving. His great hero was Mirabeau, who could not forgive because he had already forgotten. Yet, as I argued earlier, moral reasons speak against such forgetting. It is morally wrong to disregard misdeeds. Psychological reasons speak against it too. It comes too close to the counterproductive suppression against which Sigmund Freud and others have warned. To forgive is to blame, but to blame is to remember. In forgiving, we blame a person in order to release them from their debt. Similarly, in forgiving we remember the debt for a while in order to let it ultimately slip into oblivion.

Why should we let it slip into oblivion, someone may protest? When offenses are forgotten, it looks as if they never happened at all! But they *have* happened, and honesty demands that we acknowledge them. For that reason, we should remember, the argument concludes.

So what happens to the obligation to remember when we let the forgiven offense slip into oblivion? Notice that "forgetting" *follows* condemnation of sin and release from penalties and guilt, it doesn't happen apart from it, as in Nietzsche's account. When we forgive, we acknowledge the offenses and blame the perpetrator. But then we treat the person as if the offense did not happen. To forgive means most basically to give a person the gift of existing as if they had not committed the offense at all. Therefore, not remembering offenses rightly crowns forgiving.

Two things happen when we say, "I'll forgive, but I'll never forget." First, the gift of forgiveness is given in the dark wrapping paper of warning, even of threat. We keep score, and memories of transgressions become stockpiled like weapons during a cold war. And when the occasion arises, we use them to wage battle. In some cases, moreover, the memory of the offense seduces us into seeing dangers where none are lurking and justifying preventive strikes where no aggression against us is underfoot.

Second, "I'll never forget" places on the offender an indelible sign that reads "Evildoer!" Once an offender, always an offender. Memory nails offenders' identities unalterably to their misdeeds. Imagine that the murderous dictator Stalin genuinely repented, mended his ways, and landed in heaven. By some miracle, you are also there, and every time you see him, you always remember his atrocities and see a murderer on a grand scale. He would be forgiven, in a sense, but not freed from his sin.

Now, one can argue that Stalin and his ilk should not be forgiven at all. I'll turn shortly to the question of whether forgiveness has any limits and argue that it is properly given to all people. If you disagree, then you'll obviously insist that every time you think of Stalin, now consigned to hell, you'll remember his misdeeds. But *if* you think that Stalin should be forgiven if he genuinely repented, then it seems that not remembering his offenses every time you think of him should crown forgiveness. Whether by serving as a weapon or by tattooing the offender, the memory of the offense takes something away from what the forgiveness bestows.

Isn't releasing the offender from the memory of wrongdoing the ultimate victory of evil, however? Wouldn't the night of oblivion resound with the triumphant, sinister laughter of evildoers? That's one possibility, but there is another. Oblivion may deprive evil of oxygen and rob it of a future. Like many evildoers, in *Amadeus*, Salieri killed partly *in order* to be remembered. "Whenever they say Mozart with love, they'll have to say Salieri with loathing. And that's my immortality – at last!" he said to Vogler, the priest who kept urging the suicidal man to make a confession. Salieri continued, "Our names will be tied together for eternity – his in fame and mine in infamy. At least it's better than total oblivion he'd planned for me, your merciful God." Far from being a victory of evil, consigning forgiven wrongdoings to oblivion – done at the right time and in the right way – denies evil the honor and the glory of memory.

Of course, even if such oblivion crowns forgiving, in many cases it would be completely inappropriate and dangerous not to remember. Memory is a shield that protects from future harm. If Nathanael, my seven-year-old, loses control on a particular black diamond ski run and hurts himself, he'll stay away from that run for a while. He remembers and is spared repeated pain. Similarly, if someone has injured us, we remember and, if we possibly can, avoid that person or the situation in which the injury occurred. Because we remember, we can avoid falling prey, like hapless children, to offenders' violations. As long as there is potential for harm in a relationship, we *should* remember the offense. We will forgive, but the offenders' likely negligence or wickedness will prevent forgiveness from growing into its fullness. Since the potential for harm is great in our sinful world, forgiveness will mostly remain incomplete.

Still, in rare situations, forgiveness may reach completeness. Imagine that a close friend has wronged you, a friend who is deeply sorry and to whom friendship with you matters a great deal. Imagine also that you can be certain she will never wrong you that way again. You've forgiven her. As you did, you both remembered the wrongdoing, you both condemned it; you released her from punishment and guilt, and she's repented of it and thanked you for the gift.

What would *now* stand in the way of letting the forgiven offense slip into oblivion? It will always remain stored somewhere in the file system of your memory's hard drive. If at some point you want to explore whether the friend has harmed you and what that harm may have been, you could double click an icon and open the file, and there it would be for you to see. But why would you *want* to remember, when instead you can give yourself and your friend the gift of a friendship undisturbed by a past transgression? She's now your friend – not a friend who has formerly wronged you, not a forgiven friend, but a friend pure and simple, with an unburdened past. And you're her friend – not a friend whom she wronged, not a friend who has forgiven her, but a friend pure and simple.

That kind of friendship is the fruit forgiveness hopes to bear ultimately. Surprising as it may be, it often bears that fruit even now if only for brief moments. Think of reconciled friends absorbed in a common activity – playing chess, watching a movie, listening to a concert, and enjoying each other's company. Each is now outside of herself, so to speak, immersed in the common activity, and each is, just because of that, fully at one with herself. What has happened to the memory of wrongdoing? It's gone from awareness. It has slipped into oblivion, at least for a while.

Forgiveness hopes for a world – a perfect and indestructible world of love – in which such moments will be the pervasive reality. Forgiveness will then reach its own fulfillment. The forgivers and the forgiven will no longer need to remember the transgressions whose punishments forgiveness has forgone and whose guilt it has lifted.

Indiscriminate Forgiveness

God's forgiveness is indiscriminate. That's the bedrock conviction of the Christian faith. "One has died for all," wrote the apostle Paul (2 Corinthians 5:14). That simple claim has immense implications. All means all, without exception. There are no people who are sufficiently good so that God doesn't need to forgive them and Christ didn't die for them. There are no people who are too wicked for God to forgive them and for Christ to die for them. And there are no people whom God, for some inscrutable reason, decided not to forgive. Even the so-called sin against the Holy Spirit, which Jesus said would not be forgiven (Matthew 12:31 – 32), is not an exception. For that is the sin of closing oneself off to the One through whom God forgives all people and all sins. God's grace more than matches any conceivable sin. "Where sin increased," wrote the Apostle tersely but profoundly, "grace abounded all the more" (Romans 5:20).

We are so used to hearing about the indiscriminate nature of God's forgiveness that our moral sensibilities are dulled to its scandalousness. But scandalous it is. My colleague Carlos Eire, told me of a visit home to Chicago. Professor Eire often serves as a "resource person" on all matters theological for his mother and her Cuban friends. "Listen, Carlos," one of his mother's friends began a theological inquiry. "I was thinking … If by some miracle Fidel turned to God in repentance before he died, would he go to heaven?"

Not surprisingly, she and her friends dislike Fidel passionately. When he came to power and set about to weed out all the "enemies of the people" who lived comfortably under the old regime, he robbed these women of everything they had had on that beautiful island. Could that crime ever be forgiven? For Professor Eire, the answer was clear, even if it was hard to accept. "He would go to heaven," he responded. "God's grace is for all people, dictators included!" The woman paused to absorb the shock of the answer and then, slowly and deliberately, she said: "If Fidel gets to heaven, then I *don't* want to be there!" To her, Fidel should burn in hell, or he should cease to exist, or he should be banished to a planet of his own with as many cigars as he wants, whatever – but he should absolutely not be included in the company of the redeemed. He should remain unforgiven.

The scandalousness of God's indiscriminate forgiveness hits us even harder when we are called on to imitate it. When we need to forgive, most of us, perhaps unconsciously, feel entitled to draw a circle around the scope of forgiveness. We should forgive some, maybe even most, wrongdoings, but certainly not all.

Maybe we think unintentional offenses are forgivable, and deliberate ones are not. But how would we draw the line? How intentional would the offense need to be? If the offense were truly unintentional, there would be something to be sorry about but nothing to forgive; it was just an accident. Or maybe we think small offenses are forgivable, and horrendous ones are not. But again, where would we draw the line? An offense is an offense and has as much right to be forgiven as any other, which is no right at all. No line separates offenses that should be forgiven from those that should not. *There are no unforgivable sins.*

We should also forgive irrespective of who the offenders are. Maybe we think one-time offenders should be forgiven, and repeat offenders should not. One strike, even three strikes, but then you've placed yourself outside the company of those worthy of forgiveness. But why draw the line there, given that no one is *worthy* to be forgiven at all? No doubt we will want to protect ourselves – and we *should* protect ourselves – from repeat offenders. But as we have seen, we can forgive even if we restrain the offenders or demand that they be incarcerated.

Or maybe, like Jesus' disciples, we think there is a limit to the number of times we should forgive those who repent. "How often should I forgive?" inquired Peter. "As many as seven times?" "Not seven times," Jesus answered, "but I tell you, seventy times seven!" No line can be drawn between those who should be forgiven because they sin only rarely and those who shouldn't because they sin repeatedly. *There are no unforgivable people.*

Should we forgive even those who refuse to repent? Consider once again God's forgiveness, which serves as the model for ours. There are people who think that in relation to God, repentance comes before forgiveness. But that can't be right. God doesn't angrily refuse forgiveness until we show ourselves worthy of it by repentance. Instead, God loves us and forgives us before we repent. Indeed, before we even sinned, Jesus Christ died for our sins. God's forgiveness is not reactive – dependent on our repentance. It's original, preceded and conditioned by absolutely nothing on our part. We can do nothing to become worthy of it for the same reason we can do nothing to earn any of God's gifts. Before we do anything, before we even exist, God's giving and God's forgiving are already there, free of charge. God doesn't give and forgive conditionally. God's giving and forgiving are as unconditional as the sun's rays and as indiscriminate as raindrops. One died for *all*. Absolutely no one is excluded.

Why should *we* forgive unconditionally and indiscriminately? We don't do it simply because a law demands we do so. We forgive because God has already forgiven. For us to hold any offender captive to sin by refusing to forgive is to reject the reality of God's forgiving grace. Because Christ died for all, we are called to forgive everyone who offends us, without distinctions and without conditions. That hard work of indiscriminate forgiveness is what those who've been made in the likeness of the forgiving God should do. And, as we shall see in the next chapter, that hard work of forgiveness is what those who've "put on Christ" are able to do.

Those who argue that we should repent before God forgives us usually also argue that offenders should repent before we grant them forgiveness. They link our forgiveness to a prior change of heart and behavior in those who've wronged us. First the offenders must repent, which is to say that they must lay aside all excuses and explanations and say to us that they shouldn't have done what they did. The offenders must also assure us, the offended, that they are sorry, sorry not just for the pain but for the fact that they caused it. Finally, the offenders must work hard to change the way they live, continues the argument of those who view repentance as a prerequisite of forgiveness. To the extent that the offenders can, they must return what their offense has taken. They must seek to live upright lives, causing no further harm either to the person they've offended or to anybody else. From this perspective, repentance and a track record of amended life are then rewarded by forgiveness. Without repentance and changed life, forgiveness would be, as Vladimir Jankélévitch put it, "a simple buffoonery".[17]

Is it correct, however, to put repentance before forgiveness? In many ways, it may indeed be a reasonable path to take. We'd be lenient but wouldn't unduly expose ourselves to repeated transgressions. We'd be generous but wouldn't squander our gifts on irresponsible people who enjoy the fruits of their misdeeds with good digestion and undisturbed sleep. We'd be forgiving but would not waste forgiveness on those who feel entitled to receive it no matter what they have done. And yet the Christian tradition – especially Protestantism – insists that repentance doesn't precede forgiveness. What then is the place of repentance?

The Place of Repentance

From what I have said so far, it could seem that forgiveness can dispense completely with repentance. We should forgive, and whether the offender repents is irrelevant. Forgiveness is unconditional, and therefore repentance is expendable. The conclusion seems perfectly valid. Yet it's not right.

The relation between forgiveness and repentance is more complicated than such a conclusion implies. What complicates matters is that forgiveness is a *social* affair. We forgive in order to take care of a wrongdoing, but a wrongdoing always happens *between* people, not just in the thoughts or actions of an individual. Unless we are wronging ourselves, we don't just do bad things, unrelated to anyone else; we wrong others. That's why it is insufficient if forgiveness happens just in someone's mind and heart. It must happen also between people – between the offender and the offended. A person whom I've wronged doesn't just forgive; she forgives *me*. Wrongdoers, and not just those who are wronged, are always involved in forgiveness. A gift is not an object we find in a store, I've suggested in chapter 2; an object *becomes* a gift when we undertake to give it to someone as a gift. Similarly forgiveness is not just a state of our mind; it is something we give to someone else. Put differently, forgiveness is a social relationship.

Not everybody agrees. If we think the main purpose of forgiveness is to calm our raging emotions, then forgiveness is a change in feelings and happens only in the heart of the person who forgives. We were angry, now we're calm. We were plagued by resentment, now we're free of it. We suffered from intrusive memories, now we can give ourselves over undisturbed to the joys of the present and hopes for the future. All of this is important, but it is part of emotional healing that may come as a result of forgiveness. It's not forgiveness itself.

Alternatively, if we think forgiveness is just a change in the behavior of the offended party toward the offender, then again, forgiveness is something we can do on our own, without the involvement of offenders. The offenders are guilty, and they deserve to have charges pressed against them. Instead of treating them as they deserve, however, we forgive – we forgo seeking either to inflict punishment or to have it inflicted by the state; we release them from guilt, we even set ourselves on the road to letting the offense eventually slip into oblivion. We often think that that's full-fledged forgiveness. Yet it isn't. Even though this is good as far as it goes and even though this is sometimes all we can do, something is still missing. Forgiveness has not yet reached its goal.

Imagine that I tell my sister I am sending her a large gift, say, an expensive bracelet. For whatever reason, however, she's not sure she wants to accept it – maybe she thinks that I may be trying to bribe her to do something she doesn't want to do, that the gift is too large to be received without undue obligation, or that I can't afford it. Have I given her a gift? In one sense, I have. I bought it, I sent it, and the postal service delivered it. In another sense, I haven't. The gift is at her home, but she hasn't decided whether she wants to keep it. She hasn't yet received it. Given but not received, the gift is stuck somewhere in the middle between us. Forgiveness works the same way.

With this analogy in mind, consider, first, God's forgiveness. "But God proves his love for us," wrote the apostle Paul, "in that while we still were sinners Christ died for us" (Romans 5:8). God's gift was given, it was sent. But that's not enough. We need to receive it. We receive the gift by trusting that God has indeed forgiven us and by accepting both the accusation contained in forgiveness and the release from guilt and punishment. We believe and confess the wrong we've done. Without faith and repentance, we are not forgiven – God having done the forgiving notwithstanding. God has given, but we haven't received. Forgiveness is then stuck in the middle between the God who forgives and humans who don't receive.

Now apply the same analogy of a gift stuck in the middle to human forgiveness. Repentance is important, even indispensable, and it is indispensable because forgiveness is an event *between* people, not just an individual's change of feelings, attitudes, or actions. Instead of being a *condition* of forgiveness, however, repentance is its necessary *consequence*.

If they imitate the forgiving God, forgivers will keep forgiving, whether the offenders repent or not. Forgivers' forgiving is not conditioned by repentance. The offenders' *being forgiven*, however, is conditioned by repentance – just as being given a box of chocolate is conditioned by receiving that box of chocolate. Without repentance, the forgivers will keep forgiving but the offenders will remain unforgiven, in that they are untouched by that forgiveness.

Why? Because they *refuse* to be forgiven. To forgive, I've argued, is to condemn the doer and the deed – or rather, it is to condemn in the process of releasing a person from the guilt and punishment that justice would demand. Correlatively, to repent is to accept the condemnation. Not to repent is to reject the condemnation. Unrepentant offenders implicitly say: It's wrong for you to forgive me; I've done you no wrong. Or more brazenly, they say: I don't care if you forgive or not, because I don't care whether I've wronged you or not. Mostly, however, they say: I am too ashamed of the wrongdoing I've committed to repent, too afraid of the consequences that may befall me. In all three cases, forgiveness is rejected. In the first case, it is construed as a false accusation; in the second case, it is despised, and in the third case it is deemed unbearable. By refusing to acknowledge the wrongdoing, Luther rightly claimed that a transgressor himself "has changed a forgivable sin into an unforgivable one".[18]

So repentance is essential. In the process of showing that it is essential, have I given in to those who believe that repentance should *precede* forgiveness? No, it still remains true that forgiveness is not conditioned by prior repentance. Why does the Christian faith insist on this? The response to this question is the same as the response to the question about the nature of forgiveness as a whole: because that's how God forgives. But if a questioner will not let go of the issue, she may ask: *Why* does God forgive that way and why should we?

Repentance may be one of the hardest things a human being can do. What do most offenders do – whether small or large? Two top Cambodian Khmer Rouge officials, Nuon Chea and Khieu Samphan, can serve as an example of the multiple ways in which offenders often dodge responsibility. These men were in part responsible for the deaths of 1,000,000 people. What did they do when they were apprehended?[19] First, according to reports, Samphan's barely audible "sorry, very sorry" came only after relentless and aggressive questioning. As a rule offenders make no apologies until pressed hard, and then only with their backs against the wall. Second, Chea seemed more sorry that he'd been caught, maybe even sorry for the lives lost in Cambodia's civil war, but not at all repentant for his role in the ravages of the Khmer Rouge regime. When offenders reluctantly mutter their "sorry", they may be showing regret for what others have suffered, not remorse for their reprehensible behavior. Third, on the question of guilt, Samphan argued that it is difficult "to say who is wrong and who is right and who is doing this and who is doing that". When offenders do accept some responsibility, they immediately try to mitigate it by pointing to the comparable, if not greater, misdeeds of others. Finally, after admitting that some feelings of "resentment" on the part of victims are normal, Samphan remonstrated that "we have many more problems to resolve at the present and in the future, and we have to forget the past." To divert attention from their crimes, offenders often insist that it is best for all concerned not to revisit the past but instead to concentrate on the future.

That it is difficult to repent genuinely will not come as a surprise to those who have pondered the gravity and power of human sin. One of sin's most notable features is that it unfailingly refuses to acknowledge itself as sin. We usually not only refuse to admit the wrongdoing and to accept guilt, but seem neither to detest the sin committed nor feel very sorry about it. Instead, we hide our sin behind multiple walls of denial, cover-up, mitigating explanations, and claims to comparative innocence.

The accusations of others reinforce our propensity to hide sin. We usually do all we can to justify ourselves, and that reaction is understandable. We fear the consequences of sin. We may lose a good reputation or be punished. We cannot bear to face ourselves as wrongdoers. We fear that the integrity of our very selves might crumble under the weight of our offense. That's why we are often able to repent only when we are assured that our guilt will be lifted and charges will not be pressed against us. In other words, we are able to genuinely repent only when forgiveness has first been extended to us.

A friend of mine – I'll call her Esther here – was abandoned by her alcoholic mother when she was nine years old. The family never spoke about the mother and rarely heard from her. When she reached her midtwenties, Esther decided she needed to see her mother again. Though she had been deeply hurt, most of all Esther felt very guilty that she hadn't done more for her mother, that she hadn't even wanted to contact her over the years. Finally, in the little Iowa town where she had said good-bye to her mother seventeen years earlier, Esther knocked on her mother's door. It was an emotional reunion, and Esther could barely speak all afternoon as they walked around town meeting all the people who were important to Esther's mother. As they sat in the living room after dinner, Esther pulled herself together and took command of the conversation. She spoke briefly of the intervening years and then asked her mother to forgive her for not writing or calling. Esther confessed that she had broken the promise she made as a little girl never to love her mother. She told her mother how sorry she was and begged her mother's forgiveness for having neglected her for so long.

"Of course. Of course I forgive you, Esther." They both were crying now, and there was a long silence. Esther was waiting for her mother to reciprocate. Surely she would ask forgiveness for abandoning her, for all those alcoholic scenes, for the many broken promises. And Esther waited. But nothing came. Slowly Esther got up from her chair and went to sit at her mother's feet. Taking her mother's hands she said, "Mommy, I was really hurt as a little girl, and I was really, really sad. But I want you to know that I forgive you. I know that you didn't mean to hurt me. I know you loved me then and that you still love me now. And I love you. I'm okay, Mommy. My life has turned out okay, and I forgive you for everything."

"Oh, Esther! I'm so sorry. I'm so so sorry. I'm so sorry." She kept repeating it over and over, rocking back and forth, tears streaming down her face. With sudden insight Esther had realized that her mother's shame and guilt were so overwhelming, far too ugly and too painful for her to face and to bring into the open on her own. She could not even conceive of being loved and forgiven by the child she had abandoned. But hearing that indeed her daughter loved and forgave her for what she could never forgive herself, she was able to repent. And finally she was able to receive forgiveness.

Caught in the snare of a misdeed, offenders often seem unable to redeem themselves on their own. They need help from the victims of their misdeeds. By forgiving, victims enact a divine kind of love toward their enemies – and help overcome evil by the power of good. But both parties must participate in the process for it to be complete.

Though it is important to celebrate the power of forgiveness to lead offenders to repentance, it would be imprudent to overstate it. We often don't repent even when we are forgiven. We may continue to reject the claim that we've done anything wrong. We may rejoice at the gift of forgiveness without weeping over our offenses. Forgiveness does not *cause* repentance, but it does help make repentance possible.

Restitution

Since repentance is difficult, wrongdoers sometimes try alternatives. For instance, they try to deal with the problem by showering those they've wronged with gifts. Then the gifts they give – gifts they don't owe – are like checks written to cover debts they've incurred. But the debts remain unmentioned, for otherwise gifts would mutate into payments. Could such giving really take care of the wrongdoing and of the disrupted relationship, rendering forgiveness and repentance unnecessary?

If genuine, such giving will certainly help build bridges between parties separated by wrongdoing. It will show those who've been wronged that the wrongdoers are well disposed toward them now, and it will begin to build a future trust. But such giving won't do anything about the past. By definition, giving doesn't concern the past. Yet it's precisely the *past* wrongdoing that's burdening the relationship. However, if offenders aren't willing to face up to their past deeds, if they don't admit to their offense and don't ask to be forgiven, the injured person could rightly conclude that generous offenders want to make their offense disappear under a mountain of gifts. Without repentance, gift givers may end up magnifying the original wrongdoing by attempting to sweep it under the rug.

With repentance, on the other hand, gift giving becomes a form of restitution. Repentance will prove genuine only if the wrongdoer is willing to restore to the victim what wrongdoing took away. Sometimes, full restoration is impossible. A child was killed, and nothing the wrongdoer does can return that child to life. Yet some form of restitution is possible, provided the wrongdoer is willing. The child's memory can be honored in some tangible way, for instance. Or a breadwinner has been killed. Though the offender cannot restore life, she can at least soften the financial impact of the loss. Restitution is *always* possible. And it is mostly necessary too – not as a demand prior to forgiveness but as a fruit of forgiveness and a fitting sign that repentance is genuine. What kind of repentance would it be if you were willing to admit to wrong, but unwilling to cease benefiting from it or unwilling to relieve the victim's suffering?[20]

But note: We should *offer* restitution. We may not necessarily succeed at giving it. When my father was gripped by grace in the hell of a communist concentration camp, he decided that he'd go to all the people he remembered wronging, ask for forgiveness, and offer restitution. One of them was Mr Moučka, a mill owner in Sirač, a village in northwestern Croatia where my father had grown up. On his way to school, my father used to pass through Mr Moučka's orchard with his friends and occasionally steal some fruit, maybe a bit out of need but mostly out of mischief. Mr Moučka would rant and curse and try to chase the boys away. After he was released from the concentration camp, my father went to see Mr Moučka. It didn't matter to him that Mr Moučka was a prosperous man and didn't miss a few apples and pears stolen by a poor boy who grew up in a single-room house with a dirt floor. It didn't matter to him that Mr Moučka had cheated his whole life and stolen from the little grain brought by the poor, including my father's family. My father had done what was wrong, and apology and restitution were called for.

Instead of admiring my father's humility and grace, however, Mr Moučka dispatched him quickly, muttering under his breath as he was turning away, "I forgive you, I forgive you." My father sensed it was Mr Moučka's own guilt over plundering the poor that made him an uncomfortable forgiver. He wasn't sure whether he went away forgiven or not, but he went away free, whereas Mr Moučka remained bound by wrongdoing he would not confess and stolen property he would not restore.

Reconciliation

Forgiveness places us on a boundary between enmity and friendship, between exclusion and embrace. It tears down the wall of hostility that wrongdoing erects, but it doesn't take us into the territory of friendship. Should those who forgive stay in this neutral zone?

If they did, forgiveness would be the generous act of a person who wishes to stay away from the offender. Often that's all we can muster the strength to do, and all that offenders will allow us. Yet at its best, forgiveness hopes for more. In general, when we give, we hope that gifts will in some way be reciprocated and that the exchange of gifts will give birth to friendship, even to mutual delight. Giving creates and strengthens communal bonds.

Forgiveness is born on the wings of a similar hope. A wrongdoing has made a serious dent in a relationship, maybe even totaled it. We forgive in hope that it will elicit repentance and restitution, and that forgiveness will mend and restore the relationship so that gifts circulating within the community can continue to strengthen the bonds between its members.

As we seek to create communion between those whose relationship was damaged by wrongdoing, we imitate the forgiving God. "Therefore, since we are justified by faith, we have peace with God through our Lord Jesus Christ," wrote the apostle Paul (Romans 5:1). In Scripture, peace is not just the absence of war, whether the war is "hot" or "cold". Peace is not the indifference that leads each to his or her own little island, unconcerned for and unengaged with others. Peace is the flourishing of the community and of each person within it. And peace with God is our delight in communion with God. The point of God's not counting our sins is having our communion with God restored. We've been God's enemies and "were reconciled" with God through the death of Christ (Romans 5:10). Recall from chapter 4 that God forgives by indwelling us and indwells us by forgiving us. Forgiveness is one important element in the restoration of communion between God and humanity.

One way to see why those who forgive sit uncomfortably in the neutral zone between exclusion and embrace is to examine the motivation for forgiveness. Why do we forgive when we forgive as we should? As I have observed earlier, it's not primarily to benefit ourselves. We also don't forgive primarily to benefit the larger community – to help pacify it so things will function more smoothly, even though something like "communal reconciliation" may result from forgiveness. In the Christian account of things, we forgive because we love – specifically, because we love our debtors, our offenders, and even our enemies. The same love that motivates forgiveness pushes forgiveness not just from exclusion to neutrality, but from neutrality to embrace. Forgiveness between human beings is one crucial step in a larger process whose final goal is the embrace of former enemies in a community of love.

Forgiveness doesn't stand alone, as a punctual act or even as an isolated practice. That would be too passive an understanding of what forgiveness is all about. Rather, it is embedded in a way of life that is committed to overcoming evil by doing good. That's how Luther interpreted "forgetting" in the phrase "forgive and forget". Not to count the offenders guilty and not to press charges against them is important but insufficient. Luther insisted that you should "load" the enemy "with kindness so that, overcome with good [Romans 12:21], he will be kindled with love for you".[21]

Do we first forgive and then embrace the forgiven offender? Or do we start with the initial halting steps of our embrace and then let forgiveness happen when both parties are ready? No two situations are alike, and it is best not to cleave to a single inflexible rule. What's important is only to insist on the unbreakable unity of forgiveness and embrace. There can be no embrace of the former enemy without forgiveness, and forgiveness should lead beyond itself to embrace.

Ivo Markovič, a Franciscan monk from Bosnia, was caught in the whirlwind of war in the mid-1990s in which Croats, Bosnians, and Serbs were fighting each other with blood flowing and homes burning on all sides. Muslim Bosnians had massacred twenty-one men from Šušanj, the village in which Father Markovič was born. Nine of them were members of his family – all feeble senior citizens, innocent of any crimes, the youngest of whom was his seventy-one-year-old father.

Three years after the massacre, in the fall of 1996, Father Markovič visited Šušanj. Occupying the house in which his brother used to live was a fierce Muslim woman. He was warned not to go there because she brandished a rifle to protect her new home. He went anyway. As he approached the house she was waiting for him, cigarette in her mouth and rifle cocked. She barked: "Go away, or I'll shoot you." "No, you won't shoot me," said Father Markovič in a gentle but firm voice, "you'll make a cup of coffee for me." She stared at him for a while, then slowly put the rifle down and went to the kitchen. Taking the last bit of coffee she had, she mixed in some already used grounds to make enough coffee for two cups. And they, deadly enemies, began to talk as they partook in the ancient ritual of hospitality: drinking coffee together. She told him of her loneliness, of the home she had lost, of the son who never returned from the battlefield. When Father Marković returned a month later she told him: "I rejoice at seeing you as much as if my son had returned home."

Did they talk about forgiveness? I don't know. And in a sense, it doesn't matter. He, the victim, came to her asking for her hospitality in his brother's home, which she unrightfully possessed. And she responded. Though she greeted him with a rifle, she gave him a gift and came to rejoice at his presence. The humble, tenuous beginnings of a journey toward embrace were enacted through a ritual of coffee drinking. If the journey continues, it will lead through the difficult terrain of forgiveness.

Chapter 6

How Can
We Forgive?

God forgives. We should forgive. And we should forgive as God forgives. That's the simple sketch of the previous two chapters. But is it possible for us as mere humans, wounded humans, to forgive the way we should?

Giving is hard enough, as we saw in chapter 3. Laziness can get the better of us. Giving takes effort, and often we are too comfortable to extend ourselves to others. Selfishness can hold us captive. We give so as to gain an advantage for ourselves rather than to benefit others. Finally, pride can poison the gifts that indolence hasn't prevented us from giving and that selfishness hasn't transmuted into ways of benefiting ourselves. As we give, we can humiliate and manipulate the recipients. It's hard to give and to give well.

The main obstacles to giving are the ones we ourselves erect, our laziness, our selfishness, and our pride – in a word, our inordinate self-love. The recipients may be ungrateful for our gifts and careless with them, and then we find it hard to continue giving. But on the whole, the behavior and character of recipients don't stand in the way of giving. They are needy, and we give. Or we delight in them, and we give.

It's different with forgiving, and that's what makes forgiving harder than giving. Here too, of course, our self-love often stands in the way. But the greatest obstacle to forgiving comes from the deeds that need to be forgiven. Unlike gift recipients, offenders don't just stand with empty hands, waiting to receive. The empty hands of offenders have inflicted pain and are sometimes stained with blood. Injuries to forgivers' bodies and souls stand in the way of forgiving. So do smugness and enmity of the wrongdoers. The offenses and the offensiveness of wrongdoers collude with the self-love of the wronged to make it difficult to forgive, very difficult.

In the first act of Paul Simon's musical *The Capeman*, the mother of a boy who was stabbed to death struggles to forgive the perpetrator, Salvador Agron. Her sixteen-year-old son's only fault was that he happened to be in the wrong place at the wrong time, the playground on Forty-fifth Street, near Ninth Avenue in New York City, shortly after midnight on 4 April 1959. Agron was a member of the Vampires gang and known to his friends as Dracula. He stabbed the boy to death with a seven-inch dagger as other Vampires held him down. "I have to face this horror, Senora," the mother sings. "My religion asks me to pray for the murderer's soul." The well from which the prayers should flow is dry, however. "But I think you'd have to be Jesus on the cross to open your heart after such a loss," she continues. "Can I forgive him? Can I forgive him? No, I cannot."[1]

There are many reasons why it is difficult to forgive. We may find it impossible, as did the mother from the musical, or we may be unwilling to forgive. We may be frustrated by the difficulty of agreeing on the extent of the wrongdoing or by the refusal of offenders to repent. The offenders may not be around to be forgiven or they might not be able to participate in the process.

Before I examine these and similar difficulties and suggest ways to ease the hardships of forgiving, we need to consider one large obstacle to forgiveness. It's the worry that, even if we had as much goodness and inner strength as Jesus did on the cross, and even if wrongdoers did their part eagerly, for us mere humans, forgiveness might still be both impossible and inappropriate. In other words, we need to deal with the question of the power and the right to forgive.

The Power to Forgive

In his book *Ethics*, German philosopher Nicolai Hartmann stated very bluntly that forgiveness "can never remove moral guilt". True, forgiveness can do *something* with the guilt, conceded Hartmann. It can remove its sting, which is the contempt and hostility that the wronged deservedly feel toward those who have wronged them. When we forgive, we desist feeling contempt and hostility and give "the guilty the outward peace"[2], Hartmann believed. The wrongdoers' guilt remains, however.

Take God out of the picture, and Hartmann is right. In some ways, guilt is like a burden that weighs heavily on our shoulders or like a stain that mars someone's clean clothes. And yet in one crucial respect, guilt is also different from a burden or a stain. If I am bent down under the weight of a burden, a friend can come along and tell me, "This is too heavy for you. Let me help you. Put it on my truck, and I'll take it where it needs to go." Unlike a burden, however, the guilt adheres to me in such a way that no human being can remove it. Similarly, if my clothes get dirty, I can wash or dry-clean them, and they'll be clean again. Human hands cannot scrub away my guilt, however. Guilt weighs down and mars, but neither my neighbor nor I can remove it.

Recall what I wrote in chapters 4 and 5 about forgiveness. To forgive means to accuse wrongdoers while at the same time freeing them of charges against them, releasing them from guilt, and eventually letting the wrongdoing slip into oblivion. The removal of guilt is a crucial element of forgiveness. If guilt remains, forgiveness hasn't happened. But now we see that, try as we might, we cannot remove guilt on our own.

"Who can forgive sins but God alone?" murmured the scribes after seeing Jesus forgive the sins of the paralytic. Jesus didn't disagree that God alone can forgive. Instead, he contested their assumption about who he was. In response to their objection, he healed the paralytic to show that he was unique among human beings and possessed divine power to forgive (see Matthew 9:2–8; Mark 2:1–12).

Because only God can forgive, Jesus, who is divine as well as human, can forgive.

And yet we mere humans are also called to forgive. Jesus himself taught that we should. Indeed, he insisted that we should forgive as God forgives and that, if we don't forgive others, God will not forgive us. Was he requiring the impossible?

"One has died for all," wrote the apostle Paul, concluding, "therefore all have died" (2 Corinthians 5:14). As I explained in chapter 4, because all have died in Christ, wrongdoing was separated from wrongdoers, and wrongdoers' guilt was removed. God did not transfer guilt from guilty humanity to the innocent Christ who bore it for us. No such transfer is possible. In Christ's death, humanity died, and by virtue of that death, human guilt was removed. God alone has the power to make us all die and rise with Christ, even while we continue to live. God alone has the power to forgive. And in Christ, God has in fact forgiven.

Here we need to take the next step: Because God has forgiven, we also have the power to forgive. We don't forgive in our own right. We forgive by making God's forgiveness our own. And even then, we don't forgive the fact of someone's guilt, the so-called objective guilt. God has already done that. We help remove the offender's *feeling* of guilt in regard to us, the so-called *subjective* guilt. What do I do when I say to someone, "I forgive you"? In effect I tell her, "Because God in Christ doesn't count your trespasses against you and because God has removed your guilt from you, I too don't count against you the fact that you've wronged me, and I don't consider you guilty. God has made you innocent, and therefore I consider you innocent." Because God has taken away the burden of guilt, I too in my own way can lift the burden of guilt the offender rightly feels toward me, even after God has forgiven her.

Let's clarify the relationship between God's forgiveness and ours in one important regard. It's not that God forgives sins against God, and we forgive sins against us. All sins against us *are* also sins against God. Every wrong committed against a creature is a sin against the creator. God has the power to forgive all sins, as we saw in chapter 4.

On our own, we have no power to remove guilt for any wrongdoing, not even a wrongdoing committed against us personally. We have the power to remove the guilty feeling on account of such a wrongdoing only to the extent that we participate in God's forgiveness.

When God forgives, offenders need to respond in faith and repentance. But what if they don't repent? Like a package, forgiveness will then be stuck between the sender who dispatched it and the recipient who refuses to receive it. Offenders will remain unforgiven, the reality of God's forgiveness notwithstanding. The same is true when we forgive. We make God's sending of the "forgiveness package" our own. That's all we can do. And that's what we have the power to do. Whether the package will be received depends on the recipients, on whether they admit to the wrongdoing and repent.

The Right to Forgive

We have the *power* to forgive because God has already forgiven sinful humanity, the whole of it. But do we have the *right* to forgive? If I forgive, I let the offender off the hook and treat the guilty as if she were innocent. But the offender hasn't wronged just me. When we wrong people, we break moral law. Now, if moral law were just my own private set of rules, I would have the right to abrogate them and let the offender go free. I've set up the rules, and I can decide whether I want to forgive their infraction or not. But moral law is not a set of private rules I've adopted to run my life. It's also not a set of rules a community has adopted to regulate its members' interactions. In the Christian account of how things are, moral law is a *universal* set of rules, underwritten by the character and command of God.

When I visited St. Petersburg, Russia, I went to the Hermitage, a world-class museum in which, among many extraordinary objects of art, some of the glory of past Russian empires is preserved. While I was walking through the reconstructed living quarters of Russian royalty, I was told of a rule that Catherine the Great had imposed in her salon. If a subject yawned in her presence, he or she would never be admitted again. The empress considered it a personal affront if she was not interesting to everyone. I am not sure whether the anecdote is actually true, but it illustrates well the distinction between a private rule and a universal moral law. Since the rule against yawning was her private law, Catherine the Great had the right to forgive its infraction, even if, fierce as she was, she likely had no inclination to do so.

Imagine now the impossible. A general who was the empress's lover became drunk and severely abused her. In so doing, he wasn't breaking just her private rule but a universal moral law that prohibits such violation of another's body and soul. If for some strange reason the empress continued to love the man, she would have the right to exempt him from civil punishments. She was an absolute monarch after all. But would she have the right to free him from guilt? True, she had suffered the blows. But she had not created the moral law he broke. It's binding on him as well as on her. She would have the right not to feel contemptuous, resentful, and hostile toward him, hard as that is to imagine. But she would have no right to free him from guilt, even if she had the power to do so.

Of course, she could *consider* her lover as not guilty. But that wouldn't help very much in a crucial matter under consideration. It would only be her private decision to transmute "You're blameworthy for having done a bad thing" to "I don't consider you guilty anymore." Empress or not, her declaring him not guilty wouldn't change the fact that he *was* guilty. Even worse, she would be *wrong* in declaring him not guilty. He would have broken moral law when he assaulted her, and since she cannot alter moral law, she would be acting against it by declaring that, in her sight, he was not guilty. She, an absolute monarch, would have no right to place herself above moral law and suspend it, not even in the case of a man dear to her.

How can we forgive if we have no right to remove guilt? Again, God's forgiveness is the key. Just as only God ultimately has the power to forgive, only God ultimately has the *right* to forgive. In Christ, God has rightfully forgiven the sin of all human beings. And because God has forgiven, we too have the right to forgive. We don't have that right on our own. But we have the right and the obligation to make God's forgiving our own – to forgive on our part what has already been forgiven by God.

So we have both the right to forgive and, in principle, the power to forgive. In a word, we have the authority to lift the burden and wash away the stain of guilt. It's a derivative authority, dependent completely on God's. Nonetheless, it is genuine. Without such authority, Scripture could not urge us to forgive. Without such authority, the warning that God will not forgive our sins if we don't forgive the wrongs committed against us would only mock us.

The road from having the authority to forgive to actually forgiving is long and arduous. Let's examine some of the obstacles on that road and ways to remove them. The first concerns inner resistance to forgiving, which is rooted in our sense of justice.

Christ's Forgiving and Ours

Recall from the last chapter Luther's explanation of what Christ's followers' attitude should be toward those who had wronged them. They "grieve more over the sin of their offenders than over the loss or offense to themselves. And they do this that they may recall those offenders from their sin rather than avenge the wrongs they themselves have suffered."[3] This radical love of enemies which would lead us to grieve more over the sin of our offenders than over our own loss probably strikes us as otherworldly, unreachable, even a bit foolish. We find it difficult to muster the strength even for a much less saintly attitude that says, "I am utterly furious at you, but I'll forgive anyway because it's the right thing to do." We usually feel a strong inner resistance to forgiving in all forms.

Tit for tat seems to be what we are wired for. If Nathanael, my seven-year-old, is allowed to have dessert, three-year-old Aaron will want to be allowed to have dessert too. And if Aaron likes what Nathanael is having, he'll want to receive a portion as big as his older sibling's. Aaron's sense of equity for distribution of goods is acute. The same is true of his sense of equity about injuries suffered. If Nathanael tells him, "You're a meanie," Aaron will usually respond, "*You're* a meanie!" If Nathanael strikes him, he'll strike back. Once I told him, "You're a bad boy!" instead of telling him that he did a bad thing, as I ought to have done. He frowned and responded, "*Daddy is a bad boy!*" He certainly hasn't been taught to reciprocate in kind. And I am rather certain he engaged in tit for tat before he'd seen others do it.

Most of us are like Aaron. And that's not all bad. A keen sense of equity guards our dignity in a potentially hostile world. Yet to live lives in sync with who God is and who God has created us to be, we need more than just to give back measure for measure to the one who has injured us. How do we overcome our inner resistance to forgiving others and our "delight in punishments"?[4] Luther's response takes us back to the idea of the union with Christ discussed earlier. By faith, I am united with Christ, and God forgives me. One with Christ, I can boast, "Mine are Christ's living, doing, and speaking, his suffering and dying, mine as much as if I had lived, done, spoken, suffered, and died as he did."[5] Christ's presence in the soul secures God's forgiveness. And Christ's presence in the soul also sets a person on a path of forgiveness, suggested Luther.

Luther wrote often about following Christ's example. "Just as he himself did all things for us, not seeking his own good but ours only ... so he desires that we also should set the same example for our neighbors."[6] From this angle, to forgive like Christ is a requirement. But for Luther, that's not the main relationship between Christ's forgiving and ours. Christ is not just outside us, modeling forgiveness and urging us to forgive. Christ lives in us and is himself, as Luther wrote, "the basis, the cause, the source of all our own actual righteousness".[7] From Christ, we receive the power and the willingness to forgive. Christ forgives through us, and that is why we can forgive.

Just as Christ grieved more over our sin than over the injury our sin caused him, so we can grieve for others if Christ lives in us. Just as Christ overcame evil with the power of good rather than avenging himself, so can we. Just as Christ absorbed the effect of wrongdoing so as to free wrongdoers from punishment, so can we if we are united with Christ. Just as Christ lifted the guilt from their shoulders, so can we. "It is no longer I who live, but it is Christ who lives in me," wrote the apostle Paul (Galatians 2:20). Echoing those words, we can say, "It is not I who forgive, but Christ who forgives through me."

Of course, it is still we who do all the things that forgivers do – *we* desire to forgive, *we* say the words "I forgive you," *we* give up resentment, *we* don't press charges, *we* don't consider the offender guilty anymore, and *we* are even willing to let the wrongdoing slip into oblivion. And yet "behind" our doing all of this is Christ, who lives in us. In Luther's words, he is "the basis, the cause, the source" of our forgiving.

The idea of Christ living in us may seem strange. I've never seen one human being living in another, except for a brief period of gestation in mothers' wombs at the beginning of human life. Once we are born, we live next to each other, whether in deep friendship, indifference or enmity, and sometimes, it seems, in all three at the same time, sharing common language, culture, interests, likes, and dislikes. We may also acquire each other's personal traits and even bodily likeness, as longtime lovers are sometimes said to look alike. But we don't live *in* each other.

And that's how it should be in relationships between human beings. It's different in our relationship with God. We are in God in a way in which we cannot be in anybody else. And God is in us in a way nobody else can be. God is the basis, the cause, and the source of all that we are, of our whole being and all our acts. The same applies to Christ, who is one with God.

Christ's living in the depths of our souls may be beyond our imagination. But we can imagine how identification with Christ can transform us. In Nikos Kazantzakis's *The Greek Passion*, the villagers of Lycovrissi enact Christ's passion every seven years. Village leaders choose actors for the characters of the drama a year in advance, and the priest urges them to prepare themselves for the play by living out the assigned characters in their daily lives. They are John or James, Mary Magdalene or Jesus, and they should act as these characters would. The result is lives amazingly transformed, especially among those who play Christ.[8]

During one enactment of the passion play, wrote Kazantzakis, Master Charalambis, "a man of property, a good family man ... tried so hard to follow in the footsteps of Christ" that on Easter Day "he put the crown of thorns on his head, heaved the cross upon his shoulder and, abandoning everything, went off to the monastery ... and became a monk".[9] Manolios, the main character of the book assigned to act the part of Christ in a passion play, laid down his life for the survival of a group of destitute refugees. In their own way, both Charalambis and Manolios acted themselves into Christ and thus "practiced Christ".

A sense of freedom and desire to practice Christ – this is how Christ's living through human beings might feel to persons involved. At the same time, those who, indwelled by Christ, practice Christ will have a sense that it's not so much they who are acting themselves into Christ, but it's Christ who is acting through them.

Let's sum up what we've said so far about the relationship between God's forgiveness and ours. Earlier in this chapter, we saw that when we forgive we make God's forgiveness our own; God forgives, and we take that divine forgiving and, in a sense, put our own signature underneath God's. In the present section, we've seen that when we forgive it is Christ who forgives through us. Even that activity of making God's forgiveness our own is God's work. Put simply, our forgiveness is but an echo of God's. That's why we are able to forgive, and that's why our forgiving makes sense.

Forgiven Forgivers

But how can we let that echo become full of our own real voices? One part of Luther's answer to this question points to Christ's life in us. We forgive because Christ forgives through us. The other part of Luther's answer points to the experience of being forgiven. The person who has been forgiven by God, wrote Luther in *The Freedom of the Christian*, ought to think this way:

> Although I am an unworthy and condemned man, my God has given me in Christ all the riches of righteousness and salvation without any merit on my part, out of pure, free mercy,

so that from now on I need nothing except faith which believes that this is true. Why should I not therefore freely, joyfully, with all my heart, and with eager will do all things which I know are pleasing and acceptable to such a Father who has overwhelmed me with his inestimable riches? I will therefore give myself as a Christ to my neighbor, just as Christ offered himself to me.[10]

It is only fitting that being "a Christ to my neighbor" included, for Luther, taking upon oneself one's neighbor's sins. After all, Christ did not just come to give gifts to the needy; Christ came to give the gift of righteousness to a "condemned man". We forgive because Christ forgave us.

Joseph Mason of Anthony Trollope's *Orley Farm* was a man just in his dealings, or at least he endeavored to be so. "In his inner thoughts," Trollope wrote, he had "boasted to himself that he had paid all men that he owed. He had, so he thought, injured no one in any of the relations of life. His tradesmen got their money regularly. He answered every man's letter. He exacted nothing from any man for which he did not pay." Yet for all the care he took to give everyone his or her due, Mason was not a good man. "He could never forget and never forgive." He not only paid what he owed; he insisted that others pay what they owed him. "He was a man who considered that it behooved him as a man to resent all injuries, and to have his pound of flesh in all cases".[11]

If on the bottom line of our lives lies the principle that we should get what we deserve, whether good or ill, forgiveness will sit uncomfortably with us. To forgive is to give people more than their due, it's to release them from the debt they have incurred, and that's bound to mess up the books.

For a Christian, however, a bottom-line principle can never be that we should get what we deserve. Our very existence is God's gift. Our redemption from the snares of sin is God's gift. Both are undeserved, and neither could have been deserved. From start to finish, we are always given free of charge and given more than our due. It is therefore only fitting that we give others more than their due – give them gifts that satisfy their needs or delight their senses and imagination, and give them the gift of forgiveness that frees them from guilt and the obligation to pay for their misdeeds.

Likely the best novel about the power of forgiveness to transform a person into a forgiver is Victor Hugo's *Les Misérables*. Jean Valjean, an ex-convict, was given a warm reception and lodging at the house of a bishop after he was rejected by everyone else. He received the gift of hospitality but then left in the night with the bishop's silverware. Early the next day, the police stopped the fleeing Valjean, discovered the silverware, and brought him back to the bishop's residence. Instead of scolding Valjean for despising his generosity, the bishop pretended that Valjean had committed no crime and indeed chided him for having forgotten to take the silver candlesticks. As they were parting and Valjean was about to go away a free man, having been given a gift and then forgiven a crime, the bishop told him, "Jean Valjean, my brother, you no longer belong to evil, but to good. It is your soul I am buying for you; I withdraw it from dark thoughts and from the spirit of perdition, and I give it to God."[12] And so it was. Valjean became a new man, given to doing good. He even spared the life of Javert, the police officer who considered Valjean a criminal and sought to put him behind bars. Valjean forgave Javert because the bishop had transformed him by his giving and forgiving.

Not all people who experience forgiveness are transformed by it. After having been forgiven, Javert could not forgive because the rules to which he had bound himself did not allow him to be merciful. In the end, in the ultimate negation of forgiveness, he decided that all he could do was to kill himself since he had chosen not to execute absolute justice.

For some, the experience of being forgiven is humiliating. They've been found in the wrong and been forgiven. Instead of joyfully receiving the gift and passing it on, they insist on paying it back, one way or another. They dislike indebtedness. They swear to God that they will never again break a rule so as not to have to be forgiven. And in all their dealings, they are dominated by dues-paying morality, maybe a bit ruffled by grace, but ultimately untransformed by it.

It is possible to close ourselves to grace, both human and divine. But only grace can pry open the door that has been shut in its face. So God continues to give to the ungrateful and to forgive the unrepentant. Christ stands before the closed door of a grace-resistant heart and knocks gently with a nail-pierced hand.

So should we. When things go well, gifts engender gifts, and forgiveness gives birth to forgiveness. That's the power of giving and forgiving. When things go ill, gifts fall on hard soil, and forgiveness remains barren. That's the impotence of givers and forgivers, for they can only "knock at the door" by giving and forgiving. And then they must wait ... and knock again and wait – trusting that the Spirit of the resurrected Christ will make the seed of their forgiveness bear fruit.

Milk of Vengeance, Cradle of Love

A sense that people should get what they deserve isn't the only obstacle to forgiving, even if it may be the most common one. Abuse can traumatize a self so terribly that it finds the very thought of forgiveness impossible. "The rifle butt in the back," wrote Zlatko Dizdarević, an award-winning Bosnian journalist, "shatters everything civilization has ever accomplished, removes all finer human sentiments, and wipes out any sense of justice, compassion, and forgiveness."[13] He is exaggerating, but not by much.

A Muslim woman, a teacher from Bosnia, who was a victim from a recent war in that blood-soaked land, gave voice to the pain of her shattered self and to the impossibility of forgiveness. Sparsely and vividly, she told the story of how hate was born in her soul during the war:

> I am a Muslim, and I am thirty-five years old. To my second son who was just born, I have given the name "Jihad." So he would not forget the testament of his mother – revenge. The first time I put my baby at my breast I told him, "May this milk choke you if you forget." So be it. The Serbs taught me to hate. For the last two months there was nothing in me. No pain, no bitterness. Only hatred. I taught these children

to love. I did. I am a teacher of literature. I was born in Ilijas and I almost died there. My student, Zoran, the only son of my neighbor, urinated into my mouth. As the bearded hooligans standing around laughed, he told me: "You are good for nothing else, you stinking Muslim woman …" I do not know whether I first heard the yelling or felt the blow. My former colleague, a teacher of physics, was yelling like mad, "Ustasha, ustasha …" And kept hitting me. Wherever he could. I have become insensitive to pain. But my soul? It hurts. I taught them to love and all the while they made preparations to destroy everything that is not of the Orthodox faith. Jihad – war. That is the only way …[14]

What horrendous humiliation! A violation that mutes speech and makes rage glow like hot lava! Its memory must stab the victim's soul the way nails pierced the flesh of the Crucified. Can the mother of Jihad ever forgive? Can Jihad, who nursed the milk of her vengeance, ever know anything other than revenge?

Set aside for a moment the fact that the woman was a Muslim. At the end of this chapter, I'll return to the bearing my argument has on people of other faiths. For now, think only of the violence and the wound it produced. How can someone with such a wound forgive? Earlier I said that Christ is the key to our ability to forgive, just as God is the key to our power and right to forgive. We forgive because Christ has forgiven us and because Christ forgives through us. But a person with a shattered life, like the mother of Jihad, doesn't first need Christ to forgive her or to forgive through her. Before anything else, she needs Christ to cradle her, to nurse her with the milk of divine love, to hold her in his arms like an inestimable gem, to sing her songs of gentle care and firm protection, and to restore her to herself as a beloved and treasured being.

And that's what Christ does. Before Christ forgives through us, even before Christ forgives us by the Spirit, Christ comes to dwell in us by faith. Consider just one image the apostle Paul used repeatedly for God's relationship to our bodies and souls: the image of a temple. "Or do you not know that your body is a temple of the Holy Spirit within you, which you have from God," he wrote to the Corinthians who had abused their bodies (1 Corinthians 6:19). Bodies are sacred spaces. The flame of God's presence burns in them inextinguishably. Our bodies may be in ruins, they may even be desecrated by the excrement of human hatred and folly, and yet they are holy, sanctified unalterably as a dwelling place of the Holy One. The temples will be restored one day to their full splendor. The Apostle called this restoration the resurrection of the body. It will be completed in the world to come. But it starts in the here and now when, by the power of the Holy Spirit, Christ makes a dwelling place in the fragile flesh of our mortal bodies.

Indwelled by Christ, will that teacher of literature be able to forgive? She may need to rage against the perpetrators and even against God for a while. But now she will rage against perpetrators in the presence of the God who cares; and she will struggle with the God who seemed absent when she needed God most, all the while being cradled by God.

Eventually, the time to forgive may come. She may forgive with one part of her soul while desiring vengeance with another. She may forgive one moment and then take it back the next. She may forgive some lighter offenses but not the worst ones. Such ambivalent, tentative, and hesitant attempts are not yet full-fledged forgiveness, but they are a start. If she doesn't trample underfoot the tender plant of forgiveness that seeks to break through the crust of vengeance with which she has protected herself, if she waters that plant with the living water of God's goodness, one day it may grow sturdy enough to bear fruit.

Notice that the seed of forgiveness was already there when she recounted the violation and committed herself to war as the only way. She told the story a bit like a confession, though a confession bereft of repentance. Somewhere deep down, she knew that revenge was not right even if the thirst for it felt good. Paradoxically, it felt right *because* it was wrong; a wrong must be evened out by a wrong, she thought. In this implicit recognition that "the only way" was the *wrong* way, we get a glimpse of the seed of forgiveness. She also recounted twice that she was a teacher of love. She still trusted in love. She was angry at her violators that she, the teacher of love, had become a creature of hate. That's another glimpse of the seed of forgiveness that is buried under the ruins of her temple. Once the temple is rebuilt, the seed will sprout. The only question is what she will do with the tender plant. And so it is with most people who commit themselves to pursue revenge.

Intermezzo: Three Questions

If I were speaking publicly about forgiveness, right about now in my presentation I'd see a few people fidgeting restlessly, wanting to ask a question. Normally I pause to take a question or two and then continue with my talk. So let me do the same here.

"Yes, the young woman in the back ..."

"Professor Volf, you speak about the seed of forgiveness growing into a plant and the need of the forgiver to nourish the plant with the food of God's goodness. But don't perpetrators have a responsibility to tend that plant of forgiveness too? And must the forgivers do *all* the hard work of mending relationships?"

"You are right. It helps the forgiver if the offender repents. We often hesitate to forgive when we suspect that offenders might repeat the offense. All other things being equal, if they don't repent, we have little reason to think that they won't repeat the wrong. So we try to protect ourselves by withholding forgiveness. We are also reluctant to forgive when the offenders don't seem to think that they've done anything wrong. Then we want to rub their noses in their wrongdoing rather than release them from guilt and punishment.

"Yet even when offenders are unrepentant, we can and should forgive. There are better ways to protect ourselves than the refusal to forgive. And when it comes to reminding offenders that they've committed the offense, we do that precisely by forgiving. Recall that to forgive is to blame. We *do* condemn when we forgive. We do it gently and lovingly, but we still do it.

"There's no question that it is more difficult to forgive when offenders refuse to repent. Their lack of repentance is, in a sense, a continuation of their offense in a different form. But the forgiveness is unconditional, as we saw in chapter 5. It's predicated on nothing perpetrators do or fail to do. Forgiveness is not a reaction to something else. It is the beginning of something new. So we forgive, lack of repentance notwithstanding. And to be able to do it, we shield the tender plant of forgiveness from the frigid winds that blow from unrepentant perpetrators, and we nourish it with the food of God's goodness.

"Finally, to the last part of your question about the burden of mending relationships resting on the shoulders of victims. Sometimes offenders do repent first and seek reconciliation with those whom they've wronged, making the victims' burden easier to bear. When they don't, the burden is heavy. Is it fair for victims to bear it? It's not. Do they deserve to bear it? They deserve it even less than they deserved the original offense. So why should they bear it? Because that's what it means to be a follower of Christ. Forgiving the unrepentant is not an optional extra in the Christian way of life; it's the heart of the thing. Why? Because God is such a forgiver and Christ forgave in such a way. And you know what? We also bear the burden of forgiveness because when we are forgivers we are restored to our full human splendor. We were created to mirror God. Anything less is really Judas' kiss on our own cheek, a betrayal of ourselves by ourselves.

"Yes, the gentleman in the front ..."

"What about the opposite case, when the perpetrator is remorseful, even desperately in search of forgiveness, but the victim is unable or unwilling to forgive, say, because she has died or is mentally incapacitated?"

"That was the problem of the aged Salieri who, in the movie *Amadeus*, had killed young Mozart and was desperate to be forgiven. Father Vogler, the priest, sat in front of Salieri trying to take his confession and give him absolution, but Salieri wanted the impossible – forgiveness from a dead victim. If we are not angry with God, as Salieri was, we will allow ourselves to receive forgiveness from God. As I said earlier, it is always, strictly speaking, from God that we receive forgiveness because only God has the original power and the original right to forgive. When the victim is dead, or unable to respond because of mental illness, for instance, the perpetrator can be forgiven by God and be truly forgiven.

"But still, if victims don't forgive, perpetrators will remain only incompletely forgiven. As perpetrators, we need forgiveness from victims, even if victims' forgiveness is only an echo of God's. Why? Because we have wronged *them*, not just God. And we seek to restore relationship with *them*, not just with God. As long as victims don't forgive, whatever the reason may be, even if we've received God's forgiveness we will have to live with a small wound of unforgiveness.

"If we believe in the world to come, as Christians traditionally have, then we can hope that at the boundary between this world and that world of perfect love, all partial forgiveness will be made complete. Then all will forgive, and all will receive forgiveness. I'll speak about this shortly.

"One more question, and then we have to go on. The woman on the left ..."

"Sometimes I think I don't understand enough to forgive well. To forgive is to blame, you just said. So to forgive rightly is to blame correctly. But how do I know how to blame rightly? As a forgiver, I may blame more or less than is just. There are also other ways in which I may misconstrue the offense. In all these cases, I forgive wrongly, and in some of them, I may wrong the person whom I forgive because I may make her a worse offender than she in fact is!"

"An excellent question, worthy of a whole lecture in response! I'll be brief, however. We often assume that we know the extent of the blameworthiness of someone who has injured us. We don't even stop to think about the matter. But to know truly the extent of her blameworthiness, we would need fully to understand the offense – something we can never do. We'd need to know the offender and her circumstances exhaustively, and we'd need to know her relationship to us equally well. But we don't. That's why the offenders and the offended often disagree on whether the wrongdoing has occurred, and when they agree that it has occurred, they disagree about its extent. Of course, they may disagree for other reasons as well, because for instance, victims have some stake in magnifying the crime whereas offenders have some stake in diminishing it. But often we disagree simply because we don't know enough about offenses, offenders, or their relationship to victims. Indeed, we'd need to be nearly omniscient to forgive rightly – which is why we cannot forgive on our own, and when we forgive, we can forgive only in a way similar rather than identical to God.

"Earlier I mentioned Jesus' agreeing with the Jewish leaders of his day that only God can forgive. The reason was that God alone could lift the burden of guilt from the shoulders of an offender. Now we see that only God can forgive *rightly*. God alone truly knows the nature and the extent of any offense. And without that knowledge, forgiveness is bound to be at least partly wrong.

"Where does this leave us, as human forgivers? Should we then not forgive, fearful that we'll always forgive wrongly? No, we forgive by echoing God's forgiveness to the best of our ability. We don't need to know the exact nature and extent of the offense. God knows, and we join God in forgiving. The consequence for us should be humility – willingness to admit that we may have gotten the wrongdoing wrong, willingness to revise our judgment, willingness to retract it. We should always forgive humbly and provisionally. It may even turn out that what we thought was an offense against us is an offense for which we need to receive forgiveness more than we need to give it.

"Since as forgivers we don't know enough about the offense or the offenders, we should ask them and learn from them about it. True, they too may not understand either themselves or their offense sufficiently. And yet they can shed at least some light on their motives, feelings, struggles, deeds, and failures, and in the process, make us better forgivers. Forgivers need offenders' help to forgive well. Once again, forgiveness is a social relationship, not an act of a solitary individual.

"Now back to my talk."

Unforgiving Culture, Communities of Forgiving

Often the reason we don't forgive is that we live in an unforgiving culture, a culture in which it doesn't make sense to forgive. That may seem like a cop-out, but it isn't. We are deeply social beings, shaped by our surroundings to an unfathomable degree. Even when we pride ourselves on being independent, for thinking with our own heads and choosing with our own unconstrained wills, what we in fact think and choose often merely echoes the choices of a group to which we belong and a wider culture in which we live.

Does it make sense to forgive when it seems that givers are losers and forgivers are wimps? Does it make sense to forgive when, say, we've been repeatedly injured by the same person in the same way? The struggle with these questions is our own, yet even as we wage it, the voices of the community we inhabit reverberate through our own arguments.

For instance, in the United States, we live in an increasingly litigious culture. It hasn't always been that way; we've become such a culture. There are many reasons for that, which I don't need to explore here. But once a culture has become litigious, forgiveness starts making less and less sense. We can still hold onto forgiveness on our own, but we are then swimming against the stream. We start questioning our commitment to it and often give up. To forgive, we need an environment in which forgiveness is valued and nurtured.

My parents did not press charges against the soldier responsible for my brother's death. Had they lived in the United States and had my brother been killed at the beginning of the present century rather than in the middle of the last one, they might have pressed charges – and possibly walked away with a handsome sum that would have taken care of them for the rest of their lives. In the process, they might also have ruined the life of that soldier. But that would have been his tough luck. He was responsible for Daniel's death, so he should pay. Of course, it would ultimately have been my parents' personal decision, but a broader unforgiving culture would have greatly contributed to it.

As it happened, in the 1950s, they decided not to press charges but to forgive, even if the judge at the hearing about the accident underscored their right to compensation. That too was a personal decision, and yet the culture of a community to which they belonged helped shape it. I don't mean the broader culture of communist Yugoslavia in the 1950s, though that culture was much less litigious than the United States is today. It was rather the culture of the community with which they identified the most, the small Pentecostal church in Osijek, Croatia.

When I asked them why they forgave, they always said, "God's Word teaches to forgive 'one another, as God in Christ has forgiven you' (Ephesians 4:32). That's what we decided to do, each of us on our own and then both together." But why has the conviction that they should obey Scripture in this regard gotten hold of their lives so firmly that even the death of their beloved child could not shake it? Because they belonged to a community. They prayed in that community; they listened to preaching about love of enemies; they celebrated Christ's death for the ungodly as they partook of the Lord's Supper; they sang together about God's faithfulness and love; they entrusted children to God's care and dedicated them to God's service; they celebrated the baptisms of those whose sins have been washed in the blood of the Lamb; and they mourned the dead in the hope of resurrection. They forgave because they were part of a community that followed Christ and for whom Scripture wasn't an old religious book, but the life-shaping word of the living God.

I don't mean to suggest that the community made it easy for them to forgive. First, it wasn't easy. When my mother talks about the experience, she describes it as "a forgiveness which caused me a great deal of pain". The death of a five-year-old child is painful enough; forgiving the person who caused it actually increased that pain, at least for a while. A persistent shrill inner voice kept repeating angrily, "He is guilty. He should pay." But then, she said, a gentle, quiet voice barely audible to the ear of the soul would respond, "Forgive one another, as God in Christ has forgiven you." The quiet voice won out. Why? Not because she made one heroic decision and then stuck with it. She was prepared for this exceedingly difficult act of forgiveness by two decades of her own attempts – as well as failures – to "practice Christ". And she was sustained in it by life in that particular community.

A community need not be perfect to sustain us. A few people in that community made an already difficult act of forgiveness even harder. They were like Job's comforters. They knew why my brother was killed: God was punishing my parents. They also knew the reason for punishment: My father had transgressed the boundaries of the community and had gotten too cozy with the Baptists by attending their seminary! When they were most vulnerable, my parents were confronted with the image of a God who punishes the infraction of silly rules by killing what is dearest to you. On the burden of Daniel's death rested the burden of forgiving the culprit, and then on top was placed the burden of the community's condemnation! But for my parents, who became Christians less through the attractiveness of the community's life than through the power of the gospel story, that false image cast the forgiving God in even bolder relief. God forgave, so they forgave. The worst within the community served only to highlight the community's best practices rooted in the example of Christ.

Their whole life of faith and the community's best practices flowed into a single decision and made a difficult act of forgiveness possible! How does the God who forgives work in the lives of forgivers? Not through the isolated decisions of self-enclosed individuals but through a life lived in response to the God of grace and through a community that makes the practice of forgiveness meaningful. Do you want to become a forgiving person? Seek the company of forgiven forgivers!

Prideful Forgivers

So far, I have written mainly about the reluctance to forgive – about the desire to wreak revenge or insist on the demands of justice instead of offering forgiveness, about offenses that leave us incapacitated so we cannot even contemplate forgiveness, about offenders' inability or unwillingness to repent, and forgivers' inadequate knowledge of the offense. I could have also written about our reluctance to forgive because we draw a perverse strength from withholding forgiveness: We nurse our resentment; we hold the offender locked in the grip of our accusations; we feel righteous in comparison; we dream of revenge and feel the power of an avenger surging through our veins. To forgive would be to give up on all this power and pride.

Reluctance to forgive is not our only problem, however. Sometimes we are eager to forgive, but we forgive for the wrong reasons and in the wrong way. Forgiveness can be a source of inordinate pride. When we forgive, we feel we are in the right, we are superior, we are on the side of the light; the offenders are in the wrong, they are inferior, they are on the side of the darkness.

The source of such pride is usually twofold. First, we feel we've been sinned against. The act of forgiveness underscores a sense of our own innocence and the offenders' guilt, feeding our pride. Second, when we forgive, we give, and the offenders receive. Giving itself can be a source of pride, as we saw in chapter 3. A gift that, like forgiveness, underscores recipients' blameworthiness can feed our pride even more. In sum, in forgiving we sometimes put on a display of our righteousness, magnanimity, and greatness, and in the process, insult, demean, and diminish the offenders. It is possible to forgive so wrongly that it can seem that we need to be forgiven for forgiving!

It's a fine art to forgive. How do we practice that art well? How do those who forgive counter the pride engendered by their own presumed innocence? When victims declare, "We are innocent!" they may be more or less right, if we consider only the single offense in question. Broaden the field of vision, however, and it may turn out that they've committed equal or even worse offenses at other times and places. Yet they pridefully exempt themselves from the company of wrongdoers and place themselves in the exclusive company of "the good" – all because of a single offense they've suffered!

"They are guilty!" victims declare of the offenders. Again, they may be, if we consider that particular offense. Yet victims often conveniently disregard many of the offenders' good deeds, maybe even good deeds toward the victims themselves. And for the most part, victims don't even entertain the possibility that, intertwined as the lives of offenders and victims often are, they may have in some measure contributed to the offenders' misdeed. But victims *are* sometimes to blame, even though they reject the thought vehemently. Instead, they contemptuously place offenders in the exclusive category of wrong-doers, from which they conveniently exempt themselves.

As victims, when we consign the offenders to the category of wrongdoers, we often forget that evil is a formidable power that doesn't reside simply in the unconstrained will of offenders. As offenders, however, we know the power of evil. True, as offenders we *choose* to commit offenses, though more often than not, we merely fail to resist a temptation. Often we are simply blind; the good we are trying to achieve occludes the injury we are inflicting. Or we are weak; we don't want to do the bad thing but are somehow powerless to prevent sliding right into committing it. We are driven to offenses from inside, by our selfish, prideful, and slothful inclinations. We are pulled to them from outside, by the evil that surrounds us and that we mistake for good because it has donned itself with the mantle of righteousness. As offenders, we rarely simply *want* to want the evil that we want. Instead, as Luther put it, we are "confused, captivated, and dazzled by the devil".[15]

The Christian tradition has always maintained three proposi-tions simultaneously. Proposition one: No matter how good our inclinations, thoughts, deeds, or practices are, before the eyes of the all-knowing and holy God, we are always sinners, all of us, victims included. Proposition two: No matter how evil our inclinations, thoughts, deeds, or practices are, we always remain God's good crea-tures, all of us, offenders included. Proposition three: No wrongdoing is an isolated act of the pure evil will of an individual; it is nourished by our sinful inclination and reinforced by a sinful culture.

God alone is completely good. And when it comes to evil, even the Prince of Darkness isn't without any trace of goodness. When we forgive, it's good to remind ourselves that "all have sinned", that all of us sin because we are caught in sin's snare, and that none have lost basic goodness. All of us forgive as sinners, not as the righteous. All of us receive forgiveness as God's good creatures, not as despicable devils. This knowledge should counter the pride of any presumed innocence on the part of forgivers.

One Forgiveness, Two Victories

How do we counter the pride of virtuous magnanimity, the second form of pride associated with forgiving? As forgivers, we should remind ourselves that, on our own, we have neither the power nor the right to forgive and that we are neither knowledgeable nor virtuous enough to forgive well. When we forgive, we make God's forgiveness our own. And even as we do, it's Christ who forgives through us, not we who forgive on our own. Our forgiveness is proper to the extent that it reverberates with God's. When offenders thank us for forgiving, we should respond the same way we respond when recipients thank us for giving – we should deflect gratitude and direct it to God, the true source and the true agent of all forgiving. When we forgive well, there's in fact very little to be proud of. God being the source of our forgiveness, the better we forgive, the less reason there is for pride.

Prideful forgivers are bad forgivers partly because pride subverts what forgiveness seeks to achieve in the first place. As we saw in the two previous chapters, forgiveness is not a private, virtuous act. It's part of a larger strategy of overcoming evil with good and bringing about reconciliation. It doesn't just relieve us from bitterness and resentment. It enacts love for the enemy. Good forgivers can't therefore just dispense forgiveness without any regard for how it is received by the offenders. Forgiveness will help overcome evil with good if it nudges offenders to repent, reconcile, and be restored to the good. Humble forgiveness might achieve that goal. Prideful forgiveness will have the opposite effect.

Commenting on overcoming evil with good, Søren Kierkegaard spoke of two victories, not one. When we forgive, we achieve the first victory. Often that victory is not easy. We struggle, we fail, and we give up, upset – or maybe glad – that we have failed. Then we struggle again and maybe end up with little more than shards of forgiveness. Finally, one day we put all the shards together, and we forgive.

Even though we may be bruised and a bit frustrated that we've had to fight the battle in the first place, we are glad. We've won a victory! But we are not yet done, suggested Kierkegaard. One more battle to fight, one more victory to win.

"To be one who has been overcome is a humiliating feeling," wrote Kierkegaard.[16] The victors savor and flaunt their victories, and the defeated are repelled in shame. That's uniquely true when it comes to forgiveness. "The more deeply the one overcome feels his wrong and in that way also his defeat, the more he of course must feel repelled from the one who lovingly deals him this merciful blow."[17] What do those who struggle to conquer evil with good do in response? They try to win over the one who's been overcome. They fight "in love so that the other will accept forgiveness, will allow himself to be reconciled".[18] When they succeed, that's their second victory.

How is it won? Not by marching in the victory parade full of the self-satisfied pride of a grand forgiver and soaking in the accolades of cheering bystanders! "The one who loves," wrote Kierkegaard, "does not give the impression at all, nor does it occur to him that it is he who has conquered, that he is the victor – no, it is the good that has conquered."[19] God has conquered. Victory is God's. Pride is banished.

Completion

We have the power and the right to forgive – derivative power and derivative right, but still, we are authorized to forgive, to make God's forgiveness our own. That seems like a solution, but it's a problem in a sense. Since God commands us to forgive, now we actually have to get on with the business of forgiving! Are we generous enough to do it? Can we muster enough inner strength? Are we humble enough to forgive well? It helps to remember that we ourselves were forgiven, it helps to live in a community that celebrates forgiveness, and above all, it helps that it's ultimately Christ who forgives through us, that our forgiveness is an echo of God's.

This all helps, but we still have to do the forgiving. Sometimes we barely manage to make a start. In *Plan B: Further Thoughts on Faith*, Anne Lamott wrote with bold honesty about her inability to forgive her mother. "I prayed for my heart to soften," she wrote, "but my heart remained hardened toward her ... I refused to be nice to her, and didn't forgive her for being a terrified, furious, clinging, sucking maw of need and arrogance."[20] And even after Lamott took the first halting steps of forgiveness, she said, "I discovered that I had forgiven her for a number of things, although for none of the big-ticket items – like having existed at all, for instance, and then having lived so long." And then she added, "Still, the mosaic chips of forgiveness I felt that day were a start."[21]

Even when we are at our very best as forgivers, in a sense our forgiving remains only a start. I've already suggested that we don't know enough about any offense to be able to forgive well. Strange as it may sound, every act of forgiveness is also an act of injustice toward the offender, however minuscule that injustice may be. As forgivers, moreover, we are often hypocritical. We forgive with our mouths but hold onto resentment in our hearts – and beam low-grade hostility at those we have "forgiven" or attack them with clandestine acts of vengeance. We claim the high moral ground of forgivers, even as we pursue the low road of revenge.

Consider one more complication. Let's say I have forgiven a friend. He was in the wrong, I was in the right, and on top of it, I was also virtuous in forgiving him. As it turns out, however, I too have wronged him, and not just once. But he doesn't know about that – I haven't confessed it and he has not found out yet – and so I appear not to have committed a wrong in relation to him. I have also not given him a chance to display his virtue by forgiving me. I appear more virtuous than he, but I am not. My forgiveness gives a wrong impression about me and my relationship to him – it places me in comparatively better light than him and thereby wrongs him. Think for a moment about what this means: For any single wrongdoing between two people to be forgiven rightly, *all* wrongdoings between them would have to come to light, and *all* forgiven. But that's clearly impossible in the here and now.

All our forgiving is inescapably incomplete. That's why it's so crucial to see our forgiving not simply as our own act, but as participation in God's forgiving. Our forgiving is faulty; God's is faultless. Our forgiving is provisional; God's is final. We forgive tenuously and tentatively; God forgives unhesitatingly and definitively. As we forgive, we always wrong the offender by inadequate judgment and pride; God forgives with justice and genuine love. The only way we dare forgive is by making our forgiving transparent to God's and always open to revision. After all, our forgiveness is only possible as an echo of God's.

In the here and now, that echo of God's forgiveness is distorted. It can be more or less distorted, but it is inescapably distorted. One day the distortion will be removed. The apostle Paul wrote that one day we will all "appear before the judgment seat of Christ" (2 Corinthians 5:10). The day of judgment stands at the boundary between transitoriness and everlasting life, between this world of sin and the coming world of love. Mostly we think that at the judgment day we'll receive "recompense for what has been done in the body, whether good or evil", as the Apostle said. But Christ's judgment is also a judgment of grace. As a result, we'll be transformed and fully reconciled with God and one another. That's how it must be. Otherwise judgment could not be what faith claims it is – the door to the world of love.

On that day, God will condemn all sins and yet forgive them. The light of God will shine into all dark corners of our lives and our hearts, and we will know ourselves as we are known by God. The love of God will finally and definitively release us from all guilt and fear of punishment, and we will love ourselves and others as we are loved by God. Then and there, we'll make God's forgiveness of our sins fully our own. Then and there, we'll make God's forgiveness of the sins of those who have offended us fully our own. Our forgiveness, now tarnished, will then sparkle in its full splendor.

We forgive now in hope for that day.

And it is in that hope that we let the forgiven offenses against us slip out of our minds too. In chapter 5, I suggested that "forgetting" crowns forgiveness. We can forgive without consigning offenses to oblivion. Mostly we do. We don't press charges and we release a person from guilt, but we do remember. Often, we cannot help but remember. The injury was too deep, so we cannot forget. The danger often continues, so it wouldn't be wise to forget. And witnesses remember, so we keep being reminded.

And yet I've suggested that we should eventually let go of memories of wrongs, and that in the best of cases we do let go of them after we have forgiven. In the here and now, it is rare to generously release offenders from the memories of their offenses instead of engaging in self-harming and mindless forgetting. And it ought to be rare. To let go of such memories rightly requires a whole world made new – a world in which we will love God and each other in God, a world in which we will be utterly secure from all evil, a world of love that cannot be undone. With the gift of this new world, we will receive from God the gift of being unable to remember the misdeeds of our offenders anymore, and then we'll pass it on to the offenders. Then, and only then, will the work of forgiving be complete and come to its eternal rest.

A Muslim's Cup of Coffee

Much of what I have written about forgiving – indeed, much of what I have written about giving too – rests firmly on Christian convictions. God has forgiven in Christ, and therefore we have the power and the right and the obligation to forgive. Christ lives in us and forgives through us, and therefore we too can forgive. I could go on. Every step of the way, forgiving as I have described it soars on the wings of Christian convictions. Must it therefore fall without them?

What about those who don't profess Christ? What about Jews or Muslims? What about atheists who believe in no God at all? Can they walk only the paths of vengeance and justice? Is the path of forgiveness barred to them? Clearly, the answer is that they too can forgive. And obviously they *do* forgive. In fact, often non-Christians are better at forgiving than Christians.

In his moving and profound account of the war in Bosnia, Zlatko Dizdarević relates a story about the father of a three-year-old girl in Sarajevo who was hit by a sniper's bullet while playing outside her home. He writes:

> Her horrified father carries her to the hospital. Bleeding, she hovers between life and death. Only after her father, a big hulk of a man, has found a doctor to care for her does he allow himself to burst into tears. The television camera records his words. These words, every one of them, belong in an anthology of humanism, helplessness, and forgiveness at its most extreme – not so much forgiving the criminal who shot a three-year-old child, as forgiving the wild beasts for being wild beasts, for being debased by an evil that destroys every human impulse. Two of his sentences accompany thoughts that will linger long past today or tomorrow. The first comes when the stricken father invites the unknown assassin to have a cup of coffee with him so that he can tell him, like a human being, what has brought him to do such a thing. Then he says, aware that this request may not elicit any human response: "One day her tears will catch up with him."[22]

Dizdarević himself cannot identify with the girl's father. To him, the father's words reek of shameful impotence and condemnable irresponsibility. My intention here is not to enter into an argument with Dizdarević. This whole book is, in a sense, such an argument. Instead, I want to concentrate on the father. He was presumably a Muslim. His generosity was extraordinary. And what of his hope for forgiveness!? Even the blood of his own child, spilled for no other reason than the fun of a recreational killer, didn't extinguish it!

How do I account for such forgiveness on the part of a non-Christian, given what I've said about the relationship between Jesus Christ and forgiveness? One part of the answer is that every religion – every overarching interpretation of life – may have its own ways of fostering forgiveness, even a religion born with the help of violence. In Islam, for instance, that may be the mercy of Allah, invoked repeatedly by Muslims. To say that Christians forgive in a particular way is not to say that others cannot forgive in their own ways. Moreover, in light of how prominent forgiveness is in the Christian faith, Christians should take interest in highlighting the elements in all faiths that sustain forgiveness.

The second part of the answer to the question about forgiveness by non-Christians is that Christ does not need to be confessed, honored, or named to be present and to shape people's convictions and practices. A second-century church father, Justin Martyr, used to speak of the "seeds of the Word." The Word – or, in later Christian terminology, the Second of the Holy Three – "is the true light, which enlightens everyone", wrote John the Evangelist (John 1:9). By extension, the Word is also the true goodness that ennobles everyone and the true beauty that shines in everything that is fair. That Word, thought Justin Martyr, is wholly present in Jesus Christ. At the same time, the Word is scattered in the whole world, among Greek philosophers, among religious sages, among all upright people.

From a Christian perspective, there's no mystery as to why non-Christians forgive, and often forgive so impressively. They are responsive to the one Word – to the giving and forgiving God working among them and in them, mostly incognito. God may employ their religious convictions and practices, or God may work apart from those convictions and practices. And so they forgive. That's partly how the giving and forgiving God works in Christians too, often using but sometimes circumventing their convictions and practices.

A mystery remains, however – a dark and unsettling mystery. It's not why non-Christians forgive. It's why the people whose very being depends on "trust[ing] in him who justifies the ungodly" (Romans 4:5) and who pray every day "forgive us our trespasses as we forgive those who trespass against us" – why we Christians are not very good at forgiving! Some suggest that Christianity is simply a violent religion. I hope that this book has shown otherwise.

So why do so many of us take the "sword" into our hands so readily? Why do we visit vengeance upon our enemies when we should, inspired by the cross, forgive? Because we really don't identify with the deep conviction of the faith we embrace? Because we hold onto a godliness emptied of substance, to a faith that dribbled away as it was passed on to us? Because we subscribe to a thinned-out civil religion in which the God of Jesus Christ is just a semi-transparent garment covering the nakedness of the fierce goddess "the Nation"? Because we serve the god called "the Self", and therefore shamelessly take from the giving and forgiving God, and then equally shamelessly take from our neighbors and pursue them with vengeance when they've dared to take anything from us?

Why have many of our Christian fathers and mothers throughout history, greedy and vengeful as they were, left so much suffering in their trail? And why are we hardly any better, whether we are fathers and mothers, colleagues and friends, neighbors or strangers? Why do we refuse the God-given bridge that would transport us from selfishness to self-giving, from vengeance to forgiveness? That's a mystery that should make us tremble – tremble before the God who gives to the ungrateful and the God who forgives the ungodly.

POSTLUDE:
A CONVERSATION
WITH A SKEPTIC

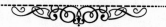

"Do you really believe all that stuff you've written about?" an acquaintance asked me.

"Stuff!? What stuff?"

"You know, all this stuff about God the giver, about how you are supposed to give as God gives, and especially that when we give it's really God giving through us. You say that Christ forgives through us, that human beings are sacred dwelling places of God, that they become fulfilled when they resonate with God's love. It seems so … unreal, like a religious fairy tale!"

"I wouldn't call it 'stuff'," I answered defensively.

"I don't mean to dis it. It's beautiful, of course, what your parents did, forgiving that soldier. It sounds beautiful to tend a single rose like the Little Prince did, and even see the stars differently as a result. Your vision of a life of generosity and forgiveness is beautiful …"

"It's not mine, you know."

"But it's beautiful as dreams are beautiful – beautifully unreal. Remember the movie *Life Is Beautiful*? In it, there was a kid in a concentration camp, Giosue, whose father created for him an illusion of living a normal life by pretending that the whole thing was an elaborate game. The life you describe is beautiful in that way, as an ingenious ruse."

"I think I know what you mean, but …"

"When I look at how we actually live," he continued, "when I think about how we are wired to live, all that talk about unselfish generosity and forgiveness makes no sense. We play a *game* of giving and forgiving, but the game was designed to mask a harsh reality that we are afraid to look at unadorned. We all just strive to maximize our 'profits', by whatever means society will let us get away with. We 'give' to get; we 'forgive' when it's in our interest. That's all there is – our profit, our interest, our insatiable egos. We are bundles of sophisticated, complex matter, each bundle hustling to survive and thrive, sometimes with others' help, but mostly at others' expense. And then we cover the tracks of our selfishness by 'giving' and 'forgiving'."

"You've stripped us naked, and with our clothes off, we're not a pretty sight," I said.

"But that's the way we *are*! What you write in this book is one long, comforting, beautiful lie."

"Lie? A strong word ..."

" ... needed to hide the brutal reality."

"I confess," I continued, speaking half to myself and half to him, "I do wake up sometimes in the middle of the night, surrounded by the darkness, and think, 'We're all a bunch of egoists, some more pleasant than others, some smart enough to be short-term altruists, but we're just stuffing ourselves and puffing ourselves up. Maybe no love has created us, no love dwells in our deceitful hearts, and no world of love will ever be given to us. We come out of inchoate darkness, and we return to inchoate darkness, and in the brief period we are alive, we are black holes of self-absorption.'"

"Now you're talking. So why did you write the book? To put yourself back to sleep and return with a good conscience to your dream world? You can't exorcise cruel reality with a pleasant dream!"

"When the dawn comes," I continued with more conviction, "and I see the huge orange ball rising over Long Island Sound, I realize that, awake in the middle of the night, I was tempted by the voices of darkness! Do you know what happens when my son Aaron climbs into my bed, looks at me with those big doe eyes of his, when he gives me one of his unforgettable smiles, mischievous and tender at the same time, when he tells me 'I love you' as he burrows his head into the pillow next to mine? Do you know what happens then? I think, 'That smile – and my failure to get angry with him for having awoken me from a short night's sleep at 5:30 a.m.! – doesn't quite fit into the story of our bottomless egotism.'"

"It's touching that you love your son and that your son loves you. But as you know, that 'love' can be explained ..."

" ... with one of those explanations that reduce complex human experiences to simple underlying causes," I said, a bit irritated. "Yes, I know such reductive explanations well. If you are smart enough and armed with a vivid imagination, you can reduce anything to anything else – well, almost anything. Marx reduced religion to the 'sigh of the oppressed creature', Nietzsche reduced morality to resentment of the weak, Freud reduced ..."

" ... you're talking about pseudo-science ..."

"There's a difference, I agree. But hard sciences also offer reductive explanations. They are right and immensely useful in their own domains, but once they leave those domains, they distort reality..."

" ... they don't distort. They explain and describe without fuzzy fluff!"

"After the hard sciences are done with their explaining, Aaron's smile will be gone as if it were wiped off his face. Of course, if, armed with scientific explanations, you took a photo of his face looking at me, it would still look exactly the same as if he were smiling, only that he wouldn't be smiling. The same facial grimace would be there, but the *smile* would be gone. A genuine smile is infused with a whole universe of meaning that the hard sciences cannot get at. The reality of that smile says to me that the world can't just be there on its own, a surd fact of matter's strange complexification, located between the Big Bang with which this universe started and the Big Whimper with which it is likely to end."

"Was that supposed to be proof of God's existence!? Aaron smiles, therefore God exists! One fine argument! It will go down in the books as 'Volf's proof of God's existence'!"

"You missed my point. No, nothing like proof of God's existence. I am inclined to think God's existence cannot be proven. Aaron's smile is more like a crack in the naturalist's 'reality'. And besides, it illustrates that what you referred to as 'fuzzy fluff' is sometimes the very best of what life is made of – a crack as a window into the true nature of reality."

"You certainly see a lot in that smile ..."

"You'd be surprised by what you can see in a single smile if you know how to look. If you look really carefully, and if you look with the eyes of the heart, you might even 'see' God. God is smiling at me in Aaron's smile. God is shining in that large orange ball just rising over the horizon."

"You said that that smile tells you the world *cannot* just be there on its own. Isn't that putting it too strongly?"

"Interpret it as 'not likely'," I said. "The smile, if you take it for what it is, tells me that it isn't likely that the world is just there. It tells me that it's more likely that the world is a gift, like that smile itself, a gift given for no other reason than God's delight is our being."

"What if your dark thoughts at night – and my sober observations! – are true? What if you are waking up to a dream?"

"Well, what?"

"You'd be wrong."

"And I would have lived the right kind of life, the life you called beautiful."

"And have lived a *false* beautiful life!" he said. "Wouldn't that matter to you? Can a false life ever be good?"

"What we *think* is a false life can be good, very good. We can always be wrong in what we think. But a life that really was false, even though beautiful, could not ultimately be good. That's presumably why you and I are arguing right now. We argue about the truth. Truth matters. But I don't think my beautiful life is false."

"You have doubts, though ..."

"I have doubts, of course. But having doubts is far from consenting to the falseness of this beautiful life."

"Don't they gnaw at you?"

"They do. But that, among many, many other things, is how I am different from God. God knows and doesn't doubt. I believe and doubt. Doubt is part of belief; it isn't contrary to it. And I don't just sometimes doubt the existence of the giving and forgiving God. I protest against that God. At times, I even scream at that God. The world doesn't often look as if such a God has created it. It can look as if God doesn't give a fig for the world. The head of my five-year-old brother was crushed."

"You make my point!"

"I don't think so. As you may remember from what I've written, I believe that you can protest against the evil in the world only if you believe in a good God. Otherwise the protest doesn't make sense. I protest with God against God."

"So, 'God, I believe, help my unbelief.'"

"And, 'Help my soul when it's angry at the world and at you, O inscrutable God.' And above all, 'Do something! Don't just sit up there!' So I doubt, protest, complain, pray, believe, and ... I think."

"Yes, it's your job to think. They pay you for that at Yale."

"I am very fortunate," I said. "But I don't think because I am paid, though being paid does give me more time to think. I think about faith because I believe. The belief in God and the way of life implied in that belief can be defended. As I've said, I don't think we can *prove* God's existence. But we can give an account of reality, an account that makes good sense in two respects. It makes good sense of the 'facts' about the universe in which you are so interested – as good as any naturalist account, I think – and it makes sense of generous giving and forgiving and of our longing for a beautiful life."

"You don't give such an account of reality in this book."

"I didn't intend to. Others have done that. I give an account of a way of life with God, from within that life, so to speak. I try to display its coherence and its beauty."

"That may not be enough to persuade a skeptic like me."

"I don't mean to insult you, but I wrote the book mainly for myself and maybe for folks like myself, not for you. Most books I write, I write for myself, as a spiritual exercise almost. And to tell you the truth, my biggest problem is not the arguments that may pull the rug from underneath the whole Christian way of life. In a sense, my biggest problem is not an argument at all."

"Something else is eating away at your beautiful life?"

"Yes, something maybe even more rapacious than the plausible arguments against it would be."

"You *are* troubled."

"Troubled? I don't know about that. That seems too psychological a way of putting it. What I am talking about goes deeper."

"Deep trouble ... You theologians are always into deep things and mysteries ..."

"You don't want to imply that you want to skate over the surfaces, do you? Even if it might be against your inclinations, do keep your mind open to true mysteries, like the mystery of love or the mystery of evil. How flat and untrue life would be without them!"

"I don't know about 'untrue'. So what is your problem?"

"I am what we Christians used to call 'a sinner', though we are now a bit embarrassed by the term."

"I remember," he mused, "reading in the Bible as a kid about a 'law in our members' – whatever that means; I always thought about sex when I heard the phrase – that's opposed to the law of God, and about being a 'wretched' man, a miserable sinner. That's in Paul, right? Your apostle. Pretty morbid stuff."

"I mention sin and you immediately think of sex! You think that what the Apostle wrote about being caught in the snares of sin is morbid? How about true?"

"I know, I know ... sin has more to do with self-love than with sex. What the apostle Paul wrote is true in the sense that we are all self-interested, even selfish creatures. But it becomes morbid when you – or Paul – call us wretched because of it."

"I'll tell you when it would be morbid. It would be morbid if you've already capitulated before you've even started the fight, or if the whole fight doesn't make sense to you at all because you believe that we are and always will remain selfish, that no redemption from selfishness is possible, and that redemption, if it were possible, would do us harm, even undo us. But look at things from my angle. I think that we should love God with all our hearts and our neighbor as ourselves. That's what Jesus said we should do. To me, that's also the flip side of the belief in the God who is love, in the God who gives and forgives, in the God who created us for love, in the God in whom we therefore find fulfillment. What I am 'troubled' about is that I so often find myself to be unloving, ungenerous, unforgiving. I find myself cheerfully taking care of my own interests at the expense of others ..."

"And you think that writing a book about giving and forgiving will cure you!?"

"If only it could! I am afraid that I need more, much more than my own book, to be cured from sin. I need daily disciplines of prayer, meditating on texts from the Holy Book, and silence. I need a community of fellow believers with whom to celebrate a vision of life that revolves around love of God and neighbor. I need friends to keep me accountable. I need my wife and my kids to hold the mirror to me and resist my selfishness, pride, and sloth. Ultimately, I need a new self and – my desires are not modest – a whole new world freed from transience and sin. Which is to say that I need God. But I also need a book. Or rather, I need a compelling sketch of a life of generosity and forgiveness. So I wrote it down."

"A book to fight the Devil and his armies in your soul, with you holding your book high like the naked St. Anthony of Salvador Dali's imagination held a slender cross against the onslaught of mighty temptations!?"

"Bring them on. Armed with my little book, I'll destroy them all ... You are a tease today. You know what one of my heroes – a hero, notwithstanding all the warts – said about those who were delighted about the success of their books? Luther advised them to grab themselves by their ears, and if they grabbed themselves well, they would discover a pair of long, shaggy donkey ears! He didn't think that an author determined the value of a book. He certainly wouldn't have thought that the market determined it, or committees who decide about awards, or even the true connoisseurs of good books. In his mind, God determines a book's value – a tough critic, but a generous one too. No, I really did write this book primarily for myself."

"To fight the Devil …"

"There you go again. I mention sin, and you go to the Devil – hooves, tail, pitchfork, and all."

"I thought sin and the Devil went together for you Christians."

"They do, but not nearly so crudely. But we are digressing. I had a strange experience after I wrote *Exclusion and Embrace*."

"What was that?"

"In the book, I argue, among other things, that we should embrace our enemies as Christ has embraced us. Well, an 'enemy' – a small one – arose in my life after I wrote the book, and I sensed in myself the propensity to return in kind and exclude rather than forgive and embrace. And then I heard myself saying, 'But you argued in your book …' It was like an academic's version of the still, small voice my wonderful and godly mother so often speaks about."

"Did that help?"

"It did! It reminded me that I was failing, that I wasn't true to God and to myself. It helped me resolve to act differently, to love my 'enemy'."

"I haven't read *Exclusion and Embrace*. But it's not a bad life that you've sketched in this book, I must admit."

"So maybe I did write the book for you too. You should try out this way of life."

"I don't believe in God."

"But you like the God who gives and forgives as a character, as an image, as a vision, right?"

"It's a pretty good god as gods go, the only trouble being that I can't believe in any of them."

"You don't need to believe in God before you can embark upon this way of life."

"What!?" he exclaimed. "I thought that everything in that way of life depended on God. God gives and forgives, and so should we. God gives and forgives – and so *can* we, not in our own right but by echoing God's giving and forgiving. Take God away and everything collapses. I got this right, didn't I?

"You did. Everything does depend on God – just not on our *belief* in God. It depends on God's presence in our life. And God is present to us whether we believe or not."

"How inconsiderate of God! Doesn't God know anything about privacy, about being left alone when you want to be alone?"

"God has an excuse. God didn't grow up in an upper-middle-class family with a bedroom of his own ... Seriously, try not to think of it as being disrespectful of your wishes but as being kind – like a lover who doesn't give up on the beloved, even though he has been betrayed, but keeps sending her a rose, or a poem, or whatever."

"But a lover should leave her alone if she writes him a note that she would rather live without his advances. And it seems to me that my belief that God doesn't exist counts as such a note."

"Does it? At any rate, God is a peculiar kind of lover ..."

"Very peculiar ..."

"God is by definition present everywhere, which makes it difficult for God to leave non-believers to themselves, to be absent from their lives. God is not like a human being, a discrete individual located in one place at any given time, a place that can be marked as distinct from any place you and I, along with everyone else in the world, find ourselves. Moreover, you and I wouldn't even be there to occupy this or that space, to believe or not to believe, if it were not for God being present in us, giving us life, one breath after another, one heartbeat after another."

"Heady stuff!"

"You don't want a plain and uncomplicated God. I guarantee you, it'll turn out being an idol."

"Still, it seems strange as a nonbeliever to take up a way of life that only makes sense if you believe in God. It's like slipping into somebody else's shoes."

"Milan Kundera, a Czech dissident writer who now lives in Paris, wrote a book three decades ago entitled *Laughable Loves*. Do you know it? It doesn't matter if you don't. It's about 'weight' and 'lightness' in our lives, the kind of stuff he explored in *The Unbearable Lightness of Being*. Edward, the hero of one part of the book, longed for something essential, that he could take truly seriously, and he couldn't find it 'in his love affairs, or in his teaching, or in his thoughts. That's why he longed for God.'"

"I can't say that I long for God."

"But you seem to long for a beautiful life – you're the one who brought up the phrase. And you also suggested between the lines that it is a life that only God can give. In any case, I don't want to compare what you want with what Kundera's Edward wanted, though the two of you may be closer than you appear to be. Edward occasionally sat in church and looked thoughtfully at the cupola. 'Let us take leave of him,' writes Kundera at the end of the book, 'at just such a time. It is afternoon, the church is quiet and empty. Edward is sitting in a pew tormented with sorrow, because God does not exist. But just at this moment his sorrow is so great that suddenly from its depth emerges the genuine *living* face of God.'"[1]

"Kundera is playing on Nietzsche's famous comment about the death of God and the churches as sepulchers of God, isn't he?"

"I think that's right. But I didn't mean for us to discuss Kundera's relation to Nietzsche ..."

"You want me to go and sit in a church?"

"I want you to slip into a way of life you say you like, as you might slip into a church building. I want you to sit in it, or rather, walk around inside it for a while. There, you just might discover a living God – not at the end of an argument, but in the midst of a life well lived."

AFTERWORD

An entire book could easily be written about what follows, but four brief observations about *Free of Charge* as a whole will have to suffice.

First, on one level, the book examines how to conceive of and live out two basic human practices, giving and forgiving. On another level, however, the two practices, as Christianity understands them, are a particular sort of lens through which we can survey the whole landscape of the Christian faith from a fresh vantage point. And since I write here as an advocate of the faith, this book is *an invitation to Christian faith*.

Second, as such an invitation, the book is also *an interpretation of the apostle Paul*, arguably the most seminal and the greatest of all Christian thinkers. Books about the Apostle seem almost as plentiful as the stars in the sky. And today, debates are raging among theologians, philosophers, and social critics about how to interpret him rightly. I enter into none of these debates here, however; I simply offer my own take on the Apostle. My excuse to the academic community – others don't need an excuse – is that this is not a scholarly book. I leave the scholarly debates about alternative perspectives aside and delve into the stuff of Paul's vision as I understand it, seeking to show its importance for us today in a style accessible to readers with little prior theological or philosophical knowledge.

Third, this book is also *a reading of Martin Luther*, the great Christian reformer of the sixteenth century. Again, scholarly work on Luther has grown into a mountain that no single human being can scale. As I do with Paul, so I do with Luther: I walk around competing interpretations and present my own. (A hint for scholars: I am closest to the Finnish interpretation of Luther, though I also depart from it in significant ways.) It's fitting for an invitation to Christian faith based on interpretation of the apostle Paul to also be offered as a reading of the great reformer. Luther, I think, got the substance of the Christian faith roughly right – or rather, the Luther who discovered the Christian faith afresh did, not the Luther concerned with preserving reformation by earthly powers. And Luther, in my judgment, also got the apostle Paul basically right. This view is not popular today, but popularity isn't an index of truthfulness.

Finally, as Archbishop of Canterbury's Lent Book for 2006, this theological text belongs roughly to the genre of spiritual writings. Some people like to keep their spirituality and theology neatly separated, the way someone may want to have the main dish and the salad served separately during a meal. I don't. Spirituality that's not theological will grope in the darkness, and theology that's not spiritual will be emptied of its most important content. For me, at any rate, thinking theologically in order to write about giving and forgiving was a spiritual exercise. I trust that the reading of it will serve the same purpose.

ACKNOWLEDGMENTS

It seems obvious to say that *I* wrote this book. Mine are its ideas, its organization, its formulations. But that's a superficial kind of "mineness". Most of what's in the book has been given to me. I don't mean it here in the sense that, as the apostle Paul reminds us, everything we have we've received as a gift from God. I was able to write this book because I've received from teachers, family, friends, students, and audiences. And I've received in such ways that I often can't tell where what's originally mine stops and where what came from others begins.

After writing *Exclusion and Embrace*, I've addressed numerous and varied audiences on the topic of forgiveness. As to giving, I've taught two seminars at Yale on the topic (one of which culminated in a Harvard-Yale doctoral students' conference that Professor Sarah Coakley from Harvard and I put together). I've given three sets of talks in churches on giving and forgiving – in Christ Episcopal Church in Guilford, Connecticut; in Christ Church Cathedral in Nashville, Tennessee; and in the Congregational Church in New Canaan, Connecticut. I also lectured in seminaries and colleges on the topic of this book – at Ashland Theological Seminary in Ashland, Ohio; Evangelical Theological Seminary in Osijek, Croatia; the Presbyterian College in Toronto, Canada; and Trinity Western University in Langley, Canada. And not to forget Martin Luther who figures prominently in this book, I regularly teach a course at Yale on Luther with my colleague Ronald Rittgers. In all these settings, I have learned a great deal, and for that I am grateful.

I have had three excellent research assistants for this project, Chris Ganski (in the initial stages) and then Peter Forrest and Sean

Larsen. Susan Richardson, my editor, did a great job at helping me craft and write a much better text than I would have on my own. My colleagues at the Yale Center for Faith and Culture, David Miller and Chris Scharen, and my friend, Cynthia Metrose offered, each from a different angle, valuable comments on the manuscript. Linda LeSourd Lader, a friend and a student, deserves special mention; virtually every page of the text I gave her came back to me covered with her wise comments.

I don't discuss many living authors in this book. My main dialogue partners are thinkers who lived centuries ago. I've learned, of course, much from my contemporaries, and those who follow the debates in theology in general or on gift giving in particular will know where I agree with them or differ. Jürgen Moltmann, my doctoral supervisor and friend, continues to exert influence on me both in style and substance of thought even though I often go my own ways.

It's hard to know exactly how to acknowledge the part one's family has played in a project like this. If this book were a plant, my family would be its sustaining environment! I've learned from my mother, Mira, much about giving and forgiving, and she continues to give me the incredible gift of daily prayer. Judy, my wife, has been a great supporter and conversation partner on matters theological over the past twenty-five years. As a specialist in the apostle Paul, she has taught me a great deal about the thought of the man whose writings are central to this book (though my comments on the Apostle should not be imputed to her, of course). As to my sons, I dedicate the book to them and mention them in the text often enough that my indebtedness to them – yes, indebtedness is the right word! – needs no further elaboration.

Yes, *I* wrote the book, but its form and content have been molded by many. My writing is in great measure a result of their giving for which I am very grateful. They'll forgive, I hope, if I've failed to receive from them as much as I maybe should have.

My final thanks goes to people who provided the impetus for the book and made its writing possible. The Rev. Norman McLeod cleared an overflow Sunday school basement room for space in which

I could write undisturbed by the delights and burdens of family life and administrative work. Yale Divinity School gave me a sabbatical and a leave of absence for the calendar year 2005, and my coworkers at Yale Center for Faith and Culture, especially the Executive Director David Miller, pitched in with enthusiasm and great competence as the Center's Director tried to make himself as scarce as possible.

The Lilly Foundation gave me a grant for "Faith as a Way of Life" – a multi-year project, superbly managed by its associate director, Christian Scharen (see www.yale.edu/faith/initiatives/fwl). My main assignment for the project was to write a book sketching Christian faith as a way of life and inviting people to embark upon it. That task is enormous and there are many dull ways of going about it. The best way I knew how to fulfill it was to expound the faith as a whole from within two of its foundational practices that are as close to its heart as anything else – giving and forgiving. I am very grateful that a generous grant made my leave of absence and my writing possible.

Finally, Archbishop Rowan Williams has honored me with the invitation to write Lent Book 2006. I could think of nothing more appropriate than to make a Lent book an invitation to faith as a way of life. I hope that it will serve to lead its readers deeper into the mystery of the gift-giving and sin-bearing Christ, the beginner and finisher of our faith.

ENDNOTES

Prelude: The Rose

1. Aristotle, *Nicomachean Ethics*, trans. H. Rackham. Loeb Classical Library (Cambridge, Mass.: Harvard UP, 1926), 483.
2. Robert Kuttner, *Everything for Sale* (New York: Alfred A. Knopf, 1996), 62–63.
3. Antoine de Saint-Exupéry, *The Little Prince*, trans. Richard Howard (San Diego: Harcourt, 2000), 71.

Chapter 1: God the Giver

1. Fyodor Dostoyevsky, *The Brothers Karamazov*, trans. Constance Garnett (New York: The Modern Library, 1996), 397.
2. Gustave Flaubert, "A Simple Heart", in *Three Tales*, trans. A. J. Krailsheimer (Oxford: Oxford UP, 1991), 31, 36, 40.
3. Peter Shaffer, *Amadeus*, All Movie Scripts: www.allmoviescripts.com/scripts/19645224413f31a892668d7.html.
4. Ibid., 196.
5. Nikos Kazantzakis, *The Greek Passion*, trans. Jonathan Griffin (New York: Simon and Schuster, 1953), 1.
6. Michael Malone, *Handling Sin* (Naperville, Ill.: Sourcebooks Landmark, 2001), 521.
7. Karl Marx, "Economic and Philosophical Manuscripts", in *Karl Marx: Selected Writings*, ed. David McLellan, 2nd ed. (Oxford: Oxford UP, 2000), 94.
8. Martin Luther, *Luther's Works (LW)*, ed. Harold J. Grimm, vol. 31, (Philadelphia: Fortress Press, 1957), 353.
9. Luther, *LW*, 31:57.
10. Karl Barth, *Church Dogmatics*, trans. G. W. Bromiley et al., vol. 11/2 (Edinburgh: T&T Clark, 1957), 142.
11. Seneca, *On Benefits*, vol. 3, *Moral Essays*, trans. John W. Basore. Loeb Classical Library (Cambridge, Mass.: Harvard UP, 1935), 1.3.2–5.
12. Luther, *LW*, 22:26.

13. Luther, *LW*, 31:353.
14. Heiko A. Oberman, *Luther: Man Between God and the Devil*, trans. Eileen Walliser-Schwarzbart (New York: Image Books, 1992), 324.
15. See Immanuel Kant, *The Metaphysics of Morals*, trans. Mary Gregor (Cambridge: Cambridge UP, 1996), 203.
16. Ralph Waldo Emerson, "Gifts", *The Logic of the Gift: Toward an Ethic of Generosity*, ed. Alan D. Schrift (New York: Routledge, 1997), 26.
17. George Appleton, ed., *The Oxford Book of Prayer* (Oxford: Oxford UP, 1989), 75.
18. Immanuel Kant, *Groundwork of the Metaphysics of Morals*, trans. Mary Gregor (Cambridge: Cambridge UP, 1998), 38.
19. Luther, *LW*, 31:57.
20. Ibid., 371.
21. Ibid., 368.
22. Ibid., 371.

Chapter 2: How Should We Give?

1. The Brothers Grimm, "The Turnip", *Grimms' Fairy Tales*, trans. E. V. Lucas, Lucy Crane, and Marian Edwards (New York: Grosset & Dunlap, 1945), 261.
2. Natalie Zemon Davies, *The Gift in Sixteenth-Century France* (Madison: University of Wisconsin Press, 2000), 9.
3. C. S. Lewis, *The Lion, the Witch, and the Wardrobe* (New York: HarperCollins, 1950), 160.
4. Gotthold Ephraim Lessing, *Nathan the Wise*, trans. Ronald Schechter (Boston: Bedford/St. Martin's, 2004), 34.
5. Étienne Gilson, *God and Philosophy*, (New Haven: Yale UP, 1941), 49–50.
6. Seneca, *On Benefits*, trans. John W. Basore (Cambridge: Harvard UP, 2001), 2.1.2.
7. Luther, *LW*, 33:65.
8. Seneca, *On Benefits.*, 3.15.4.
9. Martin Luther, *D. Martin Luther's Werke: Kritische Gesamtausgabe [WA]* (Weimar: H. Böhlau, 1883-) 36, 425.
10. Seneca, Ibid., 1.3.2.
11. See Augustine, *City of God*, trans. Henry Bettenson, intro. John O'Meara (London: Penguin, 1984), 872.
12. Tom Wolfe, *I Am Charlotte Simmons* (New York: Farrar, Straus and Giroux, 2004).
13. Ralph Waldo Emerson, "Gifts", *The Logic of the Gift: Toward an Ethic of Generosity*, ed. Alan D. Schrift (New York: Routledge, 1997), 26–27.
14. Luther, *LW*, 31:353.
15. Luther, *LW*, 14:106.

16. Lessing, Ibid., 35.
17. Jacques Derrida, *The Gift of Death*, trans. David Wills (Chicago: University of Chicago Press, 1995), 68.
18. Ibid., 96.
19. See the classic of gift literature, Marcel Maus, *The Gift: The Form and Reason for Exchange in Archaic Societies*, trans. W. D. Halls (New York: W. W. Norton, 2000).
20. Luther, *LW*, 31:351.
21. Alexander Solzhenitsyn, "Matryona's House", *We Never Make Mistakes*, trans. Paul W. Blackstock (Columbia, SC: University of South Carolina Press, 1963), 100.
22. Jacques T. Godbout (in collaboration with Alain Caillé), *The World of the Gift*, trans. Donald Winkler (Montreal & Kingston: McGill-Queen's UP, 1998), 20.
23. Seneca, Ibid., 2.18.5.
24. See, for instance, Robert Putnam, *Bowling Alone: The Collapse and Revival of American Community* (New York: Simon & Schuster, 2000), 120f.

Chapter 3: How Can We Give?

1. Dale Carnegie, *How to Win Friends and Influence People* (Pocket Books: New York, 1981). For another understanding of gift giving, I draw on Godbout (with Alain Caillé), *The World of the Gift*, 79–80.
2. Marilynne Robinson, *Gilead* (New York: Farrar, Straus and Giroux, 2004), 31.
3. Friedrich Nietzsche, *Thus Spoke Zarathustra*, in *The Viking Portable Nietzsche*, trans. and ed. Walter Kaufmann (New York: Viking, 1967), 201.
4. Luther, *LW*, 1:146.
5. For such a reading of the story of Cain and Abel, see Miroslav Volf, *Exclusion and Embrace: Theological Reflections on Identity, Otherness, and Reconciliation* (Nashville: Abingdon Press, 1996), 92–98.
6. Luther, *LW*, 1:245.
7. Joseph Conrad, *Heart of Darkness* (New York: Dover Publications, 1990), 46.
8. Luther, *WA*, 7, 212.
9. Pierre Bourdieu, "Marginalia–Some Additional Notes on the Gift", *The Logic of the Gift: Toward an Ethic of Generosity*, ed. Alan D. Schrift (New York: Routledge, 1997), 232.
10. Luther, *LW*, 44:72–73.
11. Luther, *LW*, 31:46.
12. Karl Barth, *CD*, IV/2, 403.
13. See Immanuel Kant, *Religion within the Boundaries of Mere Reason*, trans. Allen Wood and George di Giovani (Cambridge: Cambridge UP, 1998), 33–36.

14. See, for instance, Søren Kierkegaard, *Either/Or*, ed. and trans. Howard V. Hong and Edna H. Hong (Princeton: Princeton UP, 1987), 1,167–215, 213; Iris Murdoch, *The Black Prince* (New York: Penguin Classics, 1973), 192–236.

15. Kierkegaard, Ibid., 212.

16. Søren Kierkegaard, *Works of Love*, ed. and trans. Howard Hong and Edna H. Hong (Princeton: Princeton UP, 1995), 281.

17. Ronald Sider, "The Evangelical Scandal", *Christianity Today*, April 2005, 70–73.

18. See Anne Bingham, Dawn Carr, Catherine Hart, "CDW and the U.S. Market", Notre Dame Business Online: www.nd.edu/~ndbizmag/winter2005/south_africa_index.shtml.

19. Erich Fromm, *To Have or to Be?* (New York: Harper and Row, 1976), 16.

20. So Robert H. Gundry, *Matthew: A Commentary on His Literary and Theological Art* (Grand Rapids, Mich.: Eerdmans 1982), 102.

21. Lessing, 64.

22. Seneca, *On Benefits*, 1.4.5.

23. Ibid., 2.4.2.

24. Ibid., 2.1.2.

25. Ibid., 1.1.7–9.

26. Fyodor Dostoyevsky, *The Brothers Karamazov*, trans. Constance Garnett (New York: The Modern Library, 1996), 58–59.

27. Luther, *LW*, 14:106.

28. Philip Hallie, *Lest Innocent Blood Be Shed: The Story of the Village of Le Chambon, and How Goodness Happened There* (New York: Harper & Row, 1979), 20–21.

29. Luther, *LW*, 31:345.

Interlude: Daniel's Death

1. www.adamjthompson.com/thought/CreatingEthics.html.

Chapter 4: God the Forgiver

1. Ernest Hemingway, "The Capital of the World", *The Complete Short Stories of Ernest Hemingway* (New York: Charles Scribner's Sons, 1987), 29.

2. Luther, *WA*, 47, 590, 6–8.

3. Luther, *LW*, 34:336.

4. Luther, *WA*, 47, 590, 9–10.

5. Philip Roth, *The Human Stain* (New York: Vintage Books, 2000), 242.

6. Lord Byron, *Don Juan: Cantos I & II. 1819* (New York: Woodstock Books, 1992), 15.

7. Roth, Ibid., 315.

8. William Shakespeare, *Measure for Measure*, in *The Riverside Shakespeare*, ed. G. Blakemore Evans (Boston: Houghton Mifflin Company, 1974), 560.

9. Kierkegaard, *Works of Love*, 296.

10. Luther, *WA*, 101, 1, 470.

11. Luther, *LW*, 51, 92.

12. See Kant, *Religion within the Boundaries of Mere Reason*, 88–89.

13. Luther, *LW*, 26:167.

14. Ibid., 170.

15. Luther, *LW*, 31:349.

16. Luther, *LW*, 26:132–133.

17. Ibid., 133.

18. Luther, *LW*, 31:352.

19. Ibid., 127.

20. Luther, *LW*, 26:127.

21. Luther, *LW*, 21:153.

22. Ibid., 150.

Chapter 5: How Should We Forgive?

1. Miroslav Volf, *Exclusion and Embrace: Theological Reflections on Identity, Otherness, and Reconciliation* (Nashville: Abingdon, 1996).

2. Carlos Eire, *Waiting for Snow in Havana* (New York, The Free Press, 2003), 232.

3. Seth Mydans, "Cambodian Aesop Tells a Fable of Forgiveness", *New York Times*, 13 November 1997.

4. Eire, Ibid., 51.

5. Luther, *LW*, 21:149.

6. Luther, *LW*, 31:306.

7. That is why, contrary to the often-quoted saying, original sin is *not* the most empirically verifiable Christian doctrine; indeed, it's not empirically verifiable at all.

8. Luther, *LW*, 21:165.

9. Friedrich Nietzsche, *On Genealogy of Morals*, trans. Carol Diethe (Cambridge: Cambridge UP, 1994), 23–24.

10. www2.oprah.com/health/omag/health_omag_200310_philweight_g.jhtml.

11. Sophocles, *Sophocles I: Oedipus the King*, 2nd edition, ed. David Grene and Richmond Lattimore, trans. David Grene (Chicago: University of Chicago Press, 1991), 14–15.

12. James C. McKinley Jr., "As Crowds Vent Their Rage, Rwanda Publicly Executes 22", *New York Times*, 23 December 1998.

13. Leo Tolstoy, *The Complete Works*, in Russian, vol. 53, (Moscow: Terra, 1992), 197 (I owe this reference to my colleague at Yale, Professor Vladimir Alexandrov).

14. Lance Morrow, 'I spoke ... as a brother'; a pardon from the Pontiff, a lesson in forgiveness for a troubled world", *Time*, 9 January 1984.
15. Shaffer, *Amadeus*, first scene.
16. Luther, *LW*, 45:283.
17. Vladimir Jankélévitch, *Forgiveness*, trans. Andrew Kelley (Chicago: The University of Chicago Press, 2005), 157.
18. Luther, *LW*, 21:153.
19. See Seth Mydans, "Under Prodding, 2 Apologize for Cambodian Anguish", *New York Times*, 30 December 1998.
20. When God forgives, someone may protest, God doesn't demand that anything be restored. We believe and we repent, and that's the end of the matter. God has forgiven and we've received forgiveness. It's a gift that requires no return. We need to restore nothing to God. If we should forgive *as* God forgives, should we not consider restitution unnecessary?

    But why is restitution not needed in relation to God? Consider first, that by sinning we haven't taken anything from God. Yes, we've failed to honor God as the giver. But by believing, we now do precisely that—acknowledge the fact that we've received everything from God. Second, we can't give anything to God. Everything we have is from God, and God doesn't need anything. So even if there were anything to restore to God, we could only give from what God continues to give to us. Hence there is no requirement to restore things to God. What God desires of us instead is to receive divine forgiveness in faith and with recognition of our own wrongdoing.

    Our relation to human beings whom we've offended is different from our relation to God. First, we are obviously able to give restitution to our fellow human beings. We can take from our own and give to those we've offended—whether our goods, services, or funds. God has given to us, and we can give to them. Second, by offending against other people, we've taken something from them—their property, their reputation, their loved ones. It's fitting that we should return what we have illicitly taken, or its rough equivalent.
21. Luther, *LW*, 45:283.

Chapter 6: How Can We Forgive?

1. Paul Simon and Derek Wolcott, "Can I Forgive Him?" paul simon.com: www.paulsimon.com/lyrics/can_i_forgive_him.html.
2. Nicolai Hartmann, *Ethics III: Moral Freedom*, trans. Stanton Coit (London: George Allen & Unwin, 1932), 272.
3. Luther, *LW*, 31:306.
4. Ibid., 304.
5. Ibid., 297.
6. Ibid., 300.

7. Ibid., 298.

8. Kazantzakis, *The Greek Passion*, 9ff.

9. Ibid., 23.

10. Luther, *LW*, 31:367.

11. Anthony Trollope, *Orley Farm* (Oxford: Oxford UP, 1950), 63.

12. Victor Hugo, *Les Misérables*, trans. Lee Fahnestock and Norman MacAfee (New York: Signet Books, 1987), 106.

13. Zlatko Dizdarevič, *Sarajevo: A War Journal*, trans. from the French Anselm Hollo, ed. from the original Serbo-Croatian Ammiel Alcalay (New York: Fromm International, 1993), 54.

14. Željko Vukovič, *Ubijanje Sarajeva* [*The Killing of Sarajevo*] (Beograd: Kron, 1993), 134.

15. Luther, *LW*, 21:152.

16. Kierkegaard, *Works of Love*, 338.

17. Ibid., 339.

18. Ibid., 336.

19. Ibid., 339.

20. Anne Lamott, *Plan B: Further Thoughts on Faith* (New York: Riverhead Books, 2005), 46.

21. Ibid., 232.

22. Dizdarevič, *Sarajevo: A War Journal*, 15.

Postlude: A Conversation with a Skeptic

1. Milan Kundera, *Laughable Loves*, trans. Susanne Rappaport (New York: Penguin, 1975), 240.